Literature, Culture, Theory 12

❖❖❖

Theories of mimesis

Literature, Culture, Theory

General editors

RICHARD MACKSEY, *The Johns Hopkins University*
and MICHAEL SPRINKER, *State University of New York at Stony Brook*

The Cambridge *Literature, Culture, Theory* series is dedicated to theoretical studies in the human sciences that have literature and culture as their object of enquiry. Acknowledging the contemporary expansion of cultural studies and the redefinitions of literature that this has entailed, the series includes not only original works of literary theory but also monographs and essay collections on topics and seminal figures from the long history of theoretical speculation on the arts and human communication generally. The concept of theory embraced in the series is broad, including not only the classical disciplines of poetics and rhetoric, but also those of aesthetics, linguistics, psychoanalysis, semiotics, and other cognate sciences that have inflected the systematic study of literature during the past half century.

Selected recent series titles

Parody: ancient, modern, and post-modern
MARGARET A. ROSE

The poetics of personification
JAMES PAXSON

Possible worlds in literary theory
RUTH RONEN

Critical conditions: postmodernity and the question of foundations
HORACE L. FAIRLAMB

Introduction to literary hermeneutics
PETER SZONDI
(translated from the German by Martha Woodmansee)

Anti-mimesis from Plato to Hitchcock
TOM COHEN

Mikhail Bakhtin: between phenomenology and Marxism
MICHAEL F. BERNARD-DONALS

Theories of mimesis
ARNE MELBERG

Theories of mimesis

ARNE MELBERG
University of Oslo

CAMBRIDGE
UNIVERSITY PRESS

Published by the Press Syndicate of the University of Cambridge
The Pitt Building, Trumpington Street, Cambridge, CB2 1RP
40 West 20th Street, New York, NY 10011-4211, USA
10 Stamford Road, Oakleigh, Melbourne 3166, Australia

First published 1995

Printed in Great Britain at the University Press, Cambridge

A catalogue record for this book is available from the British Library

Library of Congress cataloguing in publication data applied for

ISBN 0 521 45225 2 hardback
ISBN 0 521 45856 0 paperback

Contents

❖❖

Introduction, rehearsal and repetition

❖❖

Mimesis and *repetition* are the basic terms of this book, and its basic argument is that *mimesis* turns – somehow, at some time – into *repetition*.

This statement could be developed in at least two ways, which seem like two alternative ways of describing and analysing the phenomenon of *mimesis*:

(1)   The turning of *mimesis* into *repetition* is the result of a historical process that slowly invests *mimesis* with temporal dimensions. Modernity, which can be localized as starting in the eighteenth century, is here of decisive importance; the modern development of *mimesis* results paradoxically in its fulfillment and disappearance, meaning that similarity gives way to difference.

(2)   *Mimesis* is inherently and always already a *repetition* – meaning that *mimesis* is always the meeting-place of two opposing but connected ways of thinking, acting and making: similarity and difference.

In this book I am using the second way of thinking about and discussing *mimesis*, which implies that I am always inclined to find movements of difference even in those versions of *mimesis* that suggest similarity; and even in the oldest versions of Plato and Aristotle. I do not want to discard a historical approach, however, and I am actually using one, in the simplest way possible, by arranging my four studies chronologically and not wanting to exclude a historical development between them. That means, however, that I have avoided the question of the historicity of the concept: the problems involved seemed overwhelming.

The attempt to write a full-scale history of *mimesis* has, of course, been made in the classic work by Erich Auerbach of 1946 called, simply, *Mimesis*.

Writing on *mimesis* within the tradition of literary analysis and textual analysis, one has actually to come to terms with both Plato

1

and Auerbach, so to speak: Plato for being the nearest you can come
to one responsible for the Western tradition of thinking, in which
mimesis plays such an important part; and Auerbach for being a
paradigm for the analysis of textual *mimesis*. Plato is the first author we
have all read, whether we know it or not, and Auerbach happens to be
the first author that *I* read as a literary student who left a lasting
impression.

Auerbach notably presents the history of *mimesis* in twenty
chapters in chronological order, basing each on a piece of text and
discussing its *Darstellung*, its representation of reality, as an inte-
gration of style, morality and reality. I find now that his way of
writing history is exemplary as he subordinates history to literary
texts, and always bases his analysis on the reading of this text. Yet
there are only a few of these analyses that I can follow, and no
conclusion that I can accept; and I cannot share Auerbach's idea of a
levelling of styles as the very idea of history, or his integrative pathos.
The one example from Auerbach that I discuss in my first chapter
confirms the suspicion that, despite my admiration for his scope and
reading procedures, his view of the very concept in question, *mimesis*,
is simplifying in a way that makes him blind to differential movements.
From my perspective Auerbach makes his most interesting observations on the mimetic play of similarity and difference *not* in terms
of representation, but in terms of *figura*, of figural style and figural
interpretation.[1]

Recently another admirable effort has been made to make history
out of *mimesis*: a book by Gunter Gebauer and Christoph Wulf called,
again, *Mimesis*, and broadly subtitled *Kultur – Kunst – Gesellschaft*
(Culture, Art, Society). The authors call their approach "historical
anthropology," and they manage to present an outline of the
transformations of *mimesis* from the beginning, from archaic imagery
up to modern imagination and further on into a post-historical time of
simulacrum, where a totalizing *mimesis* coincides with its disappearance: nothing is left to imitate when all is imitation and the
original is finally gone. The historical cesura comes with "modernity," here located in the aesthetic thinking of Diderot, Lessing,
Moritz and Kant. Lessing is singled out as the thinker who introduced
time into mimetic representation: "Time is discovered by Lessing as

1 As elaborated in *Mimesis* and especially in the essay "Figura," in *Neue
Dantestudien* (Istanbul, 1944).

the decisive characteristic of poetry,"[2] a "rediscovery" of "time as constitutive for poetry" that allows for his definite giving up of "similarity as the principle of Mimesis" and his modern introduction of "the idea of trace in its stead."[3]

Gebauer and Wulf's excellent analysis and the attractive perspective on *mimesis* as the beginning and end of our civilization – attractive for giving the impression of evolutionary purpose – has some drawbacks. Historicity has its costs. The major one is, in this case, that every thinker before Lessing has to be allotted temporal innocence in order to give Gebauer and Wulf the chance of letting Lessing discover the importance of time for aesthetics. And this I would call a result of a combination of analytical blindness with historical construction: it is an observation and a thesis that should be difficult to combine with the analysis of historical texts. Time is, after all, a constant problem of aesthetics already discussed by Plato and Aristotle, not to mention Augustine. Similar difficulties arise in the analysis of other concepts, used by Gebauer and Wulf as emblems of modernity: "trace" can be "traced" way back, even *simulacrum*, modern as it is, can be derived from an ancient discussion of similarity and difference – the word itself apprises us of that.

In this book I prefer to present *mimesis* and mimetic problems in terms of similarity/difference or as the meeting-place for these opposing phenomena or movements; and as including other members of the mimetical family such as proximity and distance, presence and absence. *Mimesis* is *never* a homogeneous term, and if its basic movement is towards similarity it is *always* open to the opposite. Perhaps modern theorists become modern by emphasizing the differential movements and possibilities of what earlier was called *mimesis*. But they have also been clever at finding the traces of difference in history. Heidegger, for instance, when discussing Greek, specially Platonic *mimesis*, insists that the concept is directed towards truth, but based on the *distance* from truth; imitating "representation" (*Nachahmung*) is not what it is about. On the contrary; *mimesis* is based upon the fact that the artist *cannot* reproduce the truth as similarity. It is wrong, according to Heidegger, to associate *mimesis* with

---

2 Gunter Gebauer and Christoph Wulf, *Mimesis. Kultur – Kunst – Gesellschaft* (Reinbek: Rowohlt, 1992), p. 275: "Die Zeit wird von Lessing als das entscheidende Merkmal der Dichtung entdeckt."

3 Ibid., p. 283f.: "Die Ähnlichkeit als Prinzip der Mimesis wird definitiv aufgegeben und der Gedanke der Spur an ihre Stelle gesetzt."

"primitive" imitation (*Nachbilden*). It is rather a question of "doing-after: production that comes afterwards. The *mimesis* is in its essence situated and defined through distance."[4]

Heidegger's follower H.-G. Gadamer also emphasizes *mimesis* as a productive relation of knowledge and truth, and discusses "recognition" (*Wiedererkennung*) as the best word to characterize a mimetical sense of knowledge (*Erkenntnissinn*).[5] Heidegger's "doing-after" (*Nachmachung*) as a definition of *mimesis* is, like "recognition," more productive than imitative. It is close to *repetition*, as the concept and term that inherits the burden of *mimesis* when we come to modern times, and that we find in the different strategies of repetition used by, for instance, Nietzsche, Freud and Deleuze — to mention only a few of those whom I am *not* discussing. Instead I concentrate on "*repetition* (in the Kierkegaardian sense of the term)," to use a phrase from Paul de Man that will be much in use in my last chapter, which deals with *repetition* in the versions of Kierkegaard, Heidegger, Derrida and de Man himself.

Modern theorists have become modern not only with their emphasis on repetition as difference rather than as similarity, but also in their linguistic orientation. The linguistic *turn* is the well-known *signum* of modern philosophy and literary theory, most often expressed as a discrepancy of meaning and reference. Linguistic signs refer to a reality *beyond* their own reality; but literary language, more than any other language, makes a problem of exactly this *beyond*, and of the relation between meaning and reference. The conventional and, therefore, unstable relation between sign and signified makes way for the unpleasant experience of never knowing for sure. Or, as it has been put by Paul de Man: it is "not a priori certain that literature is a reliable source of information about anything but its own language."[6]

Modern as it is, this experience has famous antecedents: Plato's dialogue *Cratylos* has, after all, the nature of the linguistic sign as its theme. My chapter on Cervantes' *Don Quijote* will expose similar

---

4 Martin Heidegger, *Nietzsche* (Pfullingen: Neste, 1961), vol. 1, p. 215: "Es ist daher irrig, wenn man der *mimesis* die Vorstellung des 'naturalistischen' und 'primitiven' Nachbildens und Abschilderns unterlegt. Nach-machung ist: nachgeordnetes Herstellen. Der *mimesis* wird in seinem Wesen durch die Stelle des Abstandes bestimmt," etc.

5 Hans-Georg Gadamer, *Wahrheit und Methode*, vol. 1 (Tübingen: Mohr, 1990 [1960]), pp. 118ff.

6 Paul de Man, *The Resistance to Theory* (Minnesota University Press, 1986), p. 11.

linguistic problems, including their relations to questions of identity. And the unreliability of signs has never been better expressed than by Shakespeare, for instance when he makes the jester, Feste, of *Twelfth Night* (iii: 1) show off his capacity as "corrupter of words" by telling Viola that *reason* cannot be yielded without words, "and words are grown so false, I am loath to prove reason with them" – as if making an early linguistic turn of the question of the reason of reason, as it was later discussed by, for instance, Leibniz and Heidegger. Feste declares that "*words are very rascals, since bonds disgraced them,*" thereby providing us with something like a motto for the linguistic aspects of the never very stable relations between sign and signified.

Shakespeare's jester even seems like an early version of the jesting spirit of today's philosophy, as personified by Jacques Derrida. *Repetition* is a major trace in his philosophy, to be followed in my last chapter. *Repetition* (and, later; *iteration*) are instrumental in his deconstructive strategies, meaning that these terms seem more important to me than his analysis of *mimesis*, developed in a couple of articles in the 1970s. As can be studied in "La Mythologie blanche" (1972) as well as in "Economimesis" (1975), Derrida regards *mimesis* as a version of classical metaphysical ontology, based on analogy, resemblance, similarity. Reading Kant (in "Economimesis"), however, opens the way for difference: Derrida's Kant finds "true *mimesis* between two producing subjects and not between two produced things," meaning that "true *mimesis*" is actually a "condemnation of the imitation" and a tribute to the creative imagination of the artist.[7] Like Heidegger, Derrida finds classical *mimesis* based in *physis*, while the modern, starting with Kant, has traveled into imagination. Derrida's own repetition is neither *physis* nor imagination, neither imitative nor productive, but a linguistically motivated mechanism working within all versions of *mimesis*.

The argument so far seems to indicate an ontological turn: the historical approach to *mimesis* outlined by Auerbach and emphasized by Gebauer and Wulf with the cesura of "modernity" has – after Nietzsche and with Heidegger and Derrida – turned into different mimetic orders; and into a mimetical order of difference. Perhaps this ontological turn in favor of difference could be summarized in J. Hillis Miller's excellent formula as "two forms of repetition." One would be

7 Jacques Derrida, "Economimesis," in *Mimesis – des articulations* (Paris: Flammarion, 1975), pp. 67ff.

heading for similarity, the other for difference.[8] Hillis Miller is able to
use his differential repetition as a tool for literary analysis in a way that
has been an inspiration for me – although my application is to the
theory itself, rather than the literature. This ontological and rhetorical
turn has so far been presented in contrast to the historical approach,
but should not, I hope, be regarded as a- or anti-historical. I would like
to emphasize here what is likely to disappear in the analyses to come:
that the ontology (and methodology and rhetoric) of *mimesis* could (or
should) open the way to aspects of temporality that are embedded in
historical time, but are nevertheless conspicuously absent from the
historical approach. I am thinking of the reversals of "making new"
studied in the chapter on Cervantes; the momentary presence
cultivated by Rousseau, and, above all, the instant or *momentum*
prefigured by Plato, conceptually developed by Kierkegaard and
explored by Heidegger, Derrida and de Man.

Walter Benjamin provides Hillis Miller with some beautiful
sentences to characterize differential repetition, and Benjamin would
perhaps be the best specimen of a modern thinker obsessed with the
possibility of evoking a time within time, a momentary presence
miraculously combining similarity and difference. Benjamin finds his
inspiration for this in Proust, among others, and, since it is a
commonplace that Proust in *A la recherche du temps perdu* demonstrates
the power of temporality to differentiate and dissociate a traditional
mimesis, thereby announcing literary modernity, I would like to finish
this introductory rehearsal with some Proustian observations. I
certainly do not want to deny the important rôle played by Time in
A la recherche, in every possible way. Then who would deny the
instrumental importance of temporality in installing distance in
mimetic similarity when we come to Lessing, Rousseau, Cervantes,
Augustine, Aristotle? In any event, this powerful differentiating
temporality coincides interestingly with what is more or less a cult of
similarity in Proust's work, and this very coincidence of the "two
forms of repetition" is what Benjamin tries to pin down.

"Zum Bilde Prousts" ("To the Image of Proust") is Benjamin's
effort to fix Proust in one of his "dialectical images," an essay written
in 1929. And *Ähnlichkeit* (similarity) is his decisive term, used to tell us
that Proust cultivates a "frenetic" and "impassioned cult of similarity,"

8   J. Hillis Miller, "Two Forms of Repetition," in *Fiction and Repetition* (Cambridge,
    Mass.: Harvard University Press, 1982).

that the world of *A la recherche* is "a world in the state of similarity governed by 'correspondances'," and that the author of this world could only be an author dominated by nostalgia "for a world displaced (*entstellt*) in the state of similarity."[9] The German *Ähnlichkeit* already indicates a kind of similarity that includes difference, and this differential aspect is emphasized by calling the "state of similarity" *entstellt*, meaning not only displaced, but also corrupted, disfigured.

I cannot fully explore Benjamin's meaning here – doing that would mean going into what he calls a *Lehre vom Ähnlichen*;[10] I can only indicate the relevance for Proust and for a modern idea of *mimesis*. And Benjamin is certainly not the only one to have observed the importance of *Ähnlichkeit* – similarity with a difference – for Proust. Georges Poulet, in his study of Proustian "space," declares *juxtaposition* to be the central device when Proust establishes his "world" of affinities and relations.[11] His observation was developed by Gérard Genette in several essays, prominently in "Métonymie chez Proust" in 1973. Genette uses terms like *rapprochement, analogie* and *concomitance* to establish the intricate and interwoven relations between metaphor and metonymy that he regards as typical of Proust. The "fundamental tendency of Proustian writing and imagination," according to Genette, is "the projection of the analogical relation on to a relation of contiguity" making metaphor, in the shape of a "following of comparisons" ("comparaisons suivies"), a *rapprochement* of two impressions or sensations by way of *analogie*, into the central figure of style and world for Proust.[12]

Proust, then, famed for his break with all traditional *mimesis* and his revolutionary use of temporality, is caught using versions of similarity as the very tool for installing temporal difference. If one were to single out one word from his work, used to initiate those endless *comparaisons suivies* that make up his text, it would simply be "*comme*": "like."

9   Walter Benjamin, "Zum Bilde Prousts," in *Gesammelte Schriften* (Frankfurt-on-Main: Suhrkamp, 1977), I: 1, p. 313 ("Prousts frenetische Studium, Sein passionierter Kultus der Ähnlichkeit"), p. 320 ("Es ist ein Welt im Stand der Ähnlichkeit und in ihr herrschen die 'Korrespondenzen'"), p. 314 ("Heimweh nach der im Stand der Ähnlichkeit entstellten Welt").

10 Walter Benjamin, *Lehre vom Ähnlichen* ("The Lesson of Similarity"), a metaphysical essay from the beginning of the 1930s, later developed into *Über das mimetische Vermögen* ("On the Mimetical Capacity").

11 Georges Poulet, *L'Espace proustien* (Paris: Gallimard, 1963), especially ch. 9.

12 Gérard Genette, "Métonymie chez Proust," in *Figures III* (Paris: Seuil, 1973), pp. 53ff.

Chains of elaborate comparisons, grown into metaphors, or at least given an air of metaphoricity, are established as Proust's method of *Recherche*; and this mingling of comparison, metonymy and metaphor may be regarded as his version of what I put broadly as a coincidence of similarity and difference.

It may seem far-fetched to use these efforts to find a formula for what is typical of Proust as a first and introductory argument in the theory of *mimesis*. Proust seems not to belong to the mimetic tradition at all, obsessed, as he was, by the difference produced by time. What interests me is his use of the mechanisms of similarity to establish this difference. His "impassioned cult of similarity," in Benjamin's words, even seems like the condition and purpose of the differentiating movements of his *Recherche*. His *comparaisons suivies*, mingling metaphor with metonymy, concentrate those "two forms of repetition" that Hillis Miller found in the novelistic tradition and that I am tempted to stretch to the tradition of *mimesis* in its ontological, as well as its historical, version.

Proust seems just as interested as his commentators to find the formula for this enigmatic mixture. Notably he (i.e. the narrator of his novel) invokes the concept of metaphor – and thereby substitution and similarity – at crucial moments in the development of the protagonist (i.e. Marcel). When he first ponders the paintings of Elstir – a major influence on the writer-to-be – he imagines he has found one of those "rare moments when one sees nature as it is, poetically"; and the painting that evokes this insight is "one of the most frequent metaphors" said to be used by Elstir: a comparison of "earth to sea, suppressing all borders between them."[13]

"Metaphor" here has apparently to do with similarity, even with the obliteration of a primary difference between earth and sea. Much later in the novel, at the decisive moment in the last part when Marcel has defined his mission (i.e. to write) and sits alone pondering how to go about it, we meet "metaphor" again. As with Elstir, it has to do with finding the correspondence of similarity between the basically different, finding "the qualities in common between two sensations,"

13 Marcel Proust, *A la recherche du temps perdu* (Paris: Gallimard Pléiade, 1991), vol. 2, p. 192: "Mais les rares moments où l'on voit la nature telle qu'elle est, poétiquement, c'était de ceux-là qu'était faite l'œuvre d'Elstir. Une de ses métaphores les plus fréquentes dans les marines qu'il avait près de lui en ce moment, était justement celle qui comparant la terre à la mer, supprimait entre elle toute démarcation."

liberating their "common essence" from the "contingencies of time." Metaphor is truth and "truth does not start until the writer takes two different objects, establishes their connection ... and encloses them in the necessary bonds of a good style."[14] Metaphor is the truth of similarity hiding in a world of difference.

This may have little to do with the actual state of this world and its history, but it summarizes a poetical impulse: the poetics of metaphorical similarity used to show a world of difference. Such a poetical impulse is not only relevant to Proust, but a vital paradox in the tradition of *mimesis*. I like to think of it as one of the reasons for *mimesis* in the shape of similarity being so amazingly long-lived when all the evidence favors difference, so to speak. Again, Proust can be used as a witness. In his *Contre Sainte-Beuve*, written as a rehearsal for the big novel, he writes in the conclusion of imagining a boy within himself and known only to himself. This *garçon* has an eye and an ear sharp enough to notice "between two impressions, between two ideas, a very subtle harmony that other people do not notice." This "harmony" is called the "general" (something I want to translate as "similarity"); and the boy can live only in the "general"; "he dies immediately in the particular" (may I read it as "difference"?). And this boy, declares Proust, "only he should write my books."[15]

My suspicion is that this mimetically sensitive boy, not very fit for the real world, but yearning for the state of similarity, has already written unbelievably much, and is still about to write.

14 *A la recherche*, vol. 4, p. 468: "la vérité ne commencera qu'au moment où l'écrivain prendra deux objets différents, posera leur rapport ... et les enfermera dans les anneaux nécessaires d'un beau style. Même, ainsi que la vie, quand rapprochant une qualité commune à deux sensations, il dégagera leur essence commune en les réunissant l'une et l'autre pour les soustraire aux contingences du temps, dans une métaphore."
15 Marcel Proust, *Contre Sainte-Beuve* (Paris: Gallimard, 1954), p. 302: "Et je pense que le garçon qui en moi s'amuse à cela doit être le même que celui qui a aussi l'oreille fine et juste pour sentir entre deux impressions, entre deux idées, une harmonie très fine que d'autres ne sentent pas", p. 303: "Il n'y a que lui qui devrait écrire mes livres."

I

Plato's "Mimesis"

Criticism

Plato rejected the poets.

The best-known *locus* for this dramatic gesture is the dialogue *Republic*, the tenth and last book, where Plato has Socrates reach the conclusion that "we can admit no poetry into our city save only hymns to the gods and the praises of good men."[1] "Our city" refers to the ideal community — *polis* — that Socrates has already sketched with the assent of his young listeners; except, in the first book, he gets some resistance from one Thrasymachos, who makes a scandalous speech in praise of injustice. This gives Socrates the opportunity to develop the connections between the true and the right and the good; his pedagogical zeal brings him on to epistemology and to statecraft, finally to poetry — and thereby to poetics and aesthetics.

The reasons poets cannot be accepted into the ideal community are both epistemological and moral, but whatever the reason they have a word in common: *mimesis*. Plato uses the word with a primarily visual significance; *mimesis* suggests image, a visual image related to imitation, re-presentation. Poetry delivers a poor and unreliable knowledge, according to Socrates — and still in the tenth book of *Republic* — since it is a second-hand imitation of an already second-hand imitation. The philosopher comes closest to first-hand knowledge of real reality: he can see the form or ideas or ideal form of things and can therefore disregard imitations. When the carpenter makes his platonic couch he has taken a step away from ideal form.

---

1 I follow, but in some cases modifying, the English translations of Plato in the Loeb Classical Library editions (1925–35), here by Paul Shorey. References will be given in my text in accordance with the pagination introduced by Stephanus in 1578. This quotation is from 607A.

And when the artist imitates the carpenter's couch we have come even further. "This, then," settles Socrates, "will apply to the maker of tragedies also, if he is an imitator [mimetes] and is in his nature three removes from the king and the truth, as are all other imitators" (597E). The poor morality of art can then be derived from its mimetic curse: art sticks, and has to stick, to the deceptive knowledge of the senses, which necessarily means that it will appeal to our worst parts, imitating "the fretful and complicated type of character" (605A) rather than the ideally calm and good, giving us a dubious "vicarious pleasure" (606B) rather than ideal and true satisfaction.

For us, today, this well-known version of "Platonism" is not only hopelessly dualistic and idealistic but also an utterly moral or moralistic approach to art, that is based on a fanciful analogy between visual imagery and the linguistic forms of poetry and drama. For Plato, the connection and the conclusions are linked to that common denominator *mimesis*: what the words make up mimetically are images, phantasies, phantoms — *phantasma* and *eidolon* are recurrent terms — and foremost in the art of words comes drama, foremost in drama comes tragedy and foremost of poets comes Homer, who, therefore, is appointed "leader" of tragedians (598D), providing Socrates with all his examples of reprehensible poetry.

And it is Homer who is rejected from the city — *if* he uses *mimesis* in his art, "if he is a *mimitis*," as Socrates put it in his epistemological investigation just quoted (597E). This little *if* may well cause some trouble for Socrates' argument, giving it first a hypothetical, and then a slippery, character: Plato has Socrates try his way with *if*, then come to a conclusion that has lost its hypothetical reservation. The tenth book of *Republic* shows this shift in the argument. It starts with Socrates reminding us and his listeners of the earlier exploration of poetical *mimesis*, mainly in the third book, and stating that he is by now confirmed in his opinion of how right he was to reject mimetic poetry, or, more exactly, "so much of it that is imitative [mimetike]" (595A). "So much of it"! Here we learn that *part* of poetry is mimetic or presupposes *mimesis* — meaning that other parts of poetry could be something else entirely, indicating that *mimesis* is a manner of poetry, one of several possible means of expression. If we only had better knowledge of poetry as a cure against mimetic poetry — a knowledge of its real nature "as an antidote [pharmakon]" (595B) — Plato/Socrates seems to consider the possibility that we could resist the mimetic seduction and maintain morals.

But after the epistemological investigation the essence of poetry appears to be *mimesis* and nothing else. Hypothetical *ifs* and other reservations of *parts* are gone and no more antidote will do; we have reached the conclusion that art is mimetic to its core and that poets *en bloc* are mimetics. "On this, then, we are fairly agreed," Socrates assures us, "that the imitator knows nothing worth mentioning of the things he imitates, but that *mimesis* is a form of play [*paidian*] not to be taken seriously, and that those who attempt tragic poetry, whether in iambics or heroic verse, are all altogether imitators [*mimetikous*]" (602B). *All altogether imitators!* None of Socrates' submissive listeners comes up with an *if* or a reminder of earlier reservations, none produces an "antidote" and nobody asks himself or us why poetic play, which cannot be taken seriously, is taken so seriously as to be rejected and expelled from the city.

This is by no means the only time or place that Plato deals with poetry – after all he rounds off the argument in *Republic* by joking about that "old quarrel between philosophy and poetry" (607B) (and it seems to me like a memento for all times that the very *first* "quarrel" known between philosophical concept and poetical expression refers to, and even quotes from, this "quarrel" as already *old*). But the famous conclusion of the tenth book of *Republic* may well be the most efficient and at least unconditional argument – if not *if* had been. There is, after all, an *if*: a built-in reservation or a kind of shift in the argument producing ambiguity not only in that central term *mimesis*, but also in surrounding concepts like image (*eidolon*), play (*paidia*), drug or antidote (*pharmakon*). And these shifts and ambiguities could perhaps be regarded as distant versions of the puzzling paradox that is never conceptually articulated, but is always present in Plato's argument against mimetic poetry: the argument is itself mimetic. Plato makes a poetic rejection of poetry – it is the poet Plato who rejects the poets.

This is a riddle that calls for a solution, a paradox that provokes each reader's urgent need for meaning: for a stable and unequivocal meaning. And the question is whether or not "Platonism" consists of solutions to riddles and paradoxes that are stored in those Platonic dialogues that make up the Platonic text. Read conceptually/ philosophically, there are at least ten divergent meanings or directions of *mimos/mimeisthai/mimetikous/mimesis* in Plato.[2] Read literally, according to Stanley Rosen,

the Plato who emerges can scarcely be regarded as a satisfactory or philosophically interesting figure, whatever standards one uses. He seems to vacillate almost from year to year on the most important matters, is so poor a thinker as continuously to be caught up in elementary fallacies, is unable to remember his line of argument for two consecutive pages, and is subject to the most vulgar superstitions of his day.[3]

Rosen recommends a reading that makes sense of Plato by way of irony and drama. I will follow his advice in my own way, meaning that I will stick to Plato's text as an ironic, poetic and dramatic text — i.e. not *only* a philosophical text (meaning also that the "old quarrel" between philosophy and literature takes place already *in* Plato's text); and I will avoid solutions according to "Platonism" and try to remember Hans-Georg Gadamer's very last words in his presentation of himself as philosopher: "daß Plato kein Platoniker war."[4]

Let us then proceed to some other instances of Plato's poetical rejection of poetry in order to come closer to the Platonic text. We go first to the second and third books of *Republic*, where we get the basis for the judgments of the tenth book, as well as a technically detailed investigation of mimetic poetry — something close to a Platonic-Socratic poetics.

It starts in morality: the effects of poetry on morals. Socrates discusses his fears about the bad effects of poetry because he has moved towards pedagogics, and naturally so after Thrasymachos' scandalous speech in praise of injustice (a speech that Socrates takes the trouble of first tearing to pieces). Tales for children must be censored, according to Socrates. Tales lie and must therefore be carefully suppressed, "especially if the lie is not a pretty one" (377D). Socrates' examples show that the untruths of tales have to do with the gods. Since the gods by definition — Plato's definition — are good, it follows that any bad tale about gods must be lying. Thus Hesiod's

---

2   The origins of the Platonic term are explored in Göran Sörbom, Mimesis and Art. Studies in the Origin and Early Development of an Aesthetic Vocabulary (Uppsala, 1966). Different meanings are systematized in Stephen Halliwell, *Aristotle's Poetics* (London: Duckworth, 1987), p. 121.

3   Stanley Rosen, *Plato's Symposion* (Yale University Press, 1968), p. xii.

4   Hans-Georg Gadamer, "Selbstdarstellung," in *Gesammelte Werke* (Tübingen: Mohr, 1986), vol. 2, p. 508.

story of the creation is a lie, since it touches on both parricide and castration (at least, Socrates does not want to mention that, but it is clear that everybody is supposed to know). The same goes for Achilles' famous lines in the last song of the *Iliad* (24: 527–32), where Zeus is said to allot "both evil and good" to man.

These two examples are also interesting in other respects: the first by touching on (but not discussing) parricide, which seems to be a recurrent, but subdued motif in Plato's text; the second by starting Plato's systematic criticism of Homer, especially the *Iliad*. As a starting-point for criticism this example is the best one possible: Achilles' line on how the "piteous mortals" by "careless gods" are doomed "to live in trouble and pain" forms the culmination and also the peaceful turning of Achilles' "wrath," which is, after all, the theme keeping the whole epos together. Plato/Socrates has with accurate critical judgment pointed to the final turning-point of the *Iliad*, which I will discuss in some detail later.

Here it is the starting-point for a first discussion on Platonic *mimesis*: on image and representation. The lies spread by tales are not authentic lies, according to Socrates, but images representing lies. Then could one perhaps credit false words – in contrast with false facts – with some pedagogical value? For instance, like a *pharmakon* preventing what is worse? Socrates puts the question (382CD), but hesitates to answer. That is, he seems at first to accept the thought that mimetic lies are a necessary evil in the world of fiction ("*to pseudos*," 382D); but when he starts comparing this with the ideal world of the gods the comparison is not to the advantage of fiction: gods or ideals are, after all, the real world, making the pseudo-world of fiction at best superfluous. "Then there is no lying poet in God," Socrates declares – and the word *pseudos* is repeated three times in this passage (382D) to signify the mimetic half-world of imaginary representation, i.e. the world mysteriously communicating between the true and the false, between Being and Nothing (to use an observation by J.-P. Vernant).[5]

This preliminary discussion leads to the drifting significance of Platonic *mimesis*, a drift indicated not only by wavering attitudes to mimetic activities, but also by terms like *pseudos* and *pharmakon*. The latter means poison as well as antidote, and Plato drifts between the oppositions indicated by the very word. That is, *mimesis* can be

5 Jean-Pierre Vernant, "Naissance d'images," in *Religions, histoires, raisons* (Paris: Maspero, 1979), pp. 111 and 131.

prescribed as a drug to be used under control and in moderation – only to be rejected in the next sentence as a dangerous poison. The pseudo-world, says Socrates a bit further on in the text, is of no interest to the gods, but it can be used by man as a *pharmakon* (389B); and he comes to the conclusion that mimetic lying should be restricted to experts who know how to handle the stuff! (The real addict was, after all, Plato himself, who stubbornly uses dialogical form – thereby mimetically creating a pseudo-world – to represent the mimetically uncontaminated world of ideas.)

This, then, was the first and hesitant step in the argument leading in the third book of *Republic* to the first rejection of the poets, a rejection that is repeated and dramatized in the tenth book as quoted above. The next step is for Socrates to enumerate examples from the *Iliad* and the *Odyssey* of tales or parts of tales that must be banished from a decent schooling. Socrates assures us that the reason for this is not that these tales are poor poetry – on the contrary, they are beautiful tales – "but because the more poetic they are the less are they suited to the ears of boys and men who are destined to be free" (387B). This is, to my knowledge, the first version of the well-known "the better, the worse" argument that recurs in moral and critical aesthetics. For instance, Rousseau in his criticism of theatrical identification (which is his imitation of Plato performed in his "Letter to M. d'Alembert") – and theatre is also a kind of *mimesis* – comes to the conclusion that the better the comedy is, the worse it is: "it follows from the principle that the more attractive and perfect the comedy is, the more its effects are disastrous for *les mœurs*."[6]

The prime example is the first hero of the *Iliad*: Achilles. I have already mentioned the denounced example of his disillusioned view of the relation between gods and humans; Socrates now condemns him generally for "two contradictory maladies, the greed that becomes no free man and at the same time overweening arrogance towards gods and men" (391C), citing his defiance against Apollo (*Iliad*, 22: 15) and Scamander (*Iliad*, 21: 130) as striking evidence. Quite as bad is Achilles' appearance in the *Odyssey*, where he famously and bitterly complains of his fate for Odysseus visiting Hades: "I would rather

6   J.-J. Rousseau, *Lettre à M. d'Alembert* (Geneva, 1948 [1758]), p. 45: "le plaisir même du comique étant fondé sur un vice de cœur humain, c'est une suite de ce principe que plus la comédie est agréable et parfaite, plus son effet est funeste aux mœurs."

follow the plow as thrall to another / man, one with no land allotted him and not much to live in, / than be a king over all the perished dead" (*Odyssey*, 11: 489–91, tr. Lattimore). Or, that he, as a still living hero, is hesitating, capricious, and – after the death of Patroclos – even upset, crying, sleepless (*Iliad*, 24: 10). Among many later examples of similar indignation one recalls Hegel's reaction to Kleist's *Prinz von Homburg*: Hegel wanted his tragic heroes clear cut, on the principle that "Cato can live only as a roman and republican"[7] – that is, an irresolute Cato would no longer be Cato – and was therefore furious about Kleist's rebellious, hesitating, death-fearing hero, who, to cap it all, walked in his sleep![8]

I will come back in some detail in this chapter to Plato's discussion of Homer and Homer's first hero, Achilles; Socrates has used these examples in *Republic* to show the topic and subject-matter (*logoi*) of tales, and he proceeds (392C) to form and diction (*lexis*). This procedure gives the literary discussion an element of reflection that transforms the argument into theory. One of Socrates' exemplary listeners complains about not understanding the distinction between the *logos* and *lexeos* – the *what* and the *how* – of tales, and thereby gives Socrates the epoch-making opportunity of taking the first steps into literary theory as a kind of "narratology."[9] Socrates shows in what way *mimesis* is not only image and/or representation, but also a way of representing. The definition is simple: it means presenting the story in a mimetic way (*dia mimeseos*), i.e. using the voice of someone else in direct speech, rather than using your own voice in direct or indirect speech, something Socrates calls "pure" or "simple" *diegesis* (392D, 394B). His example is again taken from the *Iliad*, this time the very beginning, where Homer tells us how Chryses pleads for his daughter to the affronted Agamemnon, with Homer quickly passing into that dramatized form of narration that Socrates calls mimetic. According to Socrates, Homer narrates "as if he were himself Chryses and tries as far as may be to make us feel that not Homer is the speaker, but the priest, an old man. And in this manner he has carried on nearly

---

7 G. W. F. Hegel, *Vorlesungen über die Ästhetik*, Werke 13 (Frankfurt-on-Main, 1970), p. 98: "Cato kann nur als Römer und Republikaner leben."

8 *Hegel in Berlin* (Berlin, 1981), pp. 72–79.

9 Plato was a "narratologist" long before the term was coined, since the term came into use only with French fiction analysis of structuralist inspiration in the 1960s. A short history can be found in Gérard Genette, *Nouveau discours du récit* (Paris: Seuil, 1983), pp. 10–15.

all the rest of his narration" — "this manner" meaning the imperso-
nating or mimetic or dramatized manner of narrating (393B). In order
to be even more pedagogically explicit, Socrates then narrates the
same episode "diegetically": he retells the story without direct speech
from the characters. Socrates thereby corrects and improves not only
Homer, but also, indirectly, Plato himself, who, after all, presents his
investigation of *mimesis*, including the criticism of *mimesis*, in the very
manner that he has Socrates define and criticize as mimetic.

Towards the end of Aristotle's *Poetics* we read a tribute to Homer.
Aristotle praises him for not talking excessively in his own voice, but,
"after a few words by way of preface, immediately brings on stage a
man or a woman or some other character."[10] This sounds to me more
or less like direct polemics against the part of *Republic* I have just
quoted, where Homer is blamed for the very same manner and with an
example similar to the one that he is praised for by Aristotle. Polemics
or not,[11] it is still remarkable that the two gate-posts on the road
leading into Western thinking (including its literary theory) both turn
to the same text and to the same phenomenon in this text; and that
they carry opposing views on Homeric narration, thereby opening for
a stubborn opposition in versions of *mimesis*. Modern criticism of the
art of narration, starting with Henry James, has joined the Aristotelian
camp and favored dramatized narration compared with the renarrating
Plato called pure *diégesis*. Under headings like *showing* vs. *telling*, the
Platonic distinction and Platonic–Aristotelian opposition became —
in Gérard Genette's words — "the Ormazd and the Ahriman of
novelistic aesthetics in the Anglo-American normative vulgate."[12]
And, if modern narratology has thereby turned Plato's overt
evaluation upside down in order to follow Aristotle, it has in the same
maneuver turned Platonic practice — i.e. the Platonic dialogue — into
Aristotelian analysis. Plato allows himself to criticize *mimesis* in
mimetic dialogue. This paradoxical manner and attitude indicates that
we are far from finished with Plato's evaluation of *mimesis* after having
followed Socrates' evaluations in *Republic* — and it is still an open

---

10 I use Gerald F. Else's annotated translation (*Aristotle's Poetics. The Argument*
    [Cambridge, Mass.: Harvard University Press, 1957]) and will give details in the
    text in accordance with established pagination. Here it is 24: 60a10–11.

11 It is a thesis in Gerald F. Else's *Plato and Aristotle on Poetry* (Chapel Hill, NC, 1986)
    that Aristotle created his *Poetics* in opposition to Plato's in *Republic*, and that Plato
    in his final version considered some Aristotelian views.

12 Gérard Genette, *Narrative Discourse* (Cornell University Press, 1980), p. 163.

question whether Plato or Aristotle hold narration in the highest regard; and which kind of narration that Plato values highest.

Plato's *mimesis* is, in my reading, a movable concept, and every effort to make it reasonably unambiguous would be a betrayal of that floating ambiguity. The various translations that have been offered during the long history of the concept give some clues to its possibilities, including its scenic and visual connotations, which seem constant in words like "imitation," "mirroring," "representation," or the German versions *Nachahmung* and *Darstellung*. When Plato has Socrates develop the distinction *mimesis/diegesis* in the third book of *Republic* he is also developing these visual connotations rather than restricting the term to a technical or syntactical concern with the use of direct speech; "Plato is not making such heavy weather over a grammatical distinction," as Gerald F. Else has put it.[13] And the obvious reason is the building-up of the argument that results, in the third book (398A), in the first rejection of the poets, in its turn a prelude to the general condemnation of *mimesis* in the tenth book.

On the way to the first rejection we find some curiosities. Socrates asks himself and us how much mimetic narration (in contrast to "pure" *diegesis*) could be advisable in the education of the "guardians" who are supposed to govern his ideal city: "Do we wish our guardians to be good imitators [*mimetikous*] or not?" (394E). It is easily divined that Socrates does not want any "imitators" at all in his city, but his first reason is puzzling: the guardians, who are supposed to be able to cope with anything, will still be led astray if tempted into mimetic behavior. Not even a clever "imitator" can "practice well at once even the two forms of imitation that appear most nearly akin, as the writing of tragedy and comedy" (395A).

His devoted listeners should have asked why not then. At least Plato's reader could have asked if Socrates' statement on the impossibility of combining skill in both tragedy and comedy is consistent with Socrates' statement at the end of another dialogue, *Symposium*, "that the same man could have the knowledge required for writing comedy and tragedy – that the fully skilled tragedian could be a comedian as well" (223D). The two statements are apparently not consistent, at least not as *logoi*, or statements of truth. Perhaps better as *lexis*? That is, if we go into the manner, the *how* and the way of stating of those statements – which is the very possibility

---

13 Else, *Plato and Aristotle*, p. 25.

that Plato himself opened up for us when he had Socrates make the distinction between *logos* and *lexis* in *Republic*. I will later try to use this possibility of rhetorical reflection on these passages, but can already air my suspicion that a Platonic thought can be derived from Socrates' inconsistent statements: namely, a discreet defense of Plato's own mimetic practice – the philosophical dialogue – which is apparently neither comedy nor tragedy, but another form of drama with ingredients from both.

Some more curiosities. Mimetic behavior should be avoided in education, according to Socrates, because it could easily become a habit: "Or have you not observed that imitations, if continued from youth far into life, settle down into habits and second nature in the body, the speech and the thought?" (395D). Well, Plato should know; but he should also know that the examples that he then has Socrates give to illustrate the vices of addicted imitators have little to do with drama or narration and nothing to do with Homer. Socrates indignantly counts up those things that should not be imitated, but that are still included in mimetic skill: slaves, women, horses(!), bulls(!), sheep(!), "claps of thunder and the noise of wind"(!) etc. (396AB, 397A). The better, the worse: the better the imitator, the worse the narrator, Socrates seems to mean – confronting technical skill with moral ability. "Pure" diegetical narration maintains morality, while the mimetically clever narrator is tempted into – and tempts to – the morally reprehensible; and "the more debased he is the less will he shrink from imitating anything and everything" (397A). The purely diegetical narrator is thus allowed to stay in the city while the mimetic is rejected.

Who is the target of this first rejection? We remember that Socrates' argument starts with Homer, and it ends in an imitator who shows little if any resemblance to the exalted singer, but seems closer to a *mimos*, a buffoon and a juggler with a liking for imitating animals and weather disturbances. The singer of songs seems to include a buffoon in disguise. Or the singer has two parts, a diegetical and a mimetical, and the mimetic half is rejected – with marks of respect, according to Socrates: if such a buffoon (or singer in disguise) dares to approach the ideal city, "we should fall down and worship him as a holy and wondrous and delightful creature, but should say to him that there is no man of that kind among us in the city ... and we should send him away to another city, after pouring myrrh down over his head and crowning him with fillets of wool" (398A).

Only the greasy pole is missing when Socrates rejects the imitator; meaning that his ironic celebration seems ominously like those popular rituals that we associate with king-for-a-day or other kinds of scapegoats before they are physically humiliated and thrown out or lynched. And we should not forget — Plato did not — that Homer is to be imagined as the humiliated and as the rejected! Plato has Socrates remind us of that when he comes back to the question in the tenth book and the second rejection. There the argument is resumed and reservations left aside. There we learn, as already mentioned, that poetry starts with Homer (600E), who is therefore the "leader" of tragedy (598D), and that the poets, no matter what or how they write, "are all altogether *mimetikous*" (602B). That infectious drug called *mimesis* has contaminated its environment, and no pure and diegetical narration and no knowledge and no idea were good enough as an antidote.

Vision

Poetical *mimesis* is dismissed as "juggling play", but still refuted and disputed as seriously as a matter of life and death. The reason for this is obviously that Plato's *mimesis is* a matter of life and death: behind the rejection of mimetic poetry we glimpse something I would like to call — anachronistically and preliminary — a loss of self; or rather: the fear of/longing for a loss of self. We remember that Socrates imagined Homer as the arch-imitator at the very moment that he was imitating the words of someone else, talking like someone else, becoming another. The imitator is from that moment doomed to be someone else or something other than his self. But this Self is in the same procedure doomed to seek its self in someone else, and searching can be done only mimetically, by imitation.

Plato's third rejection of the poets leads us straight into these paradoxes, but also away from those poetological — ideological trenches he was digging in *Republic*. The third rejection comes rather discreetly in the dialogue that is assumed to be his last, *Laws*, and is there articulated by the "Athenian stranger" in conversation with a man from Crete and a man from Lacedaemon, all in a pleasant setting on Crete. Socrates does not appear in this dialogue, where the topic, again, is the ideal state, now situated on Crete and populated with 5,040 happily chosen people — the number is due to its easy divisibility by most numbers, which makes this city ideally handy to administer.

The demand for poetry is slight in the divisible city, but poetry still comes up as a topic in the seventh book, where the "Athenian stranger" is suddenly struck by the thought that the discussions so far "were framed exactly like a poem" (811C). The city he has built – in his head – has imitated ideal life. It is in this sense a poetical construction on an elevated note and is therefore made as a "*mimesis* of the fairest and truest life, which is in reality, as we assert, the truest tragedy" (817B). If a poet approaches this ideal city with a tragedy in his hand he will be met with the observation that he is superfluous: those living there are already tragedians and poets in the best-constructed of all possible works of art.

This may be the first instance in the long and not always pleasant history of analogy between politics and aesthetics. Plato admits the analogy for elevated poetry. When it comes to the contemptible activity that in *Republic* was associated with mimetic buffoons and jugglers it is without political interest: "we will impose such mimicry on slaves and foreign hirelings and no serious attention shall ever be paid to it" (816E). *Mimesis* is apparently rejectable when comically imitating and superfluous when in tragic or elevated style. At the same time, *mimesis* seems like a pillar of knowledge and of the building of society: the philosophical and political program of the "Athenian stranger" has appeared as literature, i.e. as a version of a *mimesis* that has grown from the poetics of *Republic* into some kind of anthropology – nevertheless to be rejected, as long as it is literary!

But it is a rejection close to the highest recognition. And there are other similar passages in Plato's text, where mimetic activity – the transformation into someone else, the duplication – is vaguely observable as a fundamental mechanism of knowledge and reality. Furthermore, the Platonic dialogue, as I have already insisted, is a form of dramatized mimetic representation, all according to Socratic definitions of *mimesis*. The philosophical dialogue is the very form that Plato invents to make himself into someone else. I will come back later to some examples of *mimesis* as Plato's own writing practice, but will first mention some passages where *mimesis* can be glimpsed as a positive concept or an unavoidable principle for knowing.

First *Cratylos*, where Socrates speculates with company, without any particular linguistic restraint, on the nature of language and naming. Socrates cannot make himself accept what no mimetic theory or practice can easily accept: the conventional character of language and the arbitrariness of signs in relation to reference. Instead, says

Socrates, we must postulate a "natural" relation between the linguistic sign and the signified referent: the name belongs to the thing "by nature" (390E). This "nature" Socrates describes in terms of similarity; i.e. the linguistic sign shows its nature by being similar to – imitating – its referent. Socrates calls the name and the word "a vocal imitation of that which is imitated, and he who imitates with his voice names that which he imitates" (423B). Should there be any doubt about the mimetic character of language, Socrates uses four inflections of *mimesis* in this quotation and adds, furthermore, that the "name-maker" is the one who knows how to "imitate the essential nature of each thing by means of letters and syllables" (423E). (One wonders what natural essence is being imitated by the word *mimesis*.)

Yet there is some doubt about the possibility that language might carry some arbitrariness. The doubt comes partly from those amazing etymological fantasies that Socrates presents as proof of his idea of the mimetic character of language; and partly from the partner in dialogue, Cratylos himself, who evidently provokes Socrates into his ideas by resistance. The resistance consists in Cratylos' combination of an essentialistic view of the relation between names and things with a Heraclitean adherence to the movement of being – and this cannot be accepted by Socrates. At this point in the dialogue we can notice a connection in the dialogue with the philosophical problem that was already classical in Plato's time: change and movement. And in this connection we can glimpse a possibility of *mimesis* as time and movement. I will come back to that relation under a different heading – *repetition* – in my fourth chapter; here the relation is still negative, since Socrates comes up with his mimetic-linguistic speculations in contrast to the philosophy of movement that we, today, would associate with, for instance, linguistic conventionalism.

In the great dialogue on creation, *Timaeus*, Plato has the title character discuss the mimetic relations between image, imitation and time with a young and listening Socrates. And then not only does narration appear as mimetic, as in *Republic*, and not only politics, as in *Laws*, and not only language, as in *Cratylos*, but *mimesis* becomes nothing less than the formula for the creation of the world and the very form of the world. Timaeus states that the world we live in has been created in the greatest similarity to the creator himself (29E–30D). The metaphors used in this philosophical tale on creation are remarkably visual, as often with Plato, and give the impression of the first creator as a kind of pictorial artist. They could perhaps be compared with another famous visual vision: the passage on the cave in the seventh book of *Republic*, where philosophical education is likened to the capacity of the eye to endure light with its culmination in the possibility of looking into the sun; i.e. to see the non-visual being. In that passage Socrates also calls "the faculty of vision" an "imitation" of philosophical-dialectical procedure (532A); we could just as well say that Plato's idea of philosophy is based on sight, or at least has a visual orientation. And that orientation has to combine with the privileges accorded to speech and dialogue as forms of knowledge and communication. The wavering significations of Plato's *mimesis* illustrate this struggle between the faculties of vision and voice; the threefold rejection of the poets can be translated into a claim for the primacy of speech and a kind of ban directed against image. But contagious *mimesis* is not easily banned and has, in *Timaeus*, become the conquering principle. "Seeing has," as pointed out by Gerald F. Else,[14] "won out over talking, thinking, and arguing." Or, to use a thought from J.-P. Vernant, and remembering that "seeing" is connected with image and imagery and that the Platonic image is neither nothing (unreal) nor something (real), Plato's *theoria* is "the elaboration of the category of the image in Western thinking."[15]

When Timaeus states that creation was made in accordance with the principle of similarity he quickly runs into the logical problems of time. The origin that is imitated by our reality is supposedly constant and eternal, while the image, i.e. our world, is apparently a changing "flux" in the hands of time. Unfortunately, says Timaeus, it was not possible for the creator to make the image/world eternal and constant; still, he adds, the world carries traces of its constant origin as a "moving image of eternity" (37D), and what we call time is nothing but an image (*eikona*) of eternity (37D). Timaeus asks us to watch the stars: their eternal repetition of the same circuit he regards as the visual proof that "this very world must be as similar as possible to the absolute being that can be grasped by the mind and imitating its eternal nature" (39DE).

These lines are remarkable because they are the only ones, to my knowledge, where Plato discusses time-change-movement in relation to *mimesis*. *Mimesis* here becomes *repetition*. And that transformation develops into a standard in all future investigations of *mimesis* up to the latest *mimesis*-philosopher of some standing that I have come

---

14 Ibid., p. 61.   15 Vernant, "Naissance d'images," p. 120.

across, Paul Ricœur, who wants us to understand *mimesis* as a temporal concept according to the principle that "time becomes human time to the extent that it is organized after the manner of a narrative; narrative, in turn, is meaningful to the extent that it portrays the features of temporal experience."[16] One notices that, on its way to Ricœur, the Platonic conception as articulated in *Timaeus* has been turned upside down: the mimetic narration is, for Ricœur, an image of movement and change, or of "temporal experience," while Plato in *Timaeus* defines time as imitating eternity. Both have, however, the visual metaphor of imitation in common: Timaeus talks of the "similarity" between creation and origin, Ricœur of narration "portraying" time (with the reservation that "portray" is not an ideal translation of the *dessine les traits* of the original, but at least preserves the visual connotations).

Quite another way of developing the relevance and meaning of temporality out of Platonic *mimesis* is demonstrated by Martin Heidegger in *Sein und Zeit* ("Being and Time"), section 81, where the passage just quoted from *Timaeus* is used to illustrate a paradoxical version of time: the *now* of time as "entstehend-vergehende Jetztfolge," as a sequence (coming-going) that is dotted with, or interrupted by, moments of *now*.[17] This is Heidegger's way of opening a discussion of time in terms of turning, returning and repetition – his word is "Wiederholung" – and this will be recurrent also in this presentation. I will come back to Heidegger's *Wiederholung* in the last chapter. Here I will proceed to some examples of Plato's repetitive practice in some dialogues and his criticism of Homer; not just the results of Homeric *mimesis*, but also Homeric *mimesis* as a version of repetition (and in that connection I will come back to Ricœur). Here I only want to stress that a sort of temporalized and repetitive *mimesis* actually had its first hesitant introduction with Timaeus' famous definition of time, especially with his example (39D) of the stars that return repeatedly, a phenomenon in time where movement seems to coincide with an eternal return or repetition.

Plato rejected the poets in a kind of incantation of that "loss-of-self" that seems like a necessary part of the experience of imaginary doubling, the becoming another. Thus I speculated above on the

---

16 Paul Ricœur, *Time and Narrative*, tr. K. McLaughlin and D. Pellauer (Chicago University Press, 1984), vol. 1, p. 3.

17 Martin Heidegger, *Sein und Zeit* (Tübingen: Niemeyer, 1986 [1926]), p. 423.

(perhaps loose) basis of, among other things, the unexpected, unmotivated and fierce attack that Plato has Socrates direct against the juggling imitator (in *Republic*). We could also note a reminiscence of that in *Laws*, where the "Athenian stranger" scornfully rejected low and comic *mimesis*, which was ideally performed only by "slaves and foreign hirelings" (816E), i.e. by those who have no "selves" to lose. The juggler was treated with serious scorn by Plato, and the paradoxical reason seems to be the connection with *mimesis*, that contagious imaginary fantasy that always wins over the philosophical word simply because of priority. Image comes first in Plato's world, in the same way that ideal, form and being precede the phenomenal world. Platonic dialectics is a struggle against this priority, a hopeless struggle since the philosophical word, which goes in search of the ideal, meets the ideal only as an image of the ideal. *Mimesis* is, in spite of the threefold rejection, always present in the Platonic world as image and imagination.

The phenomenal world is also the world of movement, time and change; imaginary mimetic activity is unavoidably connected with repetition and, therefore, time. Plato opposes time in the sense that time for him is connected with the loss of self that, in its turn, is called death — both when he rejects mimetic activity from the ideal city and when (in *Timaeus*) he exalts *mimesis* as the very form and principle of creation. Plato's struggle against time is a hopeless project: he is in that sense not far from those Homeric heroes he makes Socrates criticize in *Republic*. The epic hero always tries to conquer death, and his real enemy is therefore called Chronos. And, as Zeus already knew when he managed to dethrone father Chronos to make himself the Olympian regent, cunning counts just as much as courage in this struggle. Time cannot be conquered, but time can be manipulated. Plato's cunning version of this manipulative trick is to create a form for narration that is not recognized as narration: the philosophical dialogue. It is a form that recreates and repeats past time in the narrative present; a mimetic construction so cleverly made that it even allows for the criticism of *mimesis*.

Dialogue

Timeless immortality, we learn from Plato, is also the aim of love. That is if love could be elevated from everyday coincidences, change and decay, yes from all that belongs to bodily life — be free to seek the good. Platonic love is, after all, a search for the good. It follows then, necessarily according to Plato, that love also seeks immortality. Such is after all the conclusion of that famous dialogue on love, *Symposium*: we must "yearn for immortality no less than for good, since love loves good to be one's own for ever. And hence it necessarily follows that love is of immortality" (207A).

Such is Plato's well-known *logos*. But what about its *lexis*? What about the *how* and the manner and the way in which we learn this *logos*? How do we reach the conclusion, who concludes and for whom? Those are, after all, the elementary questions in all that "narratology" that can be derived from Plato's *mimesis*: who is talking? who is seeing? and for whom? When Plato instituted "narratology" by having Socrates put questions of this kind in the third book of *Republic* it was from the observation that Homer had the characters of the *Iliad* talk in their "own" voices, and that narrative *mimesis* could be defined as giving voice to the other: as the capacity of the poet to talk like another. Modern narratology could be defined as the science that explores the distinction between the *what* and the *how* of narrative text, including those cracks and joints that the distinction inevitably displays. In these joints we find voice and eye and time: voice and eye, since the narrating voice and view must always reach us indirectly, characterized in the narration and by way of the characters of the narration; time, since the story has, or presupposes, a time that has to be told and plotted. Every mimetic strategy built on similarity – and that goes for Plato's *mimesis* – must handle the task of making the voice and the eye of the narrator similar to the voice and eye characterized in the story, and the time-telling compatible with the time told.

Plato's strategy is his philosophical dialogue. There he gives voice to Socrates and his partners of discussion. The relation between narrator and character, between Plato and Socrates, is difficult to judge when it comes to *logos*: interpreters have difficulty distinguishing between the voice of Plato and that of Socrates. It is easier when it comes to manner: Plato's way of telling comes *dia mimeseos*, according to the definition he had Socrates make up in order to condemn it in the third book of *Republic*. Plato gives himself the voice of another and of others. The conclusion just quoted from *Symposium* on the relation of love-the-good-immortality is voiced not by Plato but by Socrates; i.e. Plato has – mimetically – Socrates voice the conclusion.

But still not. Socrates is himself giving voice and direct speech to the woman who once taught him the logic of love: a certain Diotima. That is done as a dialogue within the dialogue, and this enclosed or framed dialogue – enclosing the quoted conclusion of the whole dialogue – starts in "pure" *diegesis* if we see it from the eye of Socrates (*dia mimeseos* seen from Plato). In other words, Socrates re-presents the story of his meeting with Diotima according to the recipe he uses in the third book of *Republic* (that Plato has him use) to improve Homer (see above). Not for long, though. Plato has Socrates of *Symposium* saying – in the face of better knowledge? or as a slip-of-the tongue? but whose tongue? – that *mimesis* comes in handier than *diegesis* when it comes to telling a story: "The readiest way, I think, will be to give my description that form of question and answer which the stranger woman used for hers that day" (201E). Thus, Socrates continues to give his story *dia mimeseos*, thereby situating his long-past meeting with Diotima in the present, in the *now* of the Platonic dialogue. The conclusion in this dialogue on the logic of love is pronounced by Diotima, i.e. Socrates has Diotima pronounce the conclusion framed in his narration, which is framed within Plato's narration.

When Plato encloses the philosophical conclusion of the dialogue in a temporally distanced, but mimetically represented, dialogue it underscores, I believe, a temporal tension. The conclusion associates love with the no-time of immortality. But this conclusion can be pronounced only with a temporal distancing that makes relative in *lexis* what was supposed to be absolute in *logos*. For the framing and time-distancing activity of mimetic narration does not end with Plato having Socrates voice his meanings, and Socrates in his turn having Diotima voice his (or Plato's) meanings. The outer frame (Agathon's feast) framing the inner (the Diotima dialogue) is also framed. The whole dialogue or narration – the text – is told *dia mimeseos* by one Apollodorus, who in his turn has the story re-presented (we do not know how) by a certain Aristodemus, who took part in the feast, which Apollodorus did not – all according to Plato. Meaning that the conclusion pronounced by the woman Diotima – on love and immortality – passes four men on its way to us: Socrates, Aristodemus, Apollodorus and Plato; and that two framed stories enclose her conclusion – the story of Apollodorus meeting a friend who wants to hear all about the feast; and the story of the feast. (There are bare outlines of other stories involving Socrates and Diotima; Socrates and Alcibiades; and perhaps is there a hint also of another story about Aristodemus, who, according to Apollodorus, was silent at the feast but outspoken afterwards – it is said to be his story, after all, that Apollodorus re-presents.)

The junctions or joints between the different levels of the story – the whole story, or the text – are marked in ways that seem like reservations undermining the credibility of parts, but perhaps making up for a sort of textual irony. I have already quoted how Socrates starts (i.e. how Plato has Socrates start) re-presenting his dialogue with Diotima by promising to use "that form of question and answer which the stranger woman used for hers that day" (201E), but ends by denying this, telling us that he had only been summing up what he had learnt from her "at various times" (207A). Socrates' great speech, including the summarized dialogue with Diotima, starts with Apollodorus reminding us of his existence (i.e. Plato has Apollodorus remind us) by informing his friend and us that Socrates started "something like this" (199C). Thus, the solemn conclusion of love and immortality, the very *logos* of the dialogue, is "something like" and therefore only approximate. If Apollodorus remembers correctly. And if, before him, Aristodemus remembered correctly. Plato cannot help reminding his readers of such subversive possibilities, as when the series of speeches in praise of love is started by Apollodorus remembering (i.e. Plato has Apollodorus remembering) that "the entire speech in each case was beyond Aristodemus' recollection, and so too the whole of what he told me is beyond mine" (178A). Apollodorus promises, however, that we will get a selection of what he values as the "most memorable" (178A).

But can we trust the choice and judgment of this Apollodorus? Well, Plato cannot resist making us suspicious. At the very beginning of the whole dialogue (the text) we are told that Apollodorus is a *manikos* – which translates as "crazy" or "fanatic" – which should warn us and put us on guard against what he says (which is the whole story); in case we believe in the characterization. But that is not obvious; it happens to be pronounced by his unknown friend and listener. About him we get to know (from Apollodorus) that he keeps to "wealthy, money-bag friends" (173C) more than to philosophers, and that could hardly be a sign of reliability in the world of Socrates and Plato.

All these discreetly ironic reminders of the different levels and possibilities of the text, and of the tensions between the story told and the telling of the story, also remind us of the displacements in time between the levels that contribute to the condensation of time within each level. A rhythm is created in this text that is something else entirely than the sequential beginning-middle-end that was soon to be recommended by Aristotle (in his *Poetics*) as the normal curve for an action (*praxis*) that the story told should imitate. The displacements in time rather introduce a kind of *staccato* shift between distance and proximity. The relations of the different levels – as framed stories within the story – also develop according to the principle of repetition: Diotima is repeated by Socrates who is repeated by Aristodemus (outside the text) who is repeated by Apollodorus. And both maneuvers of time – *staccato* and repetition – get their efficient prelude at the very start of the whole dialogue, where Apollodorus announces that he has learned the story he is about to tell "by heart" (172A; it could also be understood as Apollodorus having "rehearsed" – i.e. repeated – the text). The reason is that he has already told it for another friend, Glaucon, who had the most confused views of when the famous feast actually took place. He thought it took place the other day – i.e. in *near* time – although the host, Agathon, won his tragedy prize many years ago, "when you and I were only children" (173A) – i.e. in a time so *distant* that it is already mythical. So the story that Apollodorus has "rehearsed" – under the direction of Plato – will make the distant present for the unknown friend and for us. And this presence is the dialogue *Symposium*.

This text ends not with Socrates' speech enclosing the conclusion pronounced by Diotima on the essence of love, but with the uninvited and already drunk Alcibiades bursting in and making his own speech in honour of Socrates. First Alcibiades seems to be as ironic about Socrates as Plato is narratologically about the whole drinking-party; we learn (i.e. Plato has Apollodorus remember that Aristodemus remembered that Alcibiades said) that Socrates is by no means to be trusted (214D) since he "spends his whole life in chaffing and making game of his fellow-men" (216E), i.e. acting an *eiron*. This introduction, however, develops into a rightly famous eulogy to the unique Socrates: "you would not come anywhere near finding a comparison if you searched either among men of your day or among those of the past" (221D). The feast dissolves in general drunkenness. Plato has Apollodorus remember that Aristodemus remembered that he fell asleep but woke up again and heard Socrates still arguing with Agathon and Aristophanes. Narrative reservations are underscored: "As to most of the talk, Aristodemus had no recollection, for he had missed the beginning and was also rather drowsy; but the substance of it was, he said, that Socrates was driving them to the admission that the same man could have the knowledge required for writing comedy and tragedy — that the fully skilled tragedian could be a comedian as well" (223D).

What is actually the "substance" in this ironically presented final part of our story? The *logos* of it seems to stand, as mentioned earlier, in conspicuous opposition to the *logos* of the very same Socrates, in *Republic*, stating that no one can possibly be as good "in the two forms of imitation that appear most nearly akin, as the writing of tragedy and comedy" (395A). There are other ingredients in *Symposium*, especially towards the end, that seem playfully to oppose the poetics and aesthetics of *Republic*. Take Alcibiades. His intervention in the feast has a charm that seems to be bound up with his impudence. But the same impudence means that he is far from being the elevated and exemplary character who, according to Socrates in *Republic*, could perhaps be worth mimetic effort; rather he reminds us of the "fretful and complicated type of character" (605A) who is again condemned as unsuitable for imitation. What we know about Alcibiades from history underscores his being unsuitable for narrative representation (according to Socrates in *Republic*): at the time of the feast he was best known as a man about town, but at the time of the text — and Plato may have written it perhaps 30 years after its historic situation — he was infamous as a traitor.

It is hardly possible to harmonize these contradictions on any philosophical level, since what Socrates announces in *Republic* excludes what he is saying in *Symposium*. The only alternative to regarding Plato (and/or Socrates) as a poor or inconsistent thinker seems to be to follow the advice of Stanley Rosen, mentioned earlier, and to try to make sense of Plato by way of irony and drama: take him as a poet. That should not mean that demands for consistency are less important when it comes to poetical text than to the philosophical text. But demands are in another dimension: they have to do with the *how* of the text — its *lexis* — quite as much as with its *what*, its *logos*. Our demands on Plato's *mimesis* should take into account his mimetic practice rather than (or just as much as) his different views on the concept *mimesis*.

The narrative logic I have sketched in the dialogue *Symposium* — i.e. Plato's mimetic practice — may perhaps be called an ironic narration characterized by reservations, shifts, displacements, repetitions *in tempo staccato*. The ironic reservations are concentrated in the framework of the stories that are framed within the text and each other: Apollodorus and his unknown friend; Agathon's drinking-party; Socrates and Diotima. It is a narration marked by ironic distance when it comes to the shifting of voices and views, meaning also that it shifts between distance and proximity in time and displays an abundance of tendencies to repetition in the relation between diegetic levels: Plato re-presents what Apollodorus already has re-presented according to Aristodemus' re-presentations of Socrates' speech, which re-presented what Diotima finally and originally said.

Mimesis is, as Plato had Socrates reminding us in *Republic*, a drug (*pharmakon*) that is not always easy to handle. In *Symposium* Plato uses this glorious "drug" almost intoxicatingly, which must be regarded as mimetically reasonable in a story about a drinking-party. It is different in *Republic*, and this is perhaps as it should be in a political-pedagogical tract about the proper organization of the city. The sobriety practiced in *Republic* means no imaginary ban, but simply that Plato allows Socrates to speak for himself without using enclosed stories or intermediate, complicating and ironizing voices.

Maybe this difference in narrative logic between *Republic* and *Symposium* is the simple reason for having Socrates, in *Republic*, condemn the mixture of styles that he, as a final point, appeals to in *Symposium*? Whatever the reason, we have a movable feast in *Symposium*, a very mixed party with complicated characters – starting with the "crazy" Apollodorus and ending with drunken Alcibiades and, in between, the most complicated and framed of them all, Diotima, who is something as Platonically unlikely as a woman *and* a sage; not to mention the *eiron* Socrates and that all-pervading god of this narration, the most complicated and unreliable of them all: Eros. *Mimesis*, in Platonic practice, here means mixture to the point of confusion. No wonder that Plato ends his story by having Aristo-demus (in a mixed state) remembering (and Apollodorus remembering that Aristodemus remembered) that Socrates argued for a mixture of high tragedy and low comedy. He argued in the presence of the exclusive tragedian Agathon and the exclusive comedian Aristo-phanes. Socrates argues for the proper dispensing of the narrative drug: its calculated mixture in Platonic dialogue.

Socrates spent his life "chaffing and making games of his fellow-men" as Alcibiades puts it in his eulogy in *Symposium* (216E). And since then – or, rather, since Plato represented Socrates as *eiron* in dialogical action – his character and his "games" have fascinated, puzzled and irritated us who could not hear, but only read him. Kierkegaard raged over Socrates as the first ironic in his dissertation "On the Concept of Irony," only to become his follower in the mimetic play of similarities and pseudonyms. Heidegger, who was certainly far from ironic, could still praise Socrates as "the purest thinker of the West" and derive this exemplary "purity" from his primary philosophical virtue: "Deshalb hat er nichts geschrieben."[18]

This excellence – that Socrates had written nothing – can be conveyed to us only in writing. Heidegger therefore gets into paradoxes not unlike Kierkegaard's when he ironically tries to dissociate himself from ironic Socrates; as did Plato in his dialogues, which imitate oral dialogues in writing and mimetically dissociate themselves from *mimesis*; and as did Socrates, to judge from Plato's dialogues, since he had to use mimetic and sophistical means to criticize mimetics and sophists. Perhaps such paradoxes form the basis for what Heidegger called "Western thinking"; or perhaps this thinking consists of "conceptual monuments," in Jacques Derrida's words,[19] monumentalizing the floating shifts between phenomenal and linguistic similarities and differences. "Monument" would then imply something like a conceptual "tomb," stabilizing and fixing what in perception and creation is always on the move.

Mimesis is such a "monument." The concept occupies a monumental position in Western tradition while it accommodates – or hides? – an active, productive and highly movable paradox. When Plato in *Republic* has Socrates define the concept negatively while he (Plato) uses it positively, both monument and paradox are there, simultaneously – and oddly enough it is the famously ironic Socrates who heads for the monumental, while conservative Plato indulges in paradox. When *mimesis* in the same dialogue is associated with a drug – *pharmakon*, (e.g. 382c) – the concept itself has turned "floating," since its meaning includes its own opposite: healing as well as poisonous drug. The same pharmacological terminology is used by Plato in the dialogue *Phaedrus* in relation to his criticism of writing, and similar "floating" arguments are used by Socrates against sophists and rhetoricians in *Phaedrus*, and also in *Gorgias* and *Protagoras*.

---

18   Martin Heidegger, *Was heisst Denken?* (Tübingen: Niemeyer, 1954), p. 52.
19   Jacques Derrida, "La Pharmacie de Platon," in *La Dissémination* (Paris: Seuil, 1972), p. 122.

Jacques Derrida has once and for all – in his *Pharmacie de Platon* – analysed the connections between Plato's *pharmakon* and his mixed strategies in relation to writing, as they are developed towards the end of *Phaedrus*. The concept *pharmakon*, which is scarcely visible in *Phaedrus* – it is mentioned once at the beginning (230D) and twice in the final discussion on writing (274E, 275A) – indicates the conceptual effort involved in classifying writing (negatively) under the heading of memory/reminder, but also associates writing with arbitrariness and play: *paidia* (276B, 277E). *Pharmakon* comes out as an eminently "floating" concept – a "floating indetermination" in Derrida's words[20] – that, instead of determining the concept and idea of writing (negatively), opens it to a (positive) play of supplements, repetitions, displacements and differences: "The *pharmakon* is the movement, the locus, and the play (the production of) the difference. It is the *différence* of the difference."[21] (It should perhaps be added that Derrida's reading of *Phaedrus* has been strongly criticized, mainly for his apparent neglect of the *mania*, or divine imagination, that according to several critics – and I could mention two as different as Stanley Rosen[22] and Jesper Svenbro[23] – is the real centre of interest in *Phaedrus*. And, of course, Derrida himself comes back to the distinction between speech and writing and to Platonic "parricide" in an ironic and critical mood in *La carte postale*.)

There is no discussion of *mimesis* in *Phaedrus*, but the connection between *pharmakon* and writing is remarkably similar to the connection between *pharmakon* and *mimesis* in *Republic*. In *Phaedrus* we find another prominent concept in Platonic poetics that is absent in the sober but negative discussion in *Republic*, and that is madness or inspiration: *mania*. Plato allows Socrates two speeches on love: in the first he imitates a sophistic *mania* to promote an idea that he apparently does not believe in; and in the second (the so-called palinody) he is seized by a divinely inspired *mania* in order to reach his correct views on love, truth and memory. Moreover, the *mania* – in comparable fashion to a term like *enthousiasmos*, condescendingly

---

20 Ibid., p. 105.
21 Ibid., p. 146: "Le *pharmakon* est le mouvement, le lieu et le jeu (la production de) la différence. Il est la différence de la différence."
22 Stanley Rosen, "Platonic Reconstruction," in *Hermeneutics as Politics* (Oxford University Press, 1987).
23 Jesper Svenbro, *Phrasikleia. Anthropologie de la lecture en Grèce ancienne* (Paris, 1988).

treated in the dialogue *Ion* – is apparently a *pharmakon* that, correctly used, leads us to the loftiest truths, but in a bad dosage leads to reprehensible wrongs. Socrates' first speech is such a wrong: he is imitating a sophistic and therefore (in Platonic logic) reprehensible argument.

The two speeches stand in a kind of dialogic relation to each other, and they are framed by a witty dialogue between Socrates and Phaedrus, who has his youth and beauty mockingly admired by Socrates. We are, in other words, in quite another dramatic setting than in *Republic*, where Socrates is lecturing obedient listeners; or in the temporal and polyphonic frenzy of *Symposium*. *Phaedrus* invites us to an intimate drama, initiated by Socrates for once being tempted to leave town – he is tempted by the roll of script that he can glimpse under Phaedrus' cloak, which he calls a *pharmakon* (230D)! – for a pastoral setting for two, something that apparently inspires both speeches, the reprehensibly bad one as well as the divinely good one. We are on ground that is no longer safe: we are outside the normal situation for the dialogue, i.e. the *agora* and the city, and within a playful erotic game, close to inspiration and madness, but also close to parody and paradox (*para* signifying outside). As in *Symposium* we meet a narration with ironical distance, but distance this time has less to do with time and voice, than with view and perspective.

In both cases a kind of insecurity is produced, and in *Phaedrus* it is, for instance, more or less impossible to tell how the final dispute on writing is meant to be taken: like a new madness, divine or not, or quite seriously? And, if seriously, how do you take a repudiation of writing that is made in writing? In a text that imitates speech according to the recipe that Plato has Socrates condemn in *Republic*? If we listen carefully towards the end of the dialogue, we can perhaps – with Gerald F. Else – "detect Plato admitting to us, with a discreet smile, that his writing of dialogues is a form of play."[24] Perhaps – and anyway play (*paidia*) is one of the contagious words of the dialogue. And if we see this final part in relation to the displacements of perspective that the whole dialogue invites from the moment that Socrates is tempted to leave the city by way of Phaedrus' script, then it is difficult to avoid the impression that those final and confident statements from Socrates on writing are ironically situated in a text

24 Else, *Plato and Aristotle*, p. 58.

that does not allow any confidence at all, but invites advanced "play" with paradoxes.

The theme of the "play" is the soul, love, the truth and memory. The "play" becomes most serious – and most paradoxical – when Socrates, in his second speech, imagines the soul on the wings of love approaching the very highest and innermost essence of truth, which he calls *ousia* (247C). Plato, who consistently uses visual metaphors to imagine the adventures of the soul, proclaims an imaginary ban on this *ousia*. It cannot be seen, since it is blindingly dazzling and can be approached only *epistemis* (247D), i.e. intellectually. The soul can, after the super-sensual meeting, only remember, or be reminded of, *ousia*. And we are not surprised to learn that the philosopher is the one who is supposed to remember best, while the poet, using *mimesis*, comes only sixth in the hierarchy of memory that Socrates comes up with (248DE).

In *Republic*, as we remember, the poet was three steps away from truth. Those have now become six. In *Laws*, the poetically beautiful creation was equated with the politically righteous. And in *Timaeus*, creation itself appeared mimetic and the world an image. In *Phaedrus*, it is writing that is called image – *eidolon* (276A) – and is finally criticized as an unreliable *pharmakon*, more suitable for reminders than useful as memory. It should not be possible to extract a unified meaning or construct a stable Platonic conceptual monument out of these incompatible assertions – which has not stopped readers who cannot stand the paradoxical ambiguity from creating "Platonism." If there is no real consistency at the conceptual level, it is on the other hand to be found at the dialogical level of Platonic narration; here we find consistently a visual imagination, meaning that creation, poetry and writing are considered in terms of imagery. Plato created his dialogues *dia mimeseos*, and he seems to think of his concepts as images. And in *Phaedrus* the mimetic paradox receives its most brutal formulation, when he imagines the source and the origin, *ousia*, only to declare it inaccessible to the eye.

In *Symposium* I wanted to find the voice: who is actually speaking? In *Phaedrus* I have concentrated on the view of the eye. But Platonic dialogue does not establish any stable use of these unavoidable tools of narration, nor do the Socratic conceptual exercises result in any "Platonism." The Platonic dialogues have the habit of putting the reader in the dubious position in which Socrates puts himself after having argued with Thrasymachos in the first book of *Republic*: "for

me the present outcome of the discussion is that I know nothing"
(354C). That could hardly be called a monumental position. But if it
has anything to do with immortality, which the loving soul wants
according to *Phaedrus* and *Symposium*, it is because it invites a
discussion that never ends.

Homeric Repetition

Plato rejected the poets.

And primarily Homer, who in *Republic* is called both the leader of
the tragedians (598D) and the first poet (600E), and who is the one to
furnish Socrates with all his examples of condemnable tales and
dubious narration.

This use of Homer as an example in Plato's criticism of *mimesis* is
not surprising: Homer was for long so dominant among Greek poets
that his name was more or less synonymous with "poet." All these
examples, especially from the *Iliad*, are not surprising either: the *Iliad*
seems to have functioned as a national epic long before Greece could
be called anything like a "nation." It may be surprising that Plato, who
can sometimes appear as conservatively authoritarian, attacked the
monumental Homer with such frenzy, but part of the answer is
probably to be found in the very divided strategies and loyalties
characterizing Plato's *mimesis* as sketched above. We will now try to
get a little closer to these divisions by looking into some of the critical
examples that Plato has Socrates develop.

As already mentioned, Socrates first deals with the topics of the
tales, or their *logoi*, then their *lexis*, or manners of telling. This is done
in the second and third books of *Republic* as a basis for the summary
judgment that is pronounced first in the third book and then – with
emphasis – in the tenth. *Mimesis* has to do with both aspects: the
matter and the manner of the narration. Homer is criticized for
portraying gods and heroes as less divine or less heroic than they are
or should be, according to Plato/Socrates, *and* for his dramatized
narration: *dia mimeseos*. The first example of bad subject-matter is
taken from the last song of the *Iliad*: Achilles talking to Priam
(especially 24: 527–32). The first (and actually the only) example of a
bad manner is taken from the first song of the *Iliad*, more specifically
its transition from what Plato/Socrates calls "pure" representative
diegesis to direct speech *dia mimeseos* (392D).

There is a correspondence, often commented upon, between beginning and end in the *Iliad*. Plato, or so it seems to me, presupposes such a correspondence and, therefore, indirectly comments upon it; i.e. Plato does not develop or comment on any connections, but as the very first example of Homeric *mimesis* he chooses the two passages of the great text that not only exemplify versions of *mimesis*, but also have a sort of mimetic relation to each other. This mimetic relation, which we may call *repetition*, is the version of *mimesis* that Plato never comments upon but, instead, uses in his writing; and that all narrative text uses in degrees and versions (Plato's own versions I exemplified above in my reading of *Symposium*).

The Homeric version of narrative repetition could, in this case, be characterized as a mirroring or circular structure: the last song of the *Iliad* (or parts of it) is symmetrically inverted to the first. That can be nicely shown with the help of the two examples given by Plato/Socrates. When Achilles makes his speech in the last song, it is to give a positive answer to King Priam, who has come with the ransom for his dead son Hector. In the first song it is the priest Chryses who makes a speech in order to ransom his still living, but captured, daughter. The negative answer to Chryses is famously pronounced by Agamemnon, which means then that Agamemnon is "repeated" by Achilles, Chryses by Priam, the captured girl by the dead hero and — above all — the negative answer by the positive. Repetition repeats what has been, but turns it into something else: repetition re-presents and overcomes its origin.

Platonic criticism of this crucial passage of the *Iliad* is directed against the subject-matter as represented by the gods. When Achilles gives his speech, he tries to encourage old Priam and tell him that his son Hector will be given back to him. He starts with some observations on the gods that Plato makes Socrates quote (slightly inaccurately according to our versions of the *Iliad*) as an example of an unusually stupid Homeric "error" (379D). The complete quotation goes:

> This is the portion to piteous mortals assign'd
> By the careless Gods, to live in trouble and pain.
> For two urns stand on the floor in the palace of Zeus,
> Stor'd with the gifts he allots, both evil and good;
> For one man Zeus the Thunderer mingles his gifts,
> And he for his fortune has good, but evil as well;

> To another he metes but the evil and makes him a scorn
> Hounded by ravening hunger o'er bounteous earth,
> A waif unhonour'd of Gods and mortals alike.[25]

What, actually, is the outrageous "error" committed by Homer in these lines — according to Plato/Socrates? It appears in the context of *Republic* to be the vaguely fatalistic tone and the naming of Zeus as the one bringing man as much evil as good. Gods should, in the pedagogical frame of *Republic*, bring only good. Could the "error" also have to do with the function of this passage as a repetition? Let us remember that this speech also means the pacifying of Achilles' disastrous wrath, the very topic of the *Iliad*, the reconciliation between Achilles and Priam and the temporary armistice between Greeks and Trojans — while a couple of lines later (24: 540–41) Achilles forebodes his own death, soon to come; and thereby repeats and overcomes — overcomes by repeating — not only the choleric speech of Agamemnon in the first song, but also his own remarkable speech in the ninth song (9: 308–429).

There the situation is again similar to the situation of the last song as mentioned above: Achilles in his tent receives a call for his mercy, this time from a delegation of Greeks headed by Odysseus, who with gifts and good words tries to persuade Achilles to go back to fighting. Achilles' answer is a categorical no: he would rather go home. Death is his argument, and death seems like a mightier argument than honour:

> Fighters and stay-at-home men have an equal reward
> And for brave and coward alike one honour there is
> Since the only guerdon for doer and laggard is death.[26]

It almost appears as if Achilles here is about to decline his position as hero — line 319, at least, should not be said by any hero. Experts have furthermore suggested that the lines quoted deviate from normal Homeric syntax, meaning that Achilles is, so to speak, about to break out of heroic language.[27]

Plato/Socrates does not use this passage at all, although it could have provided a nice example of Homeric "error," so I have reason to

---

25 Homer's *Iliad*, tr. S. O. Andrew and M. J. Oakley (New York: Everyman's Library, 1963), 24: 525–33.　　26 Ibid., 9: 318–20.
27 Cf. Seth Schein, *The Mortal Hero. An Introduction to Homer's Iliad* (California University Press, 1984), pp. 91ff.

mention it only as a basis for repetitive elements in the twenty-fourth song. And to these elements belongs the topography of the two scenes: as the only ones in the *Iliad*, they take place neither on the battlefield before the walls of Troy, nor in the more "homely" setting within; instead they are situated in the tent, with the sea on one side and Troy on the other. The tent is neither house nor field, and in these two scenes the Homeric hero rests from being a hero and the war from being a war. Furthermore there is neither day nor night: they take place in the dusk and are finished by nightfall.[28]

Such are some possibilities of repetition in the twenty-fourth song of the *Iliad*. Achilles' speech — Homer's "error" according to Plato/ Socrates — initiates a repetition repeating the neither-nor of the ninth song and overcoming the antagonistic either-or of the first song. In the same movement, those "careless" gods are discreetly dethroned, and the mortals allowed to fill the scene. The famous lines I have quoted from Achilles mark the decisive step and establish the final difference: gods are immortal and can therefore take what comes with an Olympian laugh; whereas the lot of mortal man is always to "live in trouble and pain" (24: 526). With this stress on a common human cause, Achilles repeats his effort of the ninth song to break with heroism, and this time with success in the sense that his wrath is pacified and the song of the hero — the epos — can have its end. After his speech Achilles shares a meal with Priam — and no sacrifice to the gods is mentioned — culminating in full reconciliation when the Trojan patriarch admiringly seems to regard the murderer of his many sons as a new son:

> But when they had sated desire of meat and of drink,
> Dardanian Priam long at Achilles gaz'd
> Admiring his stature and beauty and aspect divine,
> And long did Achilles wonder at Dardanus' son
> Studying his kinglike mien and hearing him speak.[29]

The gaze of man — with no divine interference — is the culmination of repetition as the very moment of overcoming and of reconciliation.

Plato/Socrates points to this Homeric version of repetition with the examples given. But the phenomenon of repetition is never openly discussed, while *mimesis* is ambiguously condemned. The *mimesis* that is condemned seems to be a question of image and imitation — another

28 Cf. Michael Lynn-George, *Epos: Word, Narrative and the Iliad* (London, 1988), pp. 9–24.   29 Homer's *Iliad* 24: 628–32.

version, as it were, to the displacement in time that is the presupposition to be overcome in the movement of repetition. Plato's own mimetic practice, on the other hand, is highly, although unpredictably, repetitive and, as we have seen, his philosophical dialogues give ample scope for human voice and gaze. His own writing position in relation to Socrates – the voice – also seems repetitive in both the imitative and the overcoming sense; perhaps also as a repetition of the father–son relation that we saw idealized in the last quotation from the *Iliad*.

Is there any way of making all this clear-cut and unambiguous? Is there any formula that could capture and make sense of Platonic *mimesis*? Plato's readers have always been eager to extract one "Platonistic" voice from all the voices of the dialogues – an effort that I would think is doomed to failure. But they are necessary failures: the reader always has to try to find explanatory formulas or levels within or without Plato's text in order not to get lost in his paradoxes. Some of the efforts that are most interesting for my purposes relate to conflicting oppositions: such as the opposition between the poet (Homer) and the philosopher (Plato) – and remember that this opposition was called "an old quarrel" by Plato himself at the end of *Republic* (607B) – or between the spoken word (Socrates) and the written (Plato), or between oral culture (Homer; Socrates) and the culture of writing (Plato). Is perhaps the attack on Homeric *mimesis* that Plato has Socrates advance a part of the attack by the new written culture against the old oral culture?

Such is the argument powerfully stated by Eric A. Havelock in a series of books and primarily his *Preface to Plato*. His background is the understanding inherited from Milman Parry of Homeric poetry as an oral performance based on a repertory of formulas, set phrases and prestructured elements, a way of handling and understanding language that is generalized by Havelock as an "oral" or "Homeric state of mind."[30] Platonic criticism of Homeric *mimesis* is regarded by Havelock as an attempt to exorcize this traditional and traditionalistic "state of mind," and to promote the Platonically dialectical or philosophical mode, which Havelock associates with writing and calls analytical. In other words, Havelock constructs a meta-level that makes it possible to explain Plato's argument historically, dissolve at

30 Eric A. Havelock, *Preface to Plato* (Cambridge, Mass.: Harvard University Press, 1963), p. 41; and heading of ch. 8.

least some of his ambiguities and sort them out on either side of the threshold of civilization created by the invention of writing. He also opens the way for interesting observations on both Homeric and Platonic text, as when he argues that repetition is typical of Homeric poetry and therefore antagonistic to Platonic writing – which could explain Platonic criticism of repetition in the *Iliad* as sketched above.

If, of course, that was the same kind of repetition. But Havelock does not seem to aim at the overcoming kind of repetition that I pointed out. Havelock means something entirely different by repetition: the oral poet's active, but submissive, identification with traditional repertory and the formulaic poetry demonstrating this tradition. My example gave another picture: the Achilles character in Homer's version even seems critical of traditions of heroic behavior, and Homer also seems to stress mortality and human community considerably more than the epic tradition invited him to do. Furthermore, this Homeric version of an overcoming repetition has to do with structure and narrative logic, rather than with the formulaic repertory we associate with oral poetry. That the end of the *Iliad* repeats the beginning, including an element from the middle (or the ninth song), could by no means be explained by the definition of "formula" that Havelock presupposes and that was established by Milman Parry: "a group of words which is regularly employed under the same material conditions to express a given essential idea."[31] It might even seem as if Homer had already given a full example of the *two forms of repetition*, the one repetitive and the other renewing, that J. Hillis Miller (after Nietzsche and Deleuze) establishes as basic to the modern narrative tradition.[32]

I have neither the qualifications nor any reason to discuss the whole way of thinking that goes into Havelock's argument; I am primarily interested in Plato's *mimesis* and Platonic criticism of Homeric *mimesis*. And I have to conclude that separating Plato as the champion of writing and Homer as "oral" seems to miss the point (or one of the points) of Homeric repetition – missing the repetition that was, after all, the very starting-point for Platonic criticism of Homer. It could even look as if Plato/Socrates was criticizing not Homeric tra-

31 Milman Parry, *The Making of Homeric Verse* (Oxford University Press, 1971), p. 272.
32 J. Hillis Miller, *Fiction and Repetition* (Oxford: Blackwell, 1982), ch. 1 ("Two Forms of Repetition").

ditionalism, but, on the contrary, the overcoming of tradition indicated by the Homeric repetition as sketched above. At the same time, it is also difficult fully to accept this criticism, if one takes into consideration Plato's own repetitive practice. The suspicion is unavoidably that Plato has Socrates say something other than he – Plato – means. And, since this suspicion can never be transformed into some positive conviction – the text keeps both possibilities open – we have to confine ourselves to adding repetition to *mimesis*, and to writing in that poison cupboard of Platonic poetics: as a *pharmakon*, drug and antidote within an unruly concept.

The risk you take with thinking of Plato in terms of oppositions – such as orality/writing – is to become a Platonist. Which Plato is not. If you think of Plato as the promoter of written culture and of Homer as oral, thus arriving – with Parry – at the conclusion that "the one part of literature is oral, the other written,"[33] then you run into difficulties when it comes to explaining and understanding what seems to be common to all kinds of literature: such as repetition. Language is always a system of formulas and repetitive patterns, no literary text can avoid using these basic linguistic characteristics, and literature, in orally dominated cultures as well as in cultures dominated by writing, plays with "formulas."

If you think of Plato as a promoter of writing, there will also be difficulties in explaining the attack on writing in *Phaedrus* (although this may well be ironical). Lastly you risk idealizing oral culture as being of lost origin and a golden age. Such an idealization I would call Platonic, however much it attacks Platonic criticism of Homer.

Idealizing seems like a permanent threat to Homer's readers. In a book exploring the concept of *mimesis* I should mention one of the very best: Erich Auerbach. The first chapter of his *Mimesis* of 1946 develops an opposition between two forms of mimetic representation (*Darstellung*) of reality. The examples are Homer (taken from the *Odyssey*) and the tale from the Old Testament about Abraham and Isaac (Genesis 22). The Homeric narration is pure foreground, according to Auerbach; nothing is left undescribed or unexplained, and events occur in a simple progression in full syntactical control. The biblical narration, on the other hand, is distinguished by the unspoken, and is complicated and full of obscure background, demanding hermeneutical efforts. The beautiful observations that Auerbach is able

---

33 Parry, *Homeric Verse*, p. 377.

to make in his two examples cannot stop him from developing a binary opposition between two types of *mimesis*, which actually means that he is using an idealistic — "Platonistic" — pattern of thinking and reading. My sketch above of Homeric repetition should be enough to show that Homer too presupposes a more or less obscure background (cf. the sea-the tent-the city in my example), develops complicated characters (Achilles) and uses several versions of repetition in his narration; not to mention the fact that he calls for interpretation.

Auerbach fits well into a very German tradition. Schiller is actually mentioned in the Homer analysis and Auerbach's opposition Homer/ Bible is, in fact, a kind of repetition of Schiller's famous opposition between "naive" (pre-modern) and "sentimental" (modern) *Dichtung* — and this opposition is in turn a repetition of many efforts to separate the old from the new, the oral from the written, the epos from the novel. Such ways of thinking in oppositions could perhaps be called dialectical, and dialectics was the very "Platonism" recommended by Plato when it came to thinking. When Eric Havelock derives Platonic thinking from written culture and opposes it to oral culture, represented by Homer, he is therefore committing a "Platonism" that is structurally not unlike the one developed by Erich Auerbach as an opposition between "naive" Homer and the more or less sentimental, or at least more modern, biblical narrator. This way of thinking in oppositions is actually derived from Platonic dialectics, although Plato himself used his poetical pharmaceutics — *mimesis*, repetition, *mania*, dialogical writing — in a more playful and unpredictable way than his Platonistic followers.

Aristotelian Order

Plato the poet rejected the poets.

With Aristotle there had already appeared a philosophical literary critic who welcomed the poets. Like Plato he held Homer to be the first and greatest of poets, and I have already given an example above of how, in his *Poetics*, he praises in Homer precisely what was the starting-point for Platonic criticism in *Republic*, i.e. the dramatized narration *dia mimeseos*. As with Plato, *mimesis* is a key term in Aristotle's *Poetics* — his "master concept" according to Gerald F. Else[34]

---

34 Else, *Aristotle's Poetics*, p. 12.

— but Aristotle not only changes the Platonic evaluation of *mimesis*, he also changes the meaning of the concept, until it "ends up meaning almost the exact opposite of what Plato had meant by it," again in the words of Else.[35]

Above all, Aristotle tried to stabilize what in Plato was, as we saw, unruly, paradoxical, ambiguous. He was successful in the sense that Aristotelian *mimesis* has dominated the history of aesthetics, albeit that Platonic paradoxes seem to arise in different repetitions and disguises. Modern narratology and poetics of the novel have been thoroughly Aristotelian, and Platonic reminiscences have here been marginal. Like most critics of modern times, Aristotle is no poet rejecting poets. On the contrary, he is a philosopher welcoming the poets into his philosophical system.

It is primarily with the concepts *mythos* and *praxis* that Aristotle gives *mimesis* a new function. In the sixth chapter of his *Poetics*, the tragic drama — the highest form of art for Aristotle — is defined as an "imitation of an action" (*mimesis praxeos*; 49b24). And a bit further on in the same chapter we learn that it is the *mythos* or the "plot which is the imitation of the action" (*praxeos ho mythos he mimesis*; 50a4). The terms *mythos* and *praxis* seem very close; they even seem like "imitations" of each other. *Mythos* is the "structure of events" that Aristotle, still in the sixth chapter, calls "the soul of the tragic art" (50a38/39). Nor is *praxis* just any event or action or phenomenon; *praxis* is rather *one* event that is "serious, complete (*teleia*) and has bulk" (49b25). And in the seventh chapter we get the famous definition of *praxis* as an action "which is complete and a whole and has a certain magnitude" — which, more precisely, is a "whole" because it has "beginning, middle, and end" (50b24–27). Slightly further on in the same chapter Aristotle underscores how close *mythos* is to *praxis* by comparing both to a living body, an organically functioning whole (50b34–51a6).

This compact summary of Aristotle's compact argument should already have revealed at least three points of interest for my discussion:

(1) Aristotle's *mimesis* is defined by *mythos* and *praxis*, which brings the concept close to areas of time and action — in contrast to Platonic *mimesis*, which is closer to image, imagination and imitation.

---

35 Else, *Plato and Aristotle*, p. 74.

(2)   *Mythos* is a concept of order, which makes it possible to view literary works as structured wholes.

(3)   *Praxis* refers to already structured events or chains of events, which can be perceived as meaningful and answering a purpose.

In my commentary on these points I shall concentrate on the way in which Platonic *mimesis* is given a new function by Aristotelian *mythos* and *praxis*, and whether or not this would mean that conceptual order is established in poetics, Platonic *mimesis* being, so to speak, detoxicated.

Several commentators have emphasized that Aristotelian *mimesis* is creative and productive in comparison with the Platonic version, which is profiled as purely imitative and representative. Gerald F. Else insists that Aristotle defines art as *mimesis* and the artist as creator, thus *mimesis* is creative. The "poet is an 'imitator' in virtue of being a maker"[36] – and, again, "A poet ... is an imitator in so far as he is a maker ... Copying is after the fact; Aristotle's *mimesis* creates the fact."[37] Paul Ricœur, reading Aristotle in his *Temps et récit*, wants us to understand *mimesis* as the very activity that tears time and reality as they are experienced – "lived temporal experience"[38] – out of joint and transports them into fiction; Aristotelian *mimesis* "is the emblem of the shift [*décrochage*] that ... produces the 'literariness' of the literary work."[39] He therefore stresses Aristotelian *mimesis* as active and creative and presupposes a decisive difference from Platonic *mimesis*, which is understood as passive and imitative. Ricœur does not translate the Aristotelian constellation *mimesis* – *praxis* – *mythos* as "imitation" or as "representation," but as "emplotment" (*la mise en intrigue*): the creation of plot as the *mythos* of action.

Again, as in my discussion of Homeric repetition, we seem to have reached "two forms of repetition," with Platonic *mimesis* now playing the passive part, while the Aristotelian is active. Apparently Aristotle gives a dynamic character to *mimesis* by introducing a temporal element, which was suspiciously absent in Plato – just compare his paradoxical definition in *Timaeus*, quoted above, of time as an image of eternity (*Timaeus*, 37D). Aristotle more precisely "temporalizes" *mimesis* by imagining *mythos-praxis* as a whole structured in a sequence of beginning-middle-end, and by imagining the poetical work as an

---

36   Ibid., p. 106.   37   Else, *Aristotle's Poetics*, p. 322.
38   Paul Ricœur, *Time and Narrative*, vol. 1, p. 31; the original has "l'expérience temporelle vive."   39   Ibid., p. 45.

after that always has a *before*. This *before* is the *praxis* of action. Perhaps this *praxis* also has a *before*, since *praxis* consists of already organized events.

Before and after. The poetical work imitates or re-presents what comes prior in time, but it also has its consequence in the imitating reactions of the reader or spectator. Plato worries, as we remember, about the moral effects of poetry, while Aristotle sticks to psychology and returns repeatedly to the shuddering terror (*phobos*) and pity (*eleos*) that the tragedy is creating within the spectator, who therefore repeats or imitates what has already taken place on the stage. And that, in its turn, repeats or imitates what has already taken place as action.

The spectator repeats. It is not difficult to understand what he is repeating. The work of poetry that he watches or reads also repeats; but it is not so evident what it is that the work repeats. This belongs to the standard disputes in aesthetics – what is actually imitated in aesthetical imitation? – and the answers have varied from time to time between, for example, "ideals," "tradition," "nature," "reality." During the couple of hundred years preceding the Romantic revolution in particular, there were intense discussions on the nature of imitation and the nature of what was imitated. An important thinker on aesthetic *mimesis* in the eighteenth century, Johann Joachim Winckelmann, was in no doubt about the answer and he already indicates it in the title of an important work: "Thoughts on the Imitation of the Greek Works in Painting and Sculpture."[40] What it all came down to, according to Winckelmann, was to imitate (*nachahmen*) the old *works*. He argued against the most obvious alternative in his time – "nature" – with this beautiful example:

Nothing would more clearly show the advantages of imitating the old masters compared with imitating nature than taking two youngsters of comparable talent and have one of them study antiquity, the other pure nature. The latter would picture nature as he finds it: as an Italian he would perhaps paint figures like Caravaggio; as Dutch, if he was lucky, like Jacob Jordans; as French like Stella. But the former would picture nature according to its demands and paint figures like Raphael.[41]

40 Johann Joachim Winckelmann, *Gedanken über die Nachahmung der griechischen Werke in der Malerei und Bildhauerkunst. Kunsttheoretische Schriften* 1 (Strasbourg 1962).

41 Ibid., Introduction: "Nichts würde den Vorzug der Nachahmung der Alten vor der Nachahmung der Natur deutlicher zeigen können, als wenn man zwei junge Leute nähme von gleich schönem Talente, und den einen das Altertum, die

The art of imitation, we can observe with the help of Winckelmann, should stick to the "old masters," i.e. "antiquity," i.e. the works of art of Greek antiquity, since this model or pre-text is unprecedented – comes first and has nothing before itself – not only in art, but also in nature; only by seeing nature through classical patterns can we see it "according to its demands." Coming *after* may be the unavoidable condition for the artist: there is always both art and nature before art. Correctly understood and used, however, the coming-after is a privilege – or so I understand Winckelmann; it is the only proper way leading to "nature." Coming-after is neither a triviality nor an embarrassing destiny; rather it is the chance the artist gets to become a real artist, yes, to become a real human being, to assert himself (or, his self). Winckelmann's ingenious defence of imitation actually undermines a classical *mimesis* and paves the way for the works of Moritz and Kant, which initiate German Romanticism by transforming *mimesis* into imagination (*Einbildungskraft*).

My little detour into this early modernity has been made in order to substantiate some possibilities of the Aristotelian "temporalization" of *mimesis*. In the Aristotelian tradition, art and the poet emerge *after*, for example, "nature," "reality," "work," since the poet imitates action (*mimesis praxeos*, 49b24), but this *after* is also a privileged route to self-assertion and to the reality of *praxis*. Since I anachronistically associated Plato's *mimesis* with loss-of-self above, it is time, now, to complete the picture just as anachronistically: I associate Aristotle's *mimesis* with self-assertion, something that could easily be combined with the view just mentioned of Aristotelian *mimesis* as active and creative. The term "self-assertion" is intended not as a psychological observation, but as a small attempt to approach the phenomenology of the mimetic tradition initiated by Aristotle and characterized by a temporal element – before/after – where what comes necessarily after (the work of art) is granted a creative dimension. Aristotle made the poet into a "second maker," with the same stress on both words, to use an expression that should not be used until eighteenth-century aesthetics. The artistic "self-assertion" is an aesthetics of

---

andern die bloße Natur studieren liesse. Dieser würde die natur bilden, wie er sie findet: als ein Italiener würde er Figuren malen vielleicht wie Caravaggio; als ein Niederländer, wenn er glücklich ist, wie Jacob Jordans; als ein Franzos, wie Stella; jener aber würde die Natur bilden, wie sie es verlanget, und Figuren malen, wie Raphael."

production, but has some psychological dimensions. The Aristotelian shudder – *phobos* – is the spectator's route to himself or his self.

Plato's *mimesis* is creative too. Plato's *mimesis* can, as we remember from *Timaeus*, create a world, an imaginary world of images. But Plato's *mimesis* is also threatening: what is, after all, an Aristotelian thrill compared with the blindness that strikes the Platonic soul at its very moment of insight? Plato's *mimesis* is creative only at the expense of the creator.

Aristotle hardly thought, like Winckelmann long after him, that a work of art was the thing to imitate in a poetical *mythos*. But what kind of action – *praxis* – did he actually consider as the starting-point for the poetical *mythos*? What came *before*? Commentators seem to agree on the observation that both *mythos* and *praxis* are concepts of order; Ricœur even states that it is "the very principle of *order* that is the root of the idea of plot."[42] And Aristotle stressed, as we remember, that *praxis* is a teleological whole organized as a sequence with beginning-middle-end. It is, in other words, a question of not just any action or actions, but a chain of events that gives the impression of purposeful necessity without coincidences, chance or temporal gaps. Aristotelian *praxis*, therefore, already seems to have a narrative structure before it was narratively recycled by *mythos*. *Praxis* is, in any case, not easy to distinguish from *mythos*. Yet the difference between *mythos* and *praxis* is the very condition of narration: they relate to each other exactly like the before/after that is the Aristotelian model for creation.

The difficulty of differentiating the concepts – like their fertility – is well shown by modern narratology, which has been strongly influenced by Aristotle's proto-structuralistic view of narrative action as a purposeful whole. The coupling of *praxis/mythos* has been modernized into, for example, story/plot, *fabula/sjuzet*, *histoire/récit*, while our old *mimesis* has been swapped and diversified into a vast, confusing and complicated nomenclature describing all sorts of relations between the *before* and *after* that is presupposed by all these coupled concepts. An effort has also been made to construct a third "level" of narration called "narrative discourse" (Genette), which does not have any counterparts in Aristotle, but has a precursor in the Platonic distinction in *Republic* between the *what* and the *how* of narration.

There seems, however, to be no agreement in the conceptual

42 Ricœur, *Time and Narrative*, vol. 2, p. 7.

repertoire of the still young discipline of narratology: even the most basic terms vary from author to author, which indicates, in my view, that the basic distinction, going back to Aristotle's *praxis/mythos*, is precarious. It is as if the analysts of narration have not quite been able to decide if the *mythos* of narration refers to (or "represents" or "imitates" or "mirrors" or narrates "about") a non-narrative or not-yet-narrativized "reality" — or if, perhaps, this reality could be regarded as a projected double of narrative *mythos*. The latter alternative would, better than the first, explain the confusing terminological variety within narratology as well as the tendency among the critics to make a fresh terminological start whenever confronted with an innovating narration (which, in principle, happens every time you read a narrative text). But, if *praxis* were a projection or product of *mythos*, it would make an unendurable mess out of the order of before/after that was the temporal core of the distinction. That order invites the other alternative: with *praxis* being that which narration narrates; or: *praxis* as the not-yet-narrativized "reality" preceding the second creation of mimetic *mythos*.

The precarious balance that I have been suggesting in the distinction *praxis/mythos* is developed into full philosophical scale by Paul Ricœur in his three-volume *Temps et récit* of the 1980s. Aristotle's *mimesis* — in contrast to Plato's — is used by Ricœur, with equal relevance for the worlds of phenomena and signs, as a kind of ecumenical concept uniting the phenomenology of time, narration and hermeneutics. Ricœur insists that the *mythos* of the narration has both a *before* and an *after*. What comes *before* is suggested with terms like "lived experience" (in contrast to "historical time, and fictional time");[43] "the prenarrative quality of experience" in situations that express "a genuine demand for narrative";[44] or his standard phrase, noted above, "lived temporal experience" ("l'expérience temporelle vive").

What comes *after* the *mythos* of mimetic narration belongs to the field of hermeneutical "application" and is made real, again, in the case of written narration, by being read: "It is by way of reading that literature returns to life, that is, to the practical and affective field of existence."[45] Reading is, however, no aim in itself, and leads ideally not *into* narration, but *out* of narration and into something that Ricœur suggests by terms like "refiguration" and "reorientation": "In fact, it is what comes after reading that determines whether or not the stasis

---

43 Ibid., vol. 2, p. 5.   44 Ibid., vol. 1, p. 74.   45 Ibid., vol. 3, p. 101.

of disorientation [Ricœur's term for the state of reading] has generated a dynamics of reorientation."[46]

"Experience," "life," "practical existence" – all that comes both before narration as "pre-narrative" and after and outside narration as "practical existence" – are, however, not a chaos of phenomena and perceptions. In passages such as those quoted above, Ricœur may suggest that all that comes before and after, etc. is a state of pure experience and is therefore pre- or even un-linguistic. But he *also* insists that this field of experience or existence, derived from Aristotelian *praxis*, is *already* organized as a symbolic field: "If, in fact, human action can be narrated, it is because it is always already articulated by signs, rules, and norms."[47] *Praxis* was, in other words, "already organized in the manner of a narrative," to use Ricœur's set phrase, meaning that there was, after all, no outside to narration or nothing outside of symbolic text; what Ricœur calls "pre-narrative" experience is "always already" narrated. And yet his whole effort of developing *mimesis* from poetics into hermeneutics is based on the condition of a pre-symbolic *before* and a post-symbolic *after* to any text.

This was to show that Ricœur develops the difficulties involved in the Aristotelian distinction *praxis/mythos* into what seems to be a logical difficulty, even a regular contradiction. His high evaluation of the Aristotelian *mimesis* of narrative art is framed by a more urgent need to get away from art (and from narration, text and language) into that almost mystical state suggested by *praxis*.

But is this conflict in Ricœur's argument an inevitable consequence of tensions already to be found in Aristotle? A consequence of his effort to bring temporal order into poetical *mimesis*?

Perhaps it is. I would, however, be prepared to call it a productive tension: it expands and suspends the law of similarity that is involved in *mimesis* to the very limit that – once crossed – opens into the kingdom of difference. In Plato this threat to the law of similarity was to be found in paradox and vision; and when Aristotle tried to create temporal order out of the paradoxes of Platonic poetics he did so with Time. And then he hit upon the most differentiating of all categories, the one that was transforming – and was "always already" transforming – *mimesis* into *repetition*.

46 Ibid., vol. 3, p. 170.
47 Ibid., vol. 1, p. 57; the original has "symboliquement mediatisée" italicized.

2

Cervantes' "Imitación"

Naming

Cervantes' great novel came out in two parts, in 1605 and 1616. It lacks a title page naming it, for example, a "novel" and thereby telling us to read it like a "novel" – the name and the genre of the "novel" were not yet invented. Neither is it called a "romance of chivalry," in spite of referring constantly to this genre, which in Spain at that time was simply called *books* of knighthood ("libros de caballería"). Instead, the main character has become the title character and given the book his name – *Don Quijote* – thereby starting a long and far-reaching tradition of interchange between person and fiction. Up to our century, and formidably in the last, it was increasingly common to give a personal name or signature to the text of fiction known as "novel."

But still this book – the first book of its kind, when it comes to naming – is not called after the *real* name of its title character. The first thing we are told about Don Quijote in the first chapter of the "novel" is, after all, that he gives himself the name Don Quijote, but that *really*, i.e. in his normal or so to speak bourgeois reality, he has quite another name. And the narrator pretends not to be sure what it is: "They say that his surname was Quijada or Quesada."[1] This name will not turn up again until the very last chapter of the second part and then, again, handled by the title character, who discards his knightly name of fiction in order to recapture what, according to the very first chapter, he (hardly) was, now at last telling us his name: Alonso Quijano. This final shift of identity prepares for the real event of the very last

---

1 The chapters of *Don Quijote* are many and short, so the easiest way to keep in touch with the text is simply to cite the chapter when quoting. Here it is I: 1, i.e. the first chapter of the first book. I have used J. M. Cohen's translation in Penguin Classics, with several modifications that will be indicated by Spanish text.

51

chapter: he dies; i.e., Don Quijote discards his name and becomes Quijano (or whatever it was) in order to die.

My reading of *mimesis* as repetition and imitation in this text – book? novel? – will concentrate on the questions of naming and genre: the importance of naming for the quixotic project and Cervantes' knight-imitating hero as the hero of the genre that in both English and Spanish reads as "the new": *la novela*.

Project

Let me start with an ancient conception that crops up a couple of times in the first part of *Don Quijote* and can still be glimpsed in the second: the golden age ("la Edad de Oro").

The first time (I: 11) is when Don Quijote, together with Sancho, meets some friendly goatherds who invite them to share their meat, wine and nuts in a pastoral setting. Soon comes the time for the very first in a series of appearances of lovingly poetical shepherds, who spin out the time between the more burlesque adventures of the novel acted out by the self-styled knight. But first Don Quijote takes the opportunity of making a little speech, in which he praises those happy days called golden by the ancients: "a quien los antiguos pusieron nombre de dorados." The reason the golden age was so happy was its innocence, a state described with great eloquence. We can observe that the knight is especially interested in the innocence of wandering girls "without more clothes than were needed to cover modestly what modesty requires." His sympathy is easy to understand: free wandering is after all also the condition of the ideal life of the knight. But now, in this disgusting time of ours, the contemporary time called iron age in this topos ("la edad de hierro"), girls can no longer roam freely since they are under constant threat from erotic infection – the knight talks of "the plague of love [la amorosa pestilencia]." And he finishes by straining his argument considerably to reach the conclusion that "knights errant" are needed now too, in our age, namely to protect the girls who can no longer wander freely.

The second time the "golden age" comes up as a topic is in I: 20, this time in a more dramatic setting. Don Quijote is alone with Sancho in the dark of the night in an unknown spot and they hear frightening sounds. The knight is inspired by this nightly scenery to mount his Rocinante and make a stirring and martial speech – he talks to Sancho, but also past Sancho, into the darkness – starting by invoking the very golden age: "Sancho, my friend, you must know that, by the will of Heaven, I was born in this iron age of ours to revive the age of gold or, as it is generally called, the golden age."[2]

In the first case, among the goatherds, the knight-errant might have appeared as a passive reminiscence, a relic or a reminder or a last instance of a golden age. In the second case, in physical darkness, the term is used actively: the mission of the knight is nothing less than overcoming the symbolic darkness of his own iron age and *reviving* the golden age ("resucitar" meaning re-establish or raise from the dead). The immediate result of this heroic statement is less heroic: Sancho is not interested in any adventures in the dark, but manages to tie up Rocinante, without Don Quijote noticing, so the knight cannot plunge into any adventures of darkness at all. Not until dawn do they discover that the horrid sounds that the knight wanted to fight came from the "fulling-hammers" in a river. The episode is ambiguously concluded: Sancho laughs "violently" at the sight of the hammers and he laughingly repeats the knight's promise to "revive the golden age." But Don Quijote does not feel like laughing. He angrily gives Sancho a beating and, when Sancho defends himself by saying that he was only joking, the knight answers: "You may be joking, but I am not" (and the English cannot catch here that Don Quijote has changed his normally intimate "tu" into formal address).

The knight and his servant are acting their rôles: the knight acting adventurously, but stupidly, while the servant keeps him to realities. The imitative movements between the two are still inscribed in the inverted universe of parody. Sancho is "joking"; the knight is not. The knight takes his knighthood as well as his knightly project seriously: to re-establish a golden age. We can (with Sancho) easily laugh at his ridiculous adventures and his follies, but the knight himself is in deadly earnest. Slowly his gravity develops into melancholy – decisively from part II: 10, which is to be considered later – but he will keep on trying to "re-establish" what he then knows to be hopelessly lost: the golden age.

In the first example, showing the invocation of the golden age, we are still far from melancholy. The example deals, as already mentioned, with the innocence of the golden age, and Don Quijote's speech is an

---

2 "Sancho amigo, has de saber que yo nací, por querer del cielo, en esta nuestra edad de hierro, para resucitar en ella la de oro, o la dorada, como suele llamarse."

innocent imitation of a well-known classical theme, in literature regulated primarily by Virgil and Ovid (our knight is closest to Ovid's *Metamorphoses*, I: 89–151, although Ovid has no speculations on girls in light clothing). The comic effect of this example has nothing to do with the knight talking in "earnest," but simply with his talking above the heads of his listeners (but not his readers?); i.e. the comic effect comes from contrasts. In the second example of the heroic invocation of the golden age – to *re-establish* the golden age, raising it from the dead – the comic contrasts are sharper and the setting no longer idyllic. The ridiculous and laughable – yes, the quixotic – character of this project is immediately shown by the circumstances: the knight simply does not move from the spot and the project comes to naught, this time as every time. But his being earnest was, as mentioned, made obvious to Sancho.

Cervantes considered this golden-age revival as *the* quixotic project and therefore had to make his knight grave and earnest and Sancho his first laughing reader in order to produce the ridiculous and quixotic effect, i.e. the contrast between project and reality. This comes out everywhere in the "novel." Not only in the repeated failures of the knight's efforts or in the elaborately developed relation between Don Quijote and Sancho, with Sancho less and less laughing and, in the very last chapter, actually crying for his master; but also programmatically, as at the beginning of the second part (II: 1), where Don Quijote sits at home talking with his friends the priest and the barber. The talk is – as usual – about literature, or, more precisely, the books of chivalry. Don Quijote, who is for the moment normalized and domesticated (but remains "Don Quijote," i.e. knight-imitating), points out that he has no intention of giving up his project. He wants, or so it says, "nothing but to convince the world of its error in not reviving that most happy age [renovar en sí el felicísimo tiempo]" that was the real age of chivalry.

And he presently sets out on his third expedition.

It is apparently not enough for Don Quijote to wander around like a classical imitation or an enigmatic reminiscence from a distant or even fictitious golden age. Instead the idea is to catch up and to make it new: note that the verbs that Don Quijote are given to use when he talks in "earnest" about his golden-age project are *resucitar* (raise and revive) or (of the "happy" age) *renovar* (make new). In other words, the nub of the project is to transform fiction ("the golden age") into the here and now of reality ("the iron age").

Perhaps it can now be added that in his two invocations of the golden age, as summarized above, Don Quijote seems to be using those two versions of imitative *repetition* that I found as a conflict already in Plato's and Aristotle's handling of that repetitive, imitative and representative concept *mimesis* – all according to the analysis of chapter 1. This was a conflict between a visual-spatial order and a temporal order – and it is by developing temporality that Cervantes' *imitación* exceeds a classical *mimesis*. In later chapters I will show how temporality became a problem also for Rousseau and how *mimesis* is "modernized" into a concept for temporally renewing repetition with Kierkegaard's *gjentagelse* and Heidegger's *Wiederholung*. Here I have with some intention used the anachronistic "project" to suggest the "modernity" in the quixotic part of Don Quijote's ambitions: to wake up, re-establish, make new – to overcome time *within* time. The project is ridiculous, beyond reason and doomed to failure. But this failure of the knight makes way for the success of his author. It is in the failure – or, rather, in the combination of earnest intention, ridiculous "project" and necessary failure – that Cervantes with Don Quijote, the character and the book, still manages to create the very prototype of the new: *la novela*.

Witnesses

Cervantes' *Don Quijote* has had a remarkable aftermath. Nothing less than the "novel" itself can be seen as resulting from the quixotic project – "all prose fiction is a variation on the theme of *Don Quijote*," to use Lionel Trilling's words,[3] indicating that the imitative efforts of the knight have resulted in the more or less renovating imitations of his many servants. There are, furthermore, some moderns of genius who have developed the quixotic theme of a shift between old and new (not to mention the tensions between fiction and reality, text and body) with direct reference to or even help from our *Don Quijote*. I will here mention three such modern versions – by Miguel de Unamuno, Jorge Luis Borges and Paul Auster – called as witnesses to prove that Cervantes combines the problematic task of making new with imitation and repetition.

---

3 Lionel Trilling, "Manners, Morals, and the Novel," in *The Liberal Imagination* (New York: Doubleday, 1953), p. 209.

Miguel de Unamuno wrote several idiosyncratic commentaries on *Don Quijote*, wrote essays and an entire book on the subject, besides creating something like a new genre of philosophical fiction called *nivola*, a kind of inverted version of (the Spanish) *novela*. Here I will mention only his best-known commentary: "Life of Don Quijote and Sancho" of 1905.

This is the famous "novel" *Don Quijote* made new – or is it a remake? An innovating repetition or pure imitation? A novel, or a commentary, or what? Unamuno's method is to write the novel afresh from the start. The reason given for that odd assignment is that Cervantes did not quite understand what his novel was actually about (according to Unamuno, Cervantes is a typical example of an author inferior to his own work). Between Cervantes and his hero, or, rather, between *cervantismo* and *quijotismo*, there is a conflict as manifest as the conflict between reason and madness. Unamuno sides with madness: his often repeated aim is to defend the knight of madness against all "cervantists" of reason and to establish a good portion of poetical madness in his contemporary Spain. The aim is, to use Don Quijote's words on that happy and golden age, to re-establish ("resuscitar") and make new ("renovar").

Unamuno's program must be called an extreme version of the romantic interpretation a century earlier by Schlegel and Schelling, which made the Quijote-character into a personified idealist, with "ideal" in devastating conflict with reality, and little hope for reconciliation (or so the German Romantics have been understood – but more of them later in this chapter). In the case of Unamuno, this *quijotismo* has been mingled with Kierkegaard's existentialism as well as Nietzsche's *Lebensphilosophie* and surely some wild polemics against the Cervantes-philology of his day. In spite of (or because of) this background, Unamuno is able to express some remarkable insights into the quixotic "project" and its connections with the problems of imitation and time.

Unamuno's rewriting of *Don Quijote* transforms the original into a more intimate register, meaning that the burlesque adventures of the original have been modified or simply omitted in favor of a more elegiac, nostalgic and poetical attitude. Physical carnival has changed into discussion, and Sancho has turned philosopher. The quixotic imitation of chivalric books is replaced by Unamuno's dialogue with the knight himself; fights are replaced by polemics, often enough as furious as Don Quijote's attacks on imaginary enemies. Polemical targets are found among Unamuno's disgustingly "cervantistic" contemporaries, but the real enemy, Time, is greater than that.

The struggle for immortality, to reverse and annul time itself, is the very driving force of the quixotic project, according to Unamuno. The project is successful, he seems to imply: Quijote stays eternally the same – and dies only after having become someone else. The quixotic fiction, on the other hand, has not succeeded in transforming itself into historical reality; nothing like a golden age has been revived. On the contrary, today it is "your niece who governs", Unamuno exclaims in a bitter dialogue with Don Quijote; "it is your niece who governs your Spain; ... she who feared that you might turn to poetry, 'an incurable and catching disease'."[4] We remember that it was the niece – one of the two female members of Don Quijote's household – who was most eager to burn the books of the knight's library (i: 6), who introduces the idea that wizards are coming in his way and who has the audacity to say, before the third expedition and in front of her master, that "all you say about knights errant is fiction and lies" (ii: 6).

As an answer to this Don Quijote starts a long discussion in order to defend his project as the very road leading to what he wants to obtain: *immortalidad*. This is the cue for Unamuno. As being read and rewritten by Unamuno, Don Quijote shows the way.

Jorge Luis Borges dated his odd and often commented on short piece of text, or "story," or "fiction," *Pierre Menard, 1939*. It was created as a kind of eulogy for the diseased Menard, a minor poet in the symbolistic vein, it seems. First we get a list of his "visible" work, and one observes his interest in logical problems, for example, the classical problem of movement and who-comes-first: Achilles and the turtle. Furthermore, a fancy for creating literature on literature, like translating *Le cimetière marin* into alexandrines (when Valéry's point was not to use classical verse) or studying "metrical laws" in French prose. A remarkable lack of connection between subject, language and meaning: Menard is said to have written an "invective" proposing quite different views from those he actually held. In his "invisible"

4 Miguel de Unamuno, *Vida de Don Quijote y Sancho* (Madrid, 1966), p.222: "Es tu sobrina, Don Quijote, es tu sobrina la que hoy reina y gobierna en tu España: es tu sobrina ... lo que tenía te diese por dar en poeta, 'enfermedad incurable y pegadiza'." The allusion is to chapter i: 6 of the novel.

work, Menard goes even further in self-effacement: now the project is to write *Don Quijote*.

Not an interpretation of Quijote, not another version of Quijote and certainly not a modernization, but the Quijote itself: Menard had taken upon himself the "enigmatic task of literally reconstructing the spontaneous work of Cervantes." The eulogist-narrator sketches the enormous difficulties Menard was up against, and quotes a letter in which Menard cites "immortality" as the one condition necessary even to get started. Lastly, the narrator quotes some lines that Menard at last managed to write in his quixotic project: in literal identification with the model, these lines include some phrases on History and Truth. The narrator discusses the relation of Menard's (identical) version to Cervantes' and finds the replica superior! Menard has succeeded, we are told, in enriching "the backward and rudimentary art of reading" by way of "deliberate anachronism and erroneous attributions."[5]

This bizarre story has been called "a stupendous ... contribution to the ontology of art";[6] whatever it is, it sharpens absurdly some well-known phenomena in the quixotic tradition: reading, imitation, innovation. The story may at first seem like a heavily ironic commentary on the quixotic project – to make new – by heralding Menard's literal replica as the real innovation. The reader of Cervantes will however quickly notice that Borges has created his Menard as a commentary on the ironic discussion on authenticity and the relation between origin and imitation that is already going on in the novel. Not least, it is going on in the very passage of the novel from which Menard, according to his story, has managed to copy some lines. These happen to be taken from *Don Quijote* 1: 9, which is the chapter in which Cervantes develops a parody on the topos of the lost and found manuscript, making his narrator find the Arabic "original" of the novel and having it translated. I will comment upon this little "meta-narrative" later, and restrict myself to the conclusion here: the narrator excuses himself for possible flaws in the veracity of his narration, reminding us that the original author is an Arab – and "men

---

5   J. L. Borges, "Pierre Menard, autor del Quijote," in *Narraciones* (Madrid, 1980), p. 91: "Menard ... ha enriquecido mediante una técnica nueva el arte detenido y rudimentario de la lectura: la técnica del anacronismo deliberado y de las attribuciones erróneas."

6   A. C. Danto, *The Transfiguration of the Commonplace* (Cambridge, Mass.: Harvard University Press, 1981), p. 36.

of that nation are ready liars."[7] Then follow the phrases on History and Truth copied by Pierre Menard.

Discussions on the relation between history — narration — truth in fact recur throughout *Don Quijote,* even if the chapter quoted offers the most poignant example. I will come back to the problem later, and only want to underline here that Cervantes' use of a notoriously lying Arab historian as the very origin of his narration means that normal truth-values — true *or* false — are set aside. The lying Arab is a paradox along the lines of the classical paradox of the man from Crete stating that all men from Crete are liars: in both cases we get assertions that are *neither* true *nor* false. And, as the assertion or statement in the case of Cervantes and his Arab origin is nothing less than the whole book, the novel itself, it would mean that the neither-nor applies to everything in the book. Or, put more simply, the narration denies (or ironizes) its often repeated statements on History and its either-or Truth and establishes itself as the neither-nor of *fiction.*

Borges' *Menard* is a reminder of this Arab liar as well as of the Cretan liar; even the name sounds vaguely like "liar" in French. And Borges' story, as I read it, goes systematically (and playfully) into the world of fictional paradox and tries out on a small scale what Don Quijote had to develop in grand style, namely transforming fiction into reality. The difference is that Quijote had to get on to the road and get himself a servant in order to work out his project, while Menard stays within the library and the text.

Paul Auster wrote *The New York Trilogy* in the 1980s. It seems quite as impregnated with reading and literature as once was *Don Quijote.* The allusions to the great precursor are numerous, as when the main character of the first part is called Daniel Quinn (the initials!) and meets a door-keeper named Saavedra (like Cervantes). An important theme in this part, *City of Glass,* is the lost earthly paradise, i.e. a version of the golden age invoked by Don Quijote. With that comes the idea of fallen language and the project of re-establishing and making new — "For our words no longer correspond to the world," as the most quixotic character of this part expresses his predicament.[8] And here we can make a comparison with no less an authority than Michel Foucault, who has told us that Don Quijote paradigmatically demonstrates the

7   "siendo muy propio de los de aquella nación ser mentirosos."
8   Paul Auster, *The New York Trilogy* (London, 1988), p. 77.

crossing into modern time, when "writing and things do not get together".[9] Later we will see how Don Quijote's ambition to make new certainly included language, and that naming was his method.

Auster's trilogy thus evinces quixotic allusions and themes on several levels. I will, however, restrict myself to the passage (pp. 97–100) explicitly discussing *Don Quijote* concerning the questions, by now well known, of origin, imitation and authenticity. The situation is that Quinn, who for different reasons calls himself Paul Auster, visits the author of that name; the reader who has been through the quixotic tradition will remember that Unamuno has tried the same trick in his best-known *nivola*, called *Niebla* ("Mist," 1914), in which the main character visits "Unamuno" in order to discuss his fiction. Here Auster the writer tells Quinn/Auster that he is about to write an essay on *Don Quijote*, pretending to accept the often repeated statement by Cervantes: that his story is all true and accurate history. The starting-point is chapter I: 9, referred to above, on the found manuscript and the Arabic historian. The writer Auster comes up with the hypothesis that this Arab is actually a combination of Sancho Panza (who witnessed all adventures) and Don Quijote's literate friends, who wrote down Sancho's stories and translated them (into Arabic!). The reason for taking all this trouble is their concern for the knight: by letting him see himself in the book on himself he would be cured of his madness.

One is reminded of Kafka's two-sentences-long story "The Truth about Sancho Panza," in which Sancho is said to have given "his devil," i.e. Don Quijote, so many novels of chivalry to read that he went crazy on the road, although benevolently supervised by Sancho. Kafka, as well as Auster, demonstrates imaginative solidarity with Cervantes' own ironies. Auster develops the fact that in Cervantes' novel the friends of the knight are allowed to go remarkably far in their remedies. The mirroring motif, too, is already there; in the second part of the novel (II: 12) a friend dressed up like a "knight of mirrors" tries combat with Don Quijote in order to cure by reflection. Moreover, Auster's final point seems suitable, i.e. that Don Quijote was not mad at all, but only *acts* mad and thereby sets things going in order to test the credulity of his fellows and friends. At least it fits well

9 Michel Foucault, *Les mots et les choses* (Paris: Gallimard, 1966), p. 62: "L'écriture et les choses ne se rassemblent pas. Entres elles, Don Quichotte erre à l'aventure."

with one of the very few biographical comments we get from Don Quijote on his pre-quixotic life. This is in ii: 11, where the knight tells that "from my boyhood I have been a lover of the mask[10] and in my youth I was always a glutton for comedians."

The passage from Auster seems, however, to bear little relation to the quixotic project itself: the gravity of the knight, his ambition to reverse time and make new. I may have given the impression that Auster finds an amusingly imitative play of masks in *Don Quijote*, nothing more. The whole *New York Trilogy* makes up for this with a remarkable "existential" gravity concerning the very quixotic problems of identity, authenticity and questions of origin and truth. I cannot go into that here; I have called Auster as a witness in order to strengthen the impression that play becomes earnest in relation to fiction, reality and history in the quixotic tradition — and not least the interpretative tradition — with the tension between imitation and innovation as a common denominator.

"Imitación"

Imitation stands out as a theme in *Don Quijote*, and also as a normative and debatable concept. I will mention two occurrences.

The first is the *prólogo* of the book, a piece that parodically imitates contemporary prefaces in the learned style. This showpiece is eventually interrupted by the narrator telling of a visit from a friend who waves aside all learned efforts and instead calls for imitation: "In what you are writing you only have to make use of the imitation, and the more perfect this is, the better your writing will be."

Two circumstances should be mentioned. First, the friend, whose advice the narrator apparently wants to follow, proposes his *imitación* in opposition to the artifice of learned literature; I would say, as an anti-literary prescription. Imitation should be simple rather than conceited, amusing rather than learned and colloquial rather than solemn. As a consequence of the advice the narrator is able to start his first chapter with the famous description of everyday life of an almost nameless *hidalgo* in an anonymous village of la Mancha.

The second circumstance, which perhaps diminishes or ironizes the

---

10 Cohen has "pantomime" here, whereas Cervantes' word is "carátula," meaning mask as a synecdoche for theatre.

polemical effect, is that the friend never informs the narrator or us what the imitation is supposed to imitate. Nothing is said about, for example, *praxis*, nature, reality or classical models – to name only the most common versions of mimetic reference. There is actually nothing at all; it is the very activity *imitación* that is suggested, while its referential object is taken for granted or perhaps regarded as indifferent. The activity *imitación* is nothing but a literary activity. In other words, the anti-literary cure, *imitación*, cloaks a purely formal and literary device. Just as the narrator is able to start narrating after being given the literary signal, *imitación*, it is suggested by the same magic word that the "idle reader [desocupado lector]" famously addressed in the first line of the *prólogo*, should get busy with literature.

As a concept of poetics, imitation returns primarily towards the end of the first part, in which literature is discussed in several chapters, and in which poetics is laid down with great authority by an official and slightly pompous character, the "canon." This canon gives a lecture in I: 47 on the inferiority of the books of chivalry. His main objection is their poor and unsymmetrical composition: "I have never seen a book of chivalry," he complains, "with a whole body for a plot with all its limbs complete, so that the middle corresponds to the beginning, and the end to the beginning and the middle." His second objection is their lack of respect for verisimilitude: "plots of fiction" should instead "match the minds of their readers" in order to reach their loftiest aim, which is "to provoke admiration and delight at the same time". None of that could however be achieved by "departing from verisimilitude and imitation in which lies the perfection of all that is written."[11]

Aristotle is not far away in this lecture. The term *imitación* is close to a translation of his *mimesis* – and it is perhaps a significant detail that Aristotle's *Poetics* was introduced in Spain in 1596, the year when Cervantes was imprisoned in Seville, which is the originating moment of the great novel according to his biographers.[12] Aristotle has provided the canon with his normative comparison of a story and a harmonious body (cf. *Poetics*, 50b34–51a6), while the classicist moderation between imagination/reason and admiration/delight

---

11 "de modo que anden a un mismo paso la admiración y la alegría juntas; y todas estas cosas no podrá hacer el que huyere de la verisimilitud y de la imitación, en quien consiste la perfección de lo que se escribe."

12 Aristotelian connections are summed up in Carroll B. Johnson, *Don Quijote. The Quest for Modern Fiction* (Boston: Twayne, 1990), pp. 80ff.

seems to derive from Horace's famous formula: "aut prodesse volunt aut delectare poetae" (*Ars Poetica*, 333).

As we remember from the last chapter, Aristotle insists that *mimesis* means imitation of something coming *before* the story in time and this something-before is called action — *praxis* — and is given the characteristics of beginning-middle-end. This is echoed by Cervantes' Aristotelian canon, who, however, misses the elementary point of referential *praxis*:[13] in his lecture, as in the preface, it is the activity *imitación* that is addressed, while no referent is mentioned. Which means again that *imitación* is used as a purely literary term, and that the literary debate of the novel, reaching its Aristotelian culmination in the canon's lecture in 1: 47, is a formal debate — a debate on literary form with *imitación* as a formal master device — avoiding all reference to "reality" or "nature."

But the quasi-Aristotelian and formalistic classicism of the canon is not the poetics of Cervantes: the canon is soon refuted in the following chapters by none other than Don Quijote himself, who talks in praise of both fiction and reality — simultaneously! Having silently listened to the lecture and discussion on the books of chivalry, the knight opens his mouth and settles (in 1: 49) that the one who is "deranged and enchanted" cannot be the reader of romances, but is the honorable canon himself, who is insulting what is obviously true:

For to attempt to convince anyone that there were no such persons as Amadís and the other knights errant of whom so many records remain, would be like trying to persuade him that the sun does not shine, nor the frost chill, nor earth yield sustenance.

This invocation of reality is quite in line with what I called the quixotic project, which is not satisfied with any formalism or fiction for fiction's sake, but wants to re- establish the literary kingdom of the golden age in the here and now of reality. Furthermore, the knight continues (in 1: 50) with a striking description of the beneficial influence of fiction on life: "since I became a knight errant," i.e. since he transformed himself into fiction, "I have been valiant, courteous, liberal, well-bred, generous," etc. And, when the canon wants to

---

13   And so does his English translator Cohen: he translates the lines quoted as "imitation of nature," i.e. he adds "nature" to the "canonical" text. Furthermore, Cohen translates "admiración y alegría" in the same passage as "instruct and delight" making Cervantes more "classical" than he was.

dispute this, Don Quijote rounds off the discussion by referring to his final authority: "I do not know what more there is to say. I am guided solely by the example of the great Amadís de Gaul," etc.

It may seem logically dubious to refer to the knight Amadís as an authority to prove the existence of the very same knight; fiction itself is then a proof of its own reality as an illustration of some logical trap. This logic illustrates the paradoxically fictitious character of the quixotic enterprise, and is the very condition of its success; it is by the renovating imitation of literary examples that this book transforms itself from a book of chivalry into a "novel." This renovation is by no means an obvious result of imitation. The imitation suggested in the preface would lead to no renovation whatever, nor would the *imitación* recommended by the canon in the lecture of 1:47. The model that Don Quijote refers to as his highest authority — Amadís de Gaul — must himself be called an imitation, but his version has not led to any noticeable renovation (apart from having inspired Don Quijote). "Amadís" refers to a Spanish book of chivalry in four volumes of 1508 by Rodríguez de Montalvo, in its turn an imitation of (parts of) the medieval "Geste des Bretons," i.e. the stories centring on Artus. All these books of chivalry seem to have formed a closed world that was by no means renovated by Montalvo, who imitated in full solidarity with the tradition, although this tradition slightly later became the victim of parody with the Italian versions of Boiardo and Ariosto — the latter well read by Cervantes and Don Quijote, as it comes out in the novel.

Our knight imitates not in order to imitate or for a literary purpose, but to make new. He refers not to Amadís for the sake of Amadís, but for his own sake, and for reality and history and future history. The golden age interests him not as a literary topos, but as a possibility that should immediately be realized by himself. That is his bizarre and ridiculous project. It has been introduced in all its paradoxes by Marthe Robert in an unsurpassed way:

One fine day a middle-aged man, close to fifty, decides to leave everything and take to the road. He seems to go off quite haphazardly, but in fact he has a definite goal in mind. In the course of his adventures not the suffering that he has to endure nor any mockery can deter him from his plan: to live strictly like a book in order to discover at last what there is in the depths of literature.[14]

14 Marthe Robert, *The Old and the New. From Don Quijote to Kafka* (California University Press, 1977), p. 1; I have modified the translation.

The project or the "plan" is doomed to failure, and the failure is also the condition of most of the comical effects of the novel. But, as we remember, success is born from this failure; i.e. the paradoxical quixotic project gives *Cervantes* the opportunity of renovating and making new. Cervantes creates the book that more than any other book establishes "the new" – *la novela* – and creates in other words something more than just a name and a book, something that developed into the novel itself.

Language, naming

Don Quijote is given a precise strategy in his great project, and this strategy is developed from language as well as having linguistic consequences: by naming he transforms reality into literature.

First comes his own person. When we meet him, on the first page of the first chapter, the narrator pretends, as mentioned above, not to remember his proper name: "Quijada" or "Quesada" or "Quejana." The name of the leading character is, in other words, arbitrary, and his very first move as a character is to give himself a name that may be enigmatic and perhaps ridiculous but is certainly *not* arbitrary: Don Quijote. That is the first and decisive step in the transformation and renovation of reality. The effect is remarkable: the naming is immediately accepted by everyone within the book, the narrator included. The worried friends of our hero, the barber and the priest, try, for instance, not to remind him of his real (but arbitrary) name. Nor does the narrator ironize at the expense of Don Quijote by reminding us that the name is a fiction. That fiction has, furthermore, given a name to the final result, i.e. the novel – and nobody remembers Alonso Quijano (or whatever he was called) while everybody knows Don Quijote.

The knight continues with naming as the first move in the realization of his project. He gives Aldonza the name Dulcinea, and tries the same method on things and phenomena – the tavern is named castle and the windmill is named giant; etc. At the end of the second part he is forced to retire from chivalric life; that does not mean, however, that he gives up his project, only that he changes the setting. Now the idea is to live as a shepherd, i.e. a literary shepherd. The first move again is naming: "I will buy some sheep and everything needful for the pastoral vocation," he tells us (in II: 67); "I will call myself 'el pastor Quijotiz'." Sancho Panza has interestingly enough been allowed to keep his proper name throughout the novel (although this name may have a comic ring to us). This indicates that Sancho is the only one in the novel giving adequate resistance to the quixotic project, something shown in the dialogues between knight and squire, which move beautifully between antagonistic misunderstandings and mutual friendship. At the pastoral end, however, Sancho too is brought into fiction: Don Quijote wants to name him "el pastor Pancino." Fiction can reach no further than that, and this final naming therefore signals the end of the novel.

The method of naming demonstrates that the knight lives in exemplary fashion as a linguistic being, i.e. according to already given literary examples. This means that in every concrete situation he thinks and reacts abstractly, i.e. he never reacts spontaneously to reality without having processed reality into literature. He thinks — and thinks literarily — before acting. In some instances he is also given a purely literary existence without any embarrassing confrontations with a reluctant reality. The novel then leaves its burlesque mode to enter an almost surrealistic state.

My favorite example is the quixotic madness: I am thinking of the *literary* madness developed by the knight in 1: 25. The situation is that, as a step in his exemplary life, Don Quijote has come to a stage where he considers going mad; his mad turning-around of literature and reality has led him to literary madness. For other reasons he has also retired to the wild landscape of Sierra Morena, which gives him a setting for the purpose. The official reason must, however, be problems of the heart — knights never go mad for other reasons. Don Quijote therefore construes a situation in which he must be considered as deserted for the moment by the lady of his heart, Dulcinea. At the same time, he has to mention, for the astonished Sancho, that Dulcinea is the literary name of Aldonza Lorenzo, a peasant girl well known to both of them. As clearly as possible the knight explains to his squire that he is interested not in the real Aldonza, but only in the girl transformed into literature: "I imagine all I say to be true, neither more nor less, and in my imagination I draw her as I would have her be, both as to her beauty and her rank."

When it comes to the practical details of madness, the knight hesitates in the choice of two good literary examples: Amadís and Roland. "I intend to imitate Amadís, and to act here the desperate, raving, furious lover; at the same time following the example of the valiant Sir Roland when he found by a spring evidence that the fair Angelica had dishonoured herself with Medoro" – our knight here refers to an episode from Ariosto's *Orlando furioso*.

Amadís, in Montalvo's version, for a while considers himself deserted in love, and is, therefore, left brooding in lonely melancholy; Ariosto's Roland, on the other hand, is violent in his jealousy. Don Quijote plans to combine elements of both in making his own version: "although I do not intend to imitate Roland ... exactly in all the mad things he did, said and thought, I will sketch them as best as I can, in what appear to me to be their essentials." Sancho is the listener to these plans, and he tries as always to talk his master out of the project, without result; Don Quijote finishes his plans for a literary-inspired madness by telling Sancho to stop wasting time "advising me to give up so rare, so happy, and unprecedented an imitation." An "unprecedented imitation" – literally, a "never seen imitation [tan no vista imitación]" – seems to me like an excellent summary of the quixotic project. This project aspires, as already said, to the new and to what has never been seen before. A "never seen imitation" is no longer an "imitation" according to normal logic; but is refuting logic in order to create something new.

Don Quijote's calculated madness sticks to literature, i.e. the literary model and the linguistic examples – Amadís and Roland – as is explained in 1: 25. In the following chapter (1: 26) we get some samples of the imitative application, mainly as some sentimental verse by the knight posing as love-sick and deserted; this illustrates the assumption made by the niece (in 1: 6) that poetry would be an "incurable and catching" disease almost as dangerously contagious as the chivalric "disease." In the meantime Sancho has been sent to deliver a message concerning his love-sick master to Dulcinea, and when he comes back after some intermezzi (1: 31) we get a new and quite "surrealistic" scene without any interference from "reality". Sancho has not been near any Dulcinea, but guesses what the visit would have been like if he had visited the real model (i.e. Aldonza) – meaning that Sancho invents a kind of "realist" fiction. Don Quijote benevolently answers by correcting this fiction in every detail according to his high literary examples of visits to a beloved lady, visits as they should have taken place. Sancho's fiction is corrected by Don Quijote's fiction. The scene is actually idyllic, since no "reality" seems to threaten. Doubts about literary accuracy are easily dismissed or deferred until that magical moment when the knightly fiction necessarily has to confront reality:

when Don Quijote must meet Dulcinea in order to hand his credentials in person to the beloved.

This moment does not arrive until the second part of the novel (II: 10) and develops into an unhappily inverted repetition of the first (non-)meeting. Now Sancho is the one who tries to transform reality according to the examples given by the books of chivalry, while Don Quijote resists in the name of reality. The knight has ordered his squire to make an appointment with the beloved lady; Sancho presents the first girls he meets on the road as Dulcinea and her ladies-in-waiting, believing that the knight's never-failing literary imagination will cope with this confrontation as well as it has managed to cope with all others.

But that is not the case. "I can see nothing, said Don Quijote, but three village girls on three donkeys." It is no use Sancho trying to transform reality by depicting the girls with all the literary embellishment he has learned from his life together with the knight; Don Quijote sees nothing but reality, and this reality – with no Dulcinea – makes him call himself, in the final line of the chapter, "the most unfortunate of men [el más desdichado de los hombres]."[15]

Why is it that he cannot see what he wants to see? Why cannot he "draw her in his imagination as he would have her be" according to the method he has practiced all the time with a never-failing conviction in his capabilities of naming reality according to his wishes (see above and I: 25)?

No evident explanation can be given for this, but the situation must be discussed because this chapter functions as a turning-point for the whole novel. From this moment on Don Quijote is not only the knight of "triste figura," but a "desdichado," despairing of the possibility of realizing his project and sinking deeper and deeper into his "profunda melancolía," to use the diagnosis of a later chapter (II: 16).

The version that is given official status, i.e. the one that Don Quijote refers to and believes or wants to believe, is that wizards again have stopped his project, in the same way that they had, for instance, earlier made giants into windmills in order to deprive the knight of the honor of their defeat – or that is how Don Quijote prefers to explain the matter in I: 8. I find this difficult to accept as an explanation in this case, however, and I wonder if Don Quijote is supposed to accept it

---

15 This passage is analysed by Erich Auerbach in the chapter "Die verzauberte Dulcinea" in his *Mimesis* with almost contrary conclusions to those I make here.

either; after all, no wizard can prevent Don Quijote from calling his windmills giants and then attacking them, but here he is actually stopped from naming the peasant-girl Dulcinea.

Perhaps we should suspect that Don Quijote can accept only a literary transformation handled by himself; or at least not one as it is created by Sancho, the very principle of reality, when he is praising the peasant-girl as Dulcinea. Or perhaps the quixotic project wavers as it approaches the possibility of renewing and re-establishing by naming nothing less than the Woman – especially if one bears in mind the theories that tell us that the poor *hidalgo* transformed himself into Don Quijote and went on the road precisely in order to escape a woman.[16]

I find it difficult to choose between these speculations and will try to stick to linguistic circumstances. I am referring to the fatal consequences of Don Quijote's failure to name the anonymous peasant-girl Dulcinea. His world has, according to his own view, been put under a spell and disguised as an iron age from the beginning, or at least from the moment his library was burned (1: 6–7), and he has by pure naming tried to re-establish a golden age. Now he is forced to realize that arbitrariness or other and hostile volitions have made such a mess in the relations between things (the girl) and the sign (Dulcinea) that a naming renovation translating the girl into Dulcinea is no longer possible. The world has suddenly been transformed into a kind of allegory, open to interpretation, but closed to the immediate present.

The implications of this may be approached by something that could pompously be called a quixotic theory of words. This "theory" is diffused throughout the novel, but found concentrated in the speech on "arms and learning" that Don Quijote has the opportunity to give in the first part (1: 38) – i.e. still far from his linguistic black-out in the meeting with the peasant-girl who was not Dulcinea of the second part.

The speech is novelistically preparing for the long episode of *el cautivo*, the slave who escaped from Algiers. The speech honors arms and warfare in contrast to learned occupations, and ends with a sudden invective against modern artillery: "Blessed were the times which lacked the dreadful fury of those diabolical engines, the artillery." When the knight considers these "engines" he is almost "tempted to

---

16 Unamuno in his *Vida de Don Quijote y Sancho* imagines that Don Quijote fled his love for the peasant-girl Aldonza. Carroll B. Johnson in *Don Quijote* thinks that Don Quijote fled an inclination for his niece.

say that it grieves me to the heart to have adopted this profession of knight errantry in such a detestable age as we now live in."

We recognize the structure of the argument from the invocations of the golden age quoted earlier: on the one hand, this "happy" or "blessed" epoch called the golden age when a man was still a man, girls wandered freely and knights-errant kept things and words in order; on the other hand, our own age, called "detestable" here as well as in the chapter on the golden age (I: 11). Present time is "detestable" in matters of warfare because of artillery: the artillery bullet hits the warrior accidentally, impersonally, with no visible intention behind it and no necessary relation to the target. Artillery therefore endangers the purpose of the warrior, which is honor, personal fame, or even immortality.

Modern war is as confusingly enigmatic for the individual as the world in which it takes place; the knight can use only his old-fashioned lance and sword, both of which obey his obviously personal and necessary intention, in the same way that he uses naming to make the world intelligible. The inventor of artillery, whom Don Quijote imagines to be rightly in hell, is therefore comparable to those wizards who brought an end to the possibilities for the literary naming of the world endeavored by the knight; or, rather, who finally, in the non-meeting with Dulcinea, introduced arbitrariness into the relation between words and things.

This arbitrariness was there all along, and this example is given to show that linguistic renovation is part of the quixotic project: to re-establish the golden age. What the knight wants to re-establish is what he considers to be an unambiguous naming found in literary language. The words from the golden age have an intentional meaning quite as obvious as the lance of the knight. They are absolutely free from arbitrariness, interpretation and change; free from all that has to do with time – golden age is an age outside time.

This is the place to mention again Michel Foucault's famous analysis of Don Quijote – the novel and the character – in *Les mots et les choses*. Foucault presents Don Quijote as paradigmatic of an "epistemic" shift from similarity into representation; he is the hero of the Same, "le héros du Même."[17] He becomes Don Quijote and starts adventuring because he wants to re-establish the similarities of words in a reality where "words and things no longer go together." The

17 Foucault, *Les mots et les choses*, p. 60.

result is that he comes close to a modern poetical function, i.e. "the *allegorical* rôle" listening for that "other language" of similarity, "ressemblance."[18]

Having considered the fatal meeting between the knight and the peasant-girl who was not Dulcinea, we can now be specific about Foucault's observation: Don Quijote was, from the beginning, acting in an allegorical mode, at least if we agree with one of Walter Benjamin's tokens of baroque allegory: "Whatever it handles its Midas-hand turns into something significant. All sorts of transformation was its element; and its pattern was allegory."[19] Don Quijote's transformations of the poorest things in the world into "something significant" by using literature as an allegorical pre-text would not be less "baroque" according to the same analyst: "renaissance exploits the world, baroque the libraries." But if Don Quijote was acting allegorically all along, something fatal still happened in his non-meeting with Dulcinea: his allegory was deepened or perhaps modernized by being given a temporal dimension, that can be called *pure anteriority*, to use the term of a modern theorist on allegory, who will reappear in my last chapter.[20]

Or, to put it more dramatically, meeting the chosen woman paralyses the "Midas-hand" of the knight, making him incapable of naming her Dulcinea, i.e. transforming her into "something significant." Don Quijote's meeting with the peasant-girl who was not Dulcinea capsizes his project by introducing *distance* as a necessary part of the ideal and fictitious world and the timeless present he wanted to re-establish as the golden age. (In the next chapter we will study how the phenomenology of distance is developed by Rousseau at the very moment when presence is at hand.) When a real girl (a girl who, according to Cervante's fiction, is real) actually stands in front of Don Quijote and waits only for his naming imagination, his Midas-hand, in order to be transformed into the presence of Dulcinea, then

18 Ibid., p. 63: "Le poète assure la fonction inverse; il tient le rôle *allégorique*; sous le langage des signes et sous le jeu de leurs distinctions biens découpées, il se met à l'écoute de 'l'autre langage', celui, sans mots ni discours, de la ressemblance."

19 Walter Benjamin, *Ursprung des deutschen Trauerspiels*, in *Gesammelte Schriften*, 1 : 1 (Frankfurt-on-Main: Suhrkamp, 1974), p. 403: "Was immer sie ergreift, verwandelt ihre Midashand in ein bedeutendes. Verwandlung aller Art, das war ihr Element; und deren Schema war Allegorie."

20 Paul de Man, "The Rhetoric of Temporality," in *Blindness and Insight* (London: Methuen, 1983), p. 207.

distance in time and space is introduced. Dulcinea, who was an allegory for the golden age, is then no longer a possibility for the poor knight, who is forced to realize that the golden age needs distance in order to appear as a golden age; that the presence of Dulcinea reveals no real Dulcinea. Dulcinea in the flesh is a peasant-girl. Our time is irrevocably an iron age. Don Quijote becomes, therefore, "the most unfortunate of men." He is unable to give up a project that can no longer be realized. He has to drag melancholically on as an allegorical character in an enchanted world. Reality, which earlier was an open book to him, only waiting for his spelling of its secrets, has become an enigmatically closed "libro del mundo."

Irony, melancholy

Don Quijote dies from melancholia. Such anyway is the diagnosis of the very last chapter of the whole novel (II: 74) where the doctor called to the knight's deathbed is of the opinion "that melancholy and despondency [melancolías y desabrimientos] were bringing him to his end." Melancholia was, however, in store for him from the beginning: Sancho must have had a reason when in the first part (I: 19) he has already invented "knight of the sad countenance [el caballero de la triste figura]" as his honorary title. Melancholia is actually his dominating and often mentioned trait of character, starting from the episode discussed above, when the knight cannot give the name of Dulcinea to an arbitrary peasant-girl (II: 10); for instance, in one of the chapters where Don Quijote suffers as a guest of a duke and duchess while Sancho tries to be a governor. There the *melancolía* of the knight is observed by the duchess (II: 44, II: 48), who tries to cure it with the oddest pranks of more or less erotic significance; she even offers (in II: 44) the sad knight four of her maids, "as beautiful as flowers," for his personal service and distraction.

It goes without saying that Don Quijote categorically refuses to accept this as well as all other attacks on his virtue. Melancholia cannot be shrugged off so easily, nor can the loneliness that has distinguished his character since he named himself Don Quijote and left family, friends and all security to go on the road. Both loneliness and melancholia distingush him conspicuously from all the knights he is imitating, starting with the Spanish Amadís. The knights of the books of chivalry could be deserted by women, and they could have a touch of melancholia. But they never make themselves chaste and lonely in the same categorical way as Don Quijote, because they and their genre are simply unfamiliar with the reluctant reality that Don Quijote tries both to escape and radically to change.

The inevitable conflicts with the principle of reality may be the ultimate reason for the melancholia of Don Quijote, just as they are the very design for his novel. Which means that the sad knight Don Quijote is, from the start, haunted by premonitions of the insurpassable gap that in the second part will separate him both from Dulcinea and from the re-establishment of the golden age, i.e. the realization of his project. His author knew all along that both time and language pose formidable obstacles to such a realization. To handle this knowledge of the possible, together with the quixotic project of actually making the impossible, calls for a kind of reflective balance that Georg Lukács once named "the deepest melancholy of each genuine and great novel." The term for this balanced and reflective melancholy is *irony*. Lukács points out that such irony is not only constitutive of the novelistic genre, but also curiously self-destructive: irony demonstrates the naivety of the novelistic hero, but simultaneously turns against the conquering reality, which is exposed in its nullity, its *Nichtigkeit*.[21]

Irony, then, is somehow connected with melancholia, like both temporal and physical distance. Examples of such distancing irony flourish in our novel; and, according to Lukács, in the novelistic genre as well. In the case of Cervantes, it may at first seem as if the distance between author and hero makes the author's project simply the opposite of the knight's. It is hardly worth the effort of giving examples of the narrator handling his irony at the expense of Don Quijote, i.e. demonstrating the naivety of the hero. The well-known burlesque comedy of the novel could simply be described as if the narrator, as well as we and the whole world, knew better than the permanently naive Don Quijote. Less obvious and certainly more complicated is, perhaps, the irony that just as devastatingly turns against both the work itself and reality, or, rather, against any presumption of an absolute difference and a once-and-for-all established border-line between the real and the fictitious, the original and the copy — and the writer, the hero and the reader. Whether, however, any Lukácsian "nothingness" is "exposed" as a result of Cervantes' ironies calls for closer consideration.

---

21 Georg Lukács, *Die Theorie des Romans* (Neuwied, 1965), pp. 84f.

The first time the narrator shows an irony including a reflection on the construction of his own argument and work – a sort of extended and self-reflective irony – would be the famous ninth chapter in the first part, referred to above as a powerful inspiration for some of my "witnesses." The narrator breaks off in I: 8, complaining that his manuscript has come to an end; in I: 9 we are then told how he found the continuation. It is done as a story within the story. The narrator is walking about in the streets of Toledo and meets a boy selling "some parchments and old papers." Since the narrator confesses "a taste for reading even torn papers lying in the streets" he soon has his suspicions confirmed: he has found the original of his own broken-off story, i.e. the "History of Don Quijote de la Mancha, written by Cide Hamete Benengeli, Arabic historian." One notes that not only this fictive author, but also his fictitious original title, have a different name from the book told by the narrator and read by us, which is, after all, named exactly like its hero.

The narrator hastens to lock up a Spanish-speaking Arab who for only "fifty pounds of raisins and three bushels of wheat" translates the whole manuscript that the narrator is about to tell – but only after the already mentioned caution about possible errors due to the originator, a notoriously lying Arab.

Much of this arrangement is the result of Cervantes' intentions to produce a literary parody, which is obvious in the first portions of the book, especially the prologue. There is an element of parodical imitation too in the retrieved manuscript in relation to the books of chivalry, such as Montalvo's *Amadís de Gaul*. If Don Quijote is given the role of imitating Amadís in order to make new, then Cervantes imitates Montalvo with the explicitly opposite purpose, namely "overthrowing the ill-based fabric of these books of chivalry," as the purpose is spelled out in the prologue – and we need to know that Montalvo too used found manuscripts and fictions within fiction.

But there are also cervantic characteristics in this famous chapter that go beyond imitating parody. The lying Arab must be mentioned again, as also the intricate and extended ironic shifts that Cervantes thereby introduces between true and false and between history and fiction. This was by no means an accident; Cervantes repeatedly reminds us of his Arabic originator and historian, and on one occasion – strategically at the beginning of the second part – also insists, again, on his unreliability. This happens in II: 3, where Don Quijote himself is confronted with the story about himself (i.e. part I) and then gets worried about its truth-value considering its Arabic origin: for "he could hope for no truth of the Moors, since they are all cheats, forgers and schemers [falsarios y quimeristas]."

The lost-and-found manuscript is an often used topos; but Cervantes handles it with a flair of his own. I like especially the impression of an accident given to the narrator's wandering about in a street well known for its trading, and stumbling on a pack of writing, which, furthermore, is in Arabic — definitely a foreign language to all true believers. We are given the impression of a narrator quite as keen on reading as his too-much-read hero and as the potentially too-much-reading *desocupado lector* invoked in the prologue; and we are tempted to consider a mysterious or unknown original of the story we are reading. A script in a mother-tongue that is accessible to no Christian and with a lying father — such a story must be a foundling or a stepchild, to allude to the handling of script and writing by Plato in the dialogue *Phaedrus*, touched upon in chapter 1.

With this calculated flippancy, Cervantes has situated *three* narrators between himself and the reader: the Arabic original, the bilingual translator and then the narrator. The reader is not allowed to forget this; in the second part of the novel in particular we get complicated reminders. As when a chapter (II: 24) starts with the narrator quoting the translator of the *original* by Cide Hamete saying that in the margin he (the translator) has found handwritten commentaries by the same Cide Hamete. (Is not all we read supposed to be originally handwritten by Cide Hamete? Or are we to imagine an extra originating writer?). Or when the translator (in II: 44) is said to "interpret" the "real original [el propio original]" *not* as it was written by Cide Hamete! (Again an original before the original! And how can the narrator tell?!)

All these examples on irony ironizing over the construction of the work show an extended and reflective irony — but hardly an irony that exposes any "nothingness" of the world, to use Lukács' idea of irony again. Perhaps we rather get, in these examples, a reflective multiplicity? A laughing-mirror?

We come closer to Lukácsian irony, I think, in the second part of the novel in what comes as a result of that fatal intervention in the Cervantic project: the publication of a *false Don Quijote*, part II, written by a certain Avellaneda, a mysterious originator who has never been identified. In Cervantes' preface to his second part, and from chapter 59 to the end of the book, there are extensive allusions to this *false* Quijote. The situation is not made any clearer by Cervantes at the beginning of the second part (especially II: 3) having already used the quaint effect of letting his hero read and comment on the story about himself, i.e. part I. But now the projects of author and hero suddenly coincide: both claim to be originators. In II: 59 Don Quijote is told about the *false* story and then establishes himself as *genuine* by criticizing the *false* narrator for having mistaken the name of Sancho's wife – when, oddly enough, the source of this mistake is Cervantes' own first part (I: 7)! In II: 72 Don Quijote is then made to meet a certain Don Alvaro Tarfe, a character from Avellaneda's *false* second part. Between our *genuine* knight, whose authenticity is defined by his imitation, and whose story was anyway originally told by a notoriously lying Arab, and the *false* (many times over) character, there takes place a discussion on nothing less than the question of authenticity. Our knight wants to find out about the activities of his *false* imitator, and then wants to prove his own *genuine* identity by telling Don Alvaro Tarfe that he had certainly not (like the *false*) been to any tournament in Saragossa, but had been to Barcelona.

It may well be a point here that the meeting with Don Alvaro takes place on Don Quijote's way home from Barcelona, where he had suffered a defeat in combat, and was at least temporarily forced to rid himself of the identity as knight that defined him as "Don Quijote." This gives us an awkward situation: the knight who, according to his fiction, is but an ex-knight talks to Don Alvaro Tarfe to prove himself to be the authentic knight, Don Quijote. He even calls for the local mayor and a clerk, who happen to be in the vicinity, in order to make Don Alvaro declare his authenticity in a judicially correct manner.

If our novel, at some localizable spot, comes close to being an extended ironic exposure of what Lukács called "nothingness" – aiming at the hero as well as his fiction, reality and author – this must be the place. It occurs in a quite obvious way: the shifts between false and genuine have now accelerated; imitations, negations and doubles have accumulated to a point where normal truth-values are put aside and normal boundaries overstepped. Don Alvaro Tarfe, who was borrowed from Avellaneda's *false* second part in order to prove what was *genuine*, illustrates this effect when he, after the confrontation, "suspected that he must have been enchanted [encantado]", since he had met two different Don Quijotes – and, we may add, appeared in two different fictions. The chapter in which we were to find out what was real and what was not, had the opposite effect on the witness: he became *encantado*. This may well be read as a version of the *dizziness* that, according to expert readers, goes together with the extended irony approaching Lukácsian "nothingness."[22] If that was not enough, such ironically enchanted dizziness is most intimately related to melancholia as well as to reflection — if we are to believe the far later ironies of Baudelaire, like Cervantes a reluctant initiator of the New. For Baudelaire, "irony remains, like melancholia, and like the image reflected by mirrors, applications of Satan."[23]

The episode with Don Alvaro Tarfe shows that the levels of time and "reality" accumulated by the story seem to have entered a never-ending convolution of reflections and mirrorings. That process was started only when Cervantes came up with his combination of historian — translator — narrator in his chapter on the lost and found manuscript (I: 9). Or perhaps it was already started when Cervantes began confronting imagination and reality by combining his parody of a hero with an exposure of wordly nullity. To get rid of vertigo there is only one thing to do: make an end of the story and the narrator and the hero. Cervantes can bring his story to an end only by having his hero stop imitating, i.e. stop being a knightly hero, give up his project of immortality, become normal and die.

Mimetic infection

The quixotic project — to re-establish the golden age and bring time to an end — evidently must fail, and the narrator piles up evidence for this necessary failure. The narrator's own project is more difficult to judge. The as it were "official" Cervantic project is famously antagonistic to the quixotic project and involves "over-throwing the ill-based fabric of these books of chivalry," as it is put in the prologue. We are regularly reminded of this project, for example with the burning of Don Quijote's library (I: 6) and with several critical attacks on books of chivalry from responsible characters like the "canon" (I: 47) presented above. That Don Quijote on his death-bed (II: 74) is allowed to rid himself of his knightly name and identity, and pronounce

22 Paul de Man explores the relation of irony to dizziness in relation to Friedrich Schlegel and Baudelaire in "The Rhetoric of Temporality," pp. 215ff.
23 According to Jean Starobinski's analysis in *La mélancolie au miroir* (Paris: Gallimard, 1990), p. 32: "L'ironie, comme la mélancolie, comme l'image que renvoient les miroirs, reste des appartenances de Satan."

himself a belated "enemy of Amadís de Gaul and of all the infinite brood of his progeny," must also be seen as confirmation of the success of the project; at the end no knightly imagination is left.

Two kinds of doubt keep coming up concerning the authorial project, however. The first emanates from literary history: one wonders what is actually meant by that "infinite brood" of chivalric imitators our narrator wants to "overthrow." According to authorities on the period, the glory days for the books of chivalry had long since passed and, a century before *Don Quijote*, *Amadís* was actually one of the last before parodies took over with, for example, Ariosto. Spanish prose was dominated by picaresque novels, starting with the anonymous *Lazarillo de Tormes* (1554), ambiguously hinted at in our novel (I: 22), up to Cervantes' contemporary rivals Alemán and Quevedo.

Another doubt emanates from a remarkable phenomenon in *Don Quijote* that I prefer to call mimetic infection. We have already noted something of the kind in the previous chapter, i.e. in Plato's handling of poetry in *Republic*, where *mimesis* is presented as a disreputable drug with epidemic possibilities. The Platonic suspicion is overwhelmingly confirmed in *Don Quijote* in ways that remarkably contradict the narrator's official project: although the narrator condemns and "overthrows" the books of chivalry, they grow into models of imitation for an increasing population of his characters. The main character, Don Quijote, is mimetically defined, living fully and only in imitation of knightly literature. But his friends too, and more or less everyone he meets, accept his ideas, i.e. his imitations, and enter the mimetic game. It starts with the first tavern-keeper in the first tavern of the first expedition (I: 3), who, after having been confronted with the follies of the knight, decides to "fall in with his humour," if only − un-quixotically − "to make some sport for the night." But still: he *falls in*. It continues in the next chapter with the merchants whom Don Quijote meets on the road, and who, for no obvious reason, enter the quixotic fiction by addressing him as "señor caballero." He is, after all, called by the fictitious name "Don Quijote" by everyone, including the narrator.

Don Quijote's friends, the priest and the barber, are as eager to cure their friend of his chivalric follies as is the narrator to "overthrow" the whole genre. But the friends enter the mimetic game with an ardour that does not always appear salubrious − as at the end of the first part, when Don Quijote is transported back home in a kind of cage, and escorted by friends and friends of friends, all acting in disguise so that finally of "all those present only Sancho was in his right mind and undisguised" (I: 46).

Among these friends and helpers is the beautiful Dorotea, whose melodramatic story has earlier been mixed with Don Quijote's adventures. She is all the more willing to help since "she had read many books of chivalry, and knew the style in which afflicted maidens were accustomed to beg their boon of knights errant" (I: 29). She is not the only quixotic specimen among Don Quijote's helpers to know the "style" of chivalry. In the second part of the novel we meet the candidate Sansón Carrasco, who acts as a knight-errant himself with conviction, if only to cure Don Quijote from the same mimetic impulse; in his first (and unsuccessful) effort he also calls himself the "knight of the mirrors" (II: 12). When Don Quijote later meets a duke and his duchess, they "were most anxious to make his acquaintance, their intention being to fall in with his whimsies, to agree with him in all he said, and to treat him like a knight errant ... observing towards him all the ceremonies usual in books of knight errantry, which they had read and were very fond of" (II: 30). And so forth. At the end of the novel one gets the impression that Don Quijote is now the only one who does *not* believe in the possibility of establishing the golden age of chivalry in the contemporary here and now. Even Sancho Panza seems to side with the knight at the end, although he also prepares to go "back" to his normal reality. And, if Sancho has all the time represented the principle of reality, the steadily growing understanding and complicity between him and Don Quijote cunningly repeat and reflect the relation between the narrator and his hero: starting in opposition and ending in conciliation.

The mimetic infection — which may seem epidemic — appears like a version of the patterns of mirroring and reflection that we related to melancholic irony above, something that also hastily expands in the course of the story. The total impression of these two lines of development of the story makes me tempted to reformulate what I called the official project of the narrator — to make an end of all books of chivalry — as an unofficial project which at first may seem contradictory: the narrator both actually spreads the mimetic infection from the books of chivalry, *and* wants to make an end of all these books. In order to stop spreading infection he then has also to bring to an end the story demanding the end of the books of chivalry. The unofficial project of the narrator is, in other words, to bring his own story to an end. And, if we have reached a point where the narrator's project may seem contradictory, that would only mean that it is not so antagonistic to another contradictory project: Don Quijote's.

The kinship between the two seemingly antagonistic projects will be more obvious if we stress that both aim at the new. Both are certainly established by what was called imitation, but the aim of imitation is in both cases to re-establish, make new, "renovar." The knight demands a new golden age. The narrator demands a story to end all chivalric stories. And that story could only be created by his closing of "el libro del mundo" as it had been presented to him by tradition. In the process he opens the way to the new and unknown territory called "novela." "Like Columbus" – to use Stephen Gilman's beautiful phrase[24] – "without knowing exactly what it was, Cervantes had set foot on a new continent later to be called the novel."

Lingua romana

The mimetic infection buried in *Don Quijote* was fairly innocuous until Romanticism, when the idea started spreading of the novel as *the* new; then our book, which had been popular and read from the beginning, was suddenly exalted as an ideal of higher aesthetics. From ideal novel the step was easily taken to the Novel itself and to the very first Novel. That is not just because – as the standard explanation goes – the Romantics realized that Don Quijote was an idealist fighting a reluctant reality and, therefore, was a precursor of themselves. The main reason was that the novel as novel was now related to the new and to the newly Romantic. The novel (*Roman*) is, to paraphrase Friedrich Schlegel, a romantic book; meaning that the ideal romantic book must be a novel. Early romantic poetics was aiming precisely at the new language that Novalis amused himself by calling "lingua romana."[25]

The implications of this final *quijotismo* are enormous. I can only suggest some points in early Romanticism that made the novel as novel so important and made *Don Quijote* (together with *Wilhelm Meister*) into the recurrent and ideal example of "novel."

24 Stephen Gilman, *The Novel According to Cervantes* (California University Press, 1989), p. 184.
25 The phrase comes heavily underlined in a famous fragment on Romanticism, romantic philosophy and *Romantisierung* in *Vorarbeiten 1798* (no. 105; *Werke*, vol. 2, Darmstadt, 1978, p. 334).

(1) The "idealism" recognized by the Romantics in the character Don Quijote can be pinpointed in what I have called "naming": the attempt of the knight to form (or transform) his own (literary) reality by naming, i.e. with the power of language. If one stresses the (re)creative, (re)establishing and instituting sense of this naming activity that I have associated with the quixotic project, it fits nicely with the most revolutionary ingredient of early romantic epistemology – which was a *break* with all traditional *mimesis*. As summarized by Manfred Frank (in Heideggerian inspiration), this revolution stops thinking of "truth as re-presentation or re-production of things, it must be understood as the active positing-into-work of the Absolute."[26] Or, even more dramatically, Truth or the Absolute is what is instituted or posited – "setzen" and "stiften" are the verbs suddenly replacing all versions of imitation – in and by the performative act of the work of art. (As famously expressed by Hölderlin in the last lines of the hymn *Andenken*: "What remains / is instituted by the poets [Was bleibet aber / stiften die Dichter])."

(2) Intimately related to this epistemological revolution (less benevolent judges would call it collapse) is romantic irony, in its turn connected with well-known phenomena from *Don Quijote*: reflection, puns, allegory. The relation goes like this: the Absolute or the Truth that was ideally posited by the work of art (ideally, the novel) can, however, never be contained in the work of art; absolute truth (also called Being) is temporal and/or in other ways evasive, changing, moving. The work of art may "posit" the Absolute, but the "Absolute" still evades naming. The consequence of this is, as put by Friedrich Schlegel, that "the highest can be said only allegorically exactly because it cannot be said."[27] These Romantics seem, in other words, to have had the experience that I found in *Don Quijote*, when the knight was not able to name Dulcinea (i.e. he could not, romantically speaking, posit her as the Absolute), but saw only the peasant-girl of reality (II: 10). The difference, however, would be that Don Quijote after this falls into his "profunda melancolía," whereas the Romantics took the "same" experience as a starting-point for the

---

26 Manfred Frank, *Einführung in die frühromantische Ästhetik* (Frankfurt-on-Main: Suhrkamp, 1989), p. 124: "Wahrheit mußte aufhören, als Re-präsentation oder Re-produktion von Gegenständen gedacht zu werden, sie mußte begriffen werden als aktives Sich-ins-Werk-Setzen des Absoluten."

27 Cf. ibid., p. 293.

radically extended irony called "romantic." If we go on to Baudelaire we find the final connections between irony, allegory, reflective correspondence and melancholia. The very first connections were established by Cervantes, who, after all, used irony all along, while giving his hero the melancholia.

(3) The conflict ideality–reality can be related to the ironic epistemology as it has been sketched above, and then explained as a conflict between poetry and prose, or between poetic and prosaic language. Don Quijote's regular stumbling over a prosaic reality is well known; less evident perhaps is that "the notion of poetic idea as prose is decisive for the whole romantic art philosophy," to use a phrase in an early work by Walter Benjamin.[28] (This cryptic statement is perhaps explained in a much later essay by Theodor Adorno in which he declares that "pure language must be prose like the holy texts.")[29] To develop this idea on the conditions of romantic thought would lead us far away from all established genres and linguistic and epistemological boundaries into the new and universal language that Novalis identified with the novelistic language: "lingua romana" or, simply, "prose." It is amusing to note that this fantasy of a language beyond language started with the humble "imitación" of Cervantes.

These ideas of ironic conflicts between poetry and prose, between poetical ideals and prosaic reality, arise in more sober forms with Hegel, devoting some admiring lines of his aesthetic lectures to Cervantes, who is said to have created the novel, or at least to have introduced the novelistic ("das Romanhafte"), with his "nobly mad" hero in conflict with a "precisely represented reality":

This offers the comical contradiction of a sensible, self-ordered world and one isolated soul, who wants to create this order and permanence only by himself and chivalry, through which they can only be overthrown.[30]

---

28 Walter Benjamin, *Der Begriff der Kunstkritik in der deutschen Romantik*, in *Gesammelte Schriften*, 1: 1 (Frankfurt-on-Main: Suhrkamp, 1974), p. 103: "Die Konzeption der Idee der Poesie als der Prosa bestimmt die ganze romantische Kunstphilosophie."

29 Th. Adorno, "Parataxis. Zur späten Lyrik Hölderlins," in J. Schmidt (ed.), *Über Hölderlin* (Frankfurt-on-Main: Suhrkamp, 1970), p. 360: "Die reine Sprache ... wäre Prosa wie die heiligen Texte."

30 G. W. F. Hegel, *Vorlesungen über die Ästhetik*, in *Werke*, vol. 14 (Frankfurt-on-Main: Suhrkamp, 1970), p. 218: "Dies gibt den komischen Widerspruch einer verständigen, durch sich selbst geordneten Welt und eines isolierten Gemütes,

Heavily stylized this Hegelian and dialectic figure of thought reappears in the theory of the novel of the young Lukács, who starts from the relation between Romanticism and *Roman*; he finds this relation poignant, since "the novelistic form is, like none other, an expression of transcendental homelessness."[31] (The German "Obdachlosigkeit" sounds much better than the milder English "homelessness" and certainly fits Don Quijote, who becomes "novelistic" at the very moment when, as the anonymous man from *la Mancha*, he leaves his *Obdach* ("shelter") and goes unprotected into the unpredictable adventures of roads and taverns.)

Don Quijote then becomes Lukács' parameter for characterizing the transformation from epos into novel (which is an allegory of the tranformation into modernity and of the creation of the new out of the old), as well as the constitutive irony of the novel and its dependence on time: "Zeit." Lukács wants to explain the fact that Cervantes was capable of producing this miracle with his notion of a favorable historical moment: "His vision grew at the point where two world-epochs separated; he acknowledged and understood them and elevated the most obscure and lost problematics into the light sphere of a transcendence fully exposed as form."[32]

This seems to mean that my little excursion into romantic thought has finished at the point where it started: i.e. in the observation that Cervantes' *Don Quijote* is situated in a major historical shift. As we remember, Michel Foucault, in *Les mots et les choses*, made *Don Quijote* paradigmatic of the reluctant transformation into the proto-modern epoch of re-presentation. Hegel, Lukács and Foucault are united in this epochal thinking. And they are in good company: no less a figure than our main character and hero, Don Quijote, found himself "at the point where two world-epochs separated" and then gave himself a renovating and re-establishing mission in that "iron age" called "modernity" by later historians (following in Hegel's footsteps). The simple reason it seems so tempting to present the book on Don Quijote as new — as novel, even as *the* new and as the novel itself —

das sich diese Ordnung und Festigkeit erst durch sich und das Rittertum, durch das sie nur umgestürzt werden könnte, erschaffen will."
31 Lukács, *Die Theorie des Romans*, p. 35.
32 Ibid., p. 134: "Seine Vision erwuchs an dem Punkt, wo zwei Weltepochen sich schieden, erkannte und begriff sie und erhob die verworrenste und verlorenste Problematik in die Lichtsphäre der ganz aufgegangenen, ganz zur Form gewordenen Transzendenz."

is that this book so eminently lives and works in the problematizing and ironizing of time, for instance in the relations of old and new and in the mystery of making new out of old – by imitation.

I will finish this meditation by again calling my witnesses on the remarkable life of Don Quijote, as a character and as a story. They are all busy problematizing time and are, therefore, interested in renovation and the possibilities of the new. Unamuno insists that immortality is the ultimate aim for him, for Don Quijote and for any decent writer – while he is the one to "modernize" Cervantes most wilfully. Borges has his Pierre Menard contemptuously rejecting all modernization in favor of literal imitation – something that the narrator then pronounces to be the really new! If we endeavored to summarize the quixotic insight thereby made by Menard/Borges – in loving solidarity with the great precursor – it would be as a maxim: to make new is impossible; and it is impossible not to make new.

Novelistic history from Cervantes up to, for instance, Paul Auster indicates that this maxim, which may seem paralysing, nevertheless has an encouraging effect.

3

Rousseau's "Rêverie"

Julie: presence, distance

Letters need distance: you rarely write to someone standing at your side. Letter-writing between lovers normally does not compensate for physical intimacy and presence. In Rousseau's epistolary novel *Julie* of 1760, every participant is obsessed with love, but they write obsessively to each other because of distance. In this first section of my chapter on Rousseau dealing with *Julie* I will give some examples of his novelistic letter that carefully measure distance in time and space while powerfully expressing longing and the need for proximity, identity and simultaneity, i.e. for the presence indicated by love. These examples will revolve around Rousseau's handling of fiction and some adjoining concepts like "rêverie" and "chimère" in a dialectic of proximity and distance. This dialectic strikes me as analogous to those I have been tracing as *mimesis* in Plato and *imitación* in Cervantes, at least in the elementary meaning that the concepts involved allow for divergent readings, with Time as the point of diversion. *Mimesis* understood as imitation is an obsessive idea in Rousseau's educational mind, as shown in *Julie* and still more in *Émile*. Even more interesting is the dialectic suggested above as Rousseau – as the first, I believe – develops a phenomenology of silence and distance. I will then follow this development in Rousseau's handling of the Self and the problems of writing his Self in *Confessions*. Finally, I shall consider how in his last work, *Les Rêveries*, he tries to develop the concept of "rêverie" into a mediator between time, presence and distance. I will stick to Rousseau's works of fiction or quasi-fiction and claim the unusual concept of "rêverie" as his effort to handle the problems of fiction in a dialectical phenomenology of presence (as in sensation and memory) and distance (as in silence and forgetting).

Julie, ou la Nouvelle Héloïse was Rousseau's first and last novel and became one of the most read books of the eighteenth century. It has a not very accurate subtitle: *Lettre de deux Amans, Habitans d'une petite Ville au pied des Alpes. Recueillies et publiées par J. J. Rousseau.* By not accurate, I mean that Rousseau was a more active originator than the modest subtitle suggests; that the letters of the novel are exchanged not only between the two lovers – Julie and "Saint-Preux" – but also between connected friends and, in the last three "books," with an omnipresent husband.

And do they live at the foot of the Alps? Well, Julie lives there all the time and seems to leave her beloved Clarens for only one or two hazardous trips on Lac Léman. But "Saint-Preux" is always on the move: he comes from nowhere, approaches his beloved Julie and at the end of the first book gets as far as her bed, is exiled from bed to Paris and is exiled again when Julie finally marries, something that marks the middle point of the novel; he crosses the seas before he comes back sunburnt and pockmarked. "Saint-Preux" has no home; he is exiled from the start and, in the course of the novel he becomes a knight-errant, three or four times exiled.

He is also a stranger: "Saint-Preux" is his pseudonym. The first, and I think only, time in the text it is used is in a note to the third book, where we read that it is more or less a joke (meaning something like "holy knight") standing for a certain "S. G.". But this "real" name is never used; the letters between the two lovers are addressed to Julie or from Julie, and she is the centre – name and home and bosom – around which "Saint-Preux" and everyone else circle. Her husband's name, too, has a pseudonymous ring: Baron de Wolmar. Only late in the novel (and long after the marriage) are we and Julie informed of his background; but he does not reveal more (in IV: 12) than a romantic past of possibly noble, and certainly foreign, origin. His name is, like "Saint-Preux," an allusive *nom-de-guerre* in the war-game of love. Female names, on the other hand, are substantial. Julie's clear-sighted friend is Claire, while Julie is defined patronymically: from Julie d'Etang to Julie de Wolmar. Is that simply a development from pond ("étang") to sea ("mare," "mer")?[1]

The "two lovers" of the subtitle develop into a nest of love where

---

1 Peggy Kamuf points out that "étang" could also mean "to stop the flow of a liquid," according to her "usually blood" (*Fictions of Feminine Desire* [Nebraska University Press, 1982], p. 112).

everybody loves everybody. Or, perhaps, does everybody love Julie? Or learn to love the love that is represented by Julie? Anyway, *love* is the starting-point of the novel, the reality of love and love as presence is what it is about – and its simple action can be described as everybody slowly gathering at Clarens and around Julie as a totem of love. Julie then dies, changing her presence into definite distance. Love is the final point, as it was the axiomatic starting-point: love is a *fait accompli*, a state of affairs involving Julie and "Saint-Preux" from the very first letter, but expanding in the second half of the novel (books IV–VI) to encompass all – making first lover "Saint-Preux" more than friendly with husband Wolmar, and more or less enamoured with friend Claire. Love is there from beginning to end – but how can Rousseau elevate this feeling into an axiom and make it obvious, real, present? How is presence made present?

First, he chooses the letter as his form. The lovers themselves are to write about their love. But Rousseau's mimetic ambition is not satisfied with the letters indicating or writing *about* love; they should also express love, manifestly *be* love. An interesting introduction in the form of a dialogue, the so-called second preface, is used by Rousseau to develop a tortuous defense for his having written a love-novel. Rousseau, who had raved against novels as an expression of the decadence of the time and of manners, and the love-novels as the very worst decadence, Rousseau, the severe citizen of Geneva, had written a love-novel in six books and 600 pages, erotically steaming from the first page to the last! Rousseau's defense for this follows a well-known pattern: his novel is actually not a novel at all. The love he is "collecting and publishing" is no novelistic love, but real love. And his novelistic love-letters are no common novelistic letters, but real love-letters. A real love-letter must, Rousseau explains, be "loose" in style, "confused" in syntax, distinguished by "tedious repetitions" and even "decomposition."[2] It should, in short, give grammatical expression to the feeling that it also reports on – and the grammar of love (as presence) is antagonistic to ordinary grammar.

It comes as no surprise that several of these letters are highly strung and hyperbolic in tone: Rousseau uses what J.-L. Lecercle has characterized as "an abundance of exclamation ... especially a systematic use of paroxystic terms and of hyperboles."[3] At exciting moments Rousseau makes extensive use of the interesting trope aposiopesis in order to achieve a panting syntax, suggesting – with dashes and heavy pauses – something of what was then called "je-ne-sais-quoi"; i.e. what could be hinted and guessed at, but certainly not named.

Let me give an example. Towards the end of the first book we rapidly approach love's physical consummation – the very moment of presence! – for Julie and her eagerly courting pseudonym, "Saint-Preux." Letter I: 54 he evidently writes sitting on the bed in her room, where he has arrived by climbing a ladder and invited by herself. In other words, "Saint-Preux" is writing to Julie in her own room while she is undressing slowly enough to give him time to fantasize in writing about the "delicious imprints" of the body on the corset. He even congratulates himself for having found paper and ink, giving him the opportunity to describe expressively what he sees and feels and thereby "tempérer l'excès," (calm his violent feelings). When and how the letter is delivered does not emerge since it is interrupted by Julie's physical approach and the lover's excited exclamations. "It is she ... It is she!" he exclaims – on the paper and in the letter he is writing to her.

The next letter (I: 55) is again from the lover to Julie. It does not say where it was written, but is apparently written straight after the act of love: it starts with invitations to Julie to come "die" with him now that all "delights" are "exhausted" ("épuisé"). There then follow some lyrical descriptions of the moment, already passed, when he woke up in her arms, a moment he would dearly like to have "eternally" prolonged.

The situation may seem slightly bizarre; one might imagine that the lover in his excitement before and/or after would let go of pen and paper. But Rousseau was apparently not satisfied with having the lover, for example, report on what happened to a friend or review the event afterwards to Julie; he wants to give us the closest possible insight and impression. At the same time, he could not – for narratological as well as moral reasons – let the lover use pen and paper in the middle of the act (and certainly not to write a letter to Julie); even if he thereby would have come slightly closer to the event, the very act of love would still be separated from the act of writing.

3 Jean-Louis Lecercle, *Rousseau et l'art du roman* (Geneva: Slatkin, 1979), p. 194.

The question is whether the distinction between experience and language is not stressed or even accomplished in the effort of Rousseau to pass it by or ignore it. The text offers a lively expression of the pre-coital excitement of the lover in 1: 54 and his post-coital sentiment in 1: 55. *Between* the letters we find a so-called significant silence in the form of a void. And this void the reader can, if he so wishes, try to fill with the very act of love. That would be an effect close to a rhetorical aposiopesis, where the text, with the help of typographical signals like dashes, marks and empty spaces, tries to express a meaning beyond or above the normal meaning of signs.

Love is made present in a void.

There seems to be a kind of male logic in this: when love is to be made present, to be "consummated" as it is called, then Julie becomes silent – Julie who normally has so much to say *about* love. It is the lover who has the word both before and after the physical union. This union takes place in a void, which we can interpret as a sign (that is, a quasi-sign, since a void is nothing at all) referring to Julie (or to the actual act of love or to the part of Julie brought into use for the act) and in which the lover, as already quoted, has "exhausted" the "delights" that are foreboded by his visual fantasy in 1: 54.

This, then, is our first example of a dialectic of difference or distance: letter-writing establishes the distance that Rousseau at the same time seems to want to abolish in a gesture of aposiopesis. The two quoted letters from the lover, which frame, and in a way create, the act (the act as void), produce this effect – making love present only when the text produces absence – primarily by making the lover take his time writing letters to Julie instead of doing something else. We can apparently get an impression of Julie's physical presence only by the lover *writing* (to her) about her body and, therefore, holding the pen instead of her body in his hand (and he even writes of the "imprints" or "impressions" of her body as if to stress that the body comes to him by way of writing). The lover must make himself completely insensitive to the most basic facts of love in order to make love physically present. In other words, Rousseau must make the lover absent in order to make love present to us. A vicious logic seems close: the more Rousseau works to make love present, the more he must make the lover absent and the beloved Julie silent.

Also, for Rousseau – and not least for Rousseau – who strives after presence, writing creates difference and therefore distance. Narrative logic, i.e. the epistolary form, underlines this difference. It is, furthermore, a difference that reminds the reader of Rousseau's famous discourses on the fatal differences of *culture* in general (in comparison with the similarity and identity postulated as a state of nature); or his criticism of *language* as an obstacle to immediate communication. The vicious logic forces the enemy of novels to write a novel in order to declare his enmity. The enemy of culture must master culture. The enemy of language cannot but use language in order to establish his enmity. A recurrent theme in Rousseau's autobiographical texts is his repeated decision to quit writing – but, as Jean Starobinski points out in his great book on Rousseau, with the striking title *La transparence et l'obstacle*, he could not possibly quit writing "since writing has become absolute proof of the absence of communication."[4]

A second example. A bit earlier in the book (1: 23) the lover is at a physical distance from Julie, and, therefore has a better reason than later, in her bedroom, for writing fiery letters to her. In this one he develops a fantasy about (and to) his beloved, only to bring it to an abrupt end:

The mail is arriving, I must finish my letter and run to receive yours. How my heart will beat until that moment. Alas! I was happy in my chimeras, my happiness flies with them; what will I be in reality?[5]

I have kept the closest equivalent to Rousseau's "chimères" as the lover's term for his fantasies, since the term is important in some passages I will discuss later; and I have kept the odd construction of the last clause – "que vais-je être en realité?" – since it has something to say about the epistemological problems of the epistolary form and of fiction in general.

What is actually the "reality" for "Saint-Preux" here? The passage gives the impression that he has written with such enthusiasm about Julie that she and the letter have developed into chimeric fantasy; when the mail arrives, fantasies are interrupted by "reality." "Reality" is what makes him end his letter and, with the letter, his fantasy; Julie comes closer in the shape of a new letter. Julie as fantasy is interrupted by Julie as reality – and reality here is nothing but the text of a letter.

4 I will follow Arthur Goldhammer's translation of Jean Starobinski, *Transparency and Obstruction* (Chicago University Press, 1988) with slight modifications. Here, it is p. 141.
5 Rousseau, *Julie*, p. 84: "La post arrive, il faut finir ma lettre, et courir recevoir la votre. Que le coeur me bat jusqu'à ce moment! Helas! j'étois heureux dans mes chimères: mon bonheur fuit avec elles; que vais-je être en realité?"

This interruption provokes the melancholy of the lover ("Alas!"): even before he has finished his letter he mourns as lost the fantasy he had created in writing. "Saint-Preux" seems to prefer his fantastic Julie to the real. Or does he prefer his text to hers (since both fantasy and reality are in this case produced as text)? Or is the odd choice created by the narratological predicament of the epistolary form?

Glancing out of the window to see the mail arriving seems like a standard device in the epistolary novel of the period to create change and development of time. The effect is mimetic or at least scenic: we are reminded of the very act of writing also in the letter-writing, which is otherwise necessarily retrospective. The implicit temporal conflict between *now* and *then* that is manifested could be poignant for an author like Rousseau with ambitions to make the text into reality and a permanent *now*. He surely chooses the epistolary form when writing his great novel on love because letters give the feeling of intimate presence and of reality. His mail arriving comes *as* reality and *with* reality! But it also interrupts the lover's letter and his fiction as an efficient reminder that love-letters are still different from love; at the decisive moment the lover has to put down his pen (even if he is able to hold on to it longer than should be possible, according to my previous example). But even the first letter of the first book has as its very condition that love has *already* happened, and this can be lamented or celebrated only by the letters. The second letter of the first book then laments the first! And the third letter laments all that already has happened! Yes, there would be no reason whatsoever to write all these letters if love had not *already* happened before the letters. The letters also appear, as has been commented, "to be reflective and retrospective musings, interpretations of events rather than being themselves the events."[6]

And what else could they possibly be? The events themselves — reality itself — necessarily come before the letters or take place between the letters or after the letters. "The whole text," according to another commentator, "carries a title evoking the mediaeval past, and an epigraph from a long-dead poet mourning one who is gone before him. What follows, six hundred pages, is monument."[7] Well, such

---

6 Paul de Man, "Allegory (Julie)," in *Allegories of Reading* (Yale University Press, 1979), p. 194.
7 R. J. Howells, *Rousseau, La nouvelle Héloïse* (London: Grant and Cutler, 1986), p. 52.

categorical judgments invite modification. Rousseau has, after all, his devices for producing an effect of presence in the text: aposiopesis and adjoining rhetorical tropes make small-scale what the letter-writer's glance through the window – "The mail arrives" – produces as scenic effect. In both cases the textual effect must be called interruption: the epistolary text is interrupted to give way to the imaginary (or, should one say, negative?) presence of a void, and, by this interruption, presence becomes dependent on absence.

The temporal sequence of the whole novel illustrates a similar phenomenology: it spans a long period of time while celebrating the disruptive and extraordinary moment – the very moment that "Saint-Preux" in I: 55 wanted to stick to eternally as a permanent presence of love. The moment or instant and the presence – they are the breaks or interruptions of time, the temporal cesuras that the letters all aim for; while the letters nevertheless build a "novel" in vast narrative and temporal sequence. The moment escapes the letter and the narration and the language – like the moment of love, which has already happened when the letters and the novel start, or which happens in the breaks between the letters; or like the moment of death: in the sixth book Wolmar reports extensively on Julie's death (after it has happened) and Julie herself can forebode this death, but the moment of death comes in between.

The letters, therefore, underscore the predicament of writing and language: they measure the void between the phenomenal world and the textual world. As text, the letters deal with phenomena like love and death while drawing a boundary and thereby establishing distance, void.

But Rousseau unwillingly dispenses with his hope for a world without voids and boundaries, and he reluctantly abandons his hope for a language of love as presence. An example of his hopes is that Rousseau has provided a piece of text *before* the text in analogy to love as something that has *already* happened as a condition of the text getting started. This is the epigraph or pre-text from the "long-dead poet," who is Petrarch. Italian quotations – from Metastasio, Tasso but above all Petrarch, who "became Virgil for this new Dante," to quote another commentary[8] – precede and introduce the text and make themselves noticed throughout the novel. For the French, the

---

8 Bernard Gagnebin in the commentary on Rousseau's *Julie*, p. 1340: Petrarch "fut le Virgile de ce nouveau Dante."

Italian sounds foreign and archaic, but is still recognizable and can be understood as a language of authenticity with direct communication to love and death – as a kind of language before language and, therefore, a language that can immediately and really name and mean. Unless you start reading this language in the same way that you read the language of the letters: the pre-text from Petrarch (*Rime* 188) then definitely expresses distance and difference – it is in the past tense and describes the mourning of the poet after the loss of the woman he once "knew"; while alluding, as far as I understand it, to another and still earlier biblical text.

We glimpsed another attempt to handle the voids of language and suggest a state without difference and borders at the end of letter I: 23 as quoted above. "Saint-Preux" imagines his beloved Julie, but interrupts himself writing: "I was happy in my *chimères*, my happiness flies with them." The situation is odd: it is as if "Saint-Preux" prefers Julie as a fantasy to the reality coming as a letter to him, as if fantasy is more real than reality. Yet, the happily chimeric fantasy is quite as much a part of a letter as the "reality" announcing its presence. In his fantasy the lover can forget the social and practical circumstances that prevent the presence of his love, i.e. his possession of Julie. To those circumstances belong, however, a factor that could not be eliminated: time. His fantasy, as it developed in the letter to Julie – remember that he is writing *to* Julie *about* Julie – before our quotation, is therefore about a timeless life with Julie, life in an eternal now. And if the mail had not arrived he would still have been writing his fantasy – since time was excluded.

Yet the quoted passage seems to demonstrate that the conditions for his fantasy are exactly those circumstances that the fantasy excludes: time (i.e. distance) and language (needed to write the fantasy). Distance in time and space is needed for the lover to get started with his writing, and he must start writing in order to reach his fantasy. The fantasy about Julie's presence is provoked in writing – and in a letter to the same Julie, a letter that has her absence as its first condition, and in which she can read about herself as eternally present. But, at the very moment that presence gets close, the letter-writing is interrupted. The mail is arriving! The delightful *chimères* of the lover not only seem to have distance and language as necessary conditions, but they also lead to and call to mind their own boundaries, which are the boundaries of the letter and of the writing of the letter. When "Saint-Preux" in the written fantasy re-presents and re-establishes his love as passion he also establishes the boundaries of passion.[9]

"Rêverie" is the term used elsewhere by Rousseau to name that unnameable state beyond borders and differences. The term and phenomenon crop up everywhere in his writings, not least in his autobiographical writings and primarily in his last work: *Les rêveries du promeneur solitaire.* I will have every opportunity of going into the term when I come to this text in the last section of this chapter, so here I will mention only its significance for Rousseau's fiction. The term is close to the *chimères* demonstrated above as being tempting to the lover "Saint-Preux," but problematic since they suggested a conflict with "reality" — no matter if "reality" was Julie's text or her person. As a contrast I will continue with an example of *rêverie* that seems excitingly and unproblematically happy.

To be sure, we know nothing of the content of this fantasy, but all the more about its circumstances and setting. We are now approaching Julie's famous *Elysée*, extensively described by "Saint-Preux" in a letter to a friend in the fourth book, i.e. at the beginning of the second half of the novel (IV: 11). (Again the lover is the dreamer; that seems to be his privilege.) The novelistic situation is that time has passed: the novel has passed its turning-point, "Saint-Preux" has sailed the seas, Julie has become Mme. de Wolmar complete with children, and after consulting her husband she invites the ex-lover on a sublimating cure at Clarens, where earthly love is practiced as social utopia under the supervision of the Baron of Wolmar. Near to the estate is her garden, where an impressed "Saint-Preux" is taken on a guided tour by husband and wife. At the first sight he becomes "motionless," and then cries out in "involuntary enthusiasm" (p. 471) — the reason seems to be the wonderfully thick and rich green foliage. The cause of its richness is an equally wonderful watering system: the garden is crossed by channels in which the water winds easily or "bubbles up" or miraculously "cascades" out of the earth (p. 474). At the sight of these charms "Saint-Preux" wants instantly to fall into a *rêverie*, but he is prevented from that by Julie, who "drags" him out of his dreams by

---

9 Cf. Robert J. Morrissey, *La Rêverie jusqu'à Rousseau. Recherches sur un topos littéraire* (Lexington, Mass., 1984), p. 143: "Revivre la passion, c'est surtout revivre les limites de la passion. Et celle expérience angoissante des limites, Saint-Preux la fera en rêvant."

informing him that purely vegetative nature invites melancholy on inspection and that he first must watch the population of the garden, i.e. the fishes and the birds (p. 475). The next time "Saint-Preux" visits the garden he is alone and nothing can stop him: "I had promised myself a pleasant *rêverie,*" he writes. "I dreamed there more agreeably than I had expected. In this Elysium I spent two hours that I prefer to any other time of my life."[10]

True, we are not informed about the contents of this remarkable *rêverie*. But the garden! It is, we can soon see, a piece of perfect nature that impresses "Saint-Preux" and invites his dreaming just because of its abundantly green perfection. The letter he writes about this gives partly a description of the garden, partly explanations of its origin and lastly a more philosophical and political reflection on gardening (and no reader is surprised to learn that the English natural garden is praised at the expense of the French clipped one). Finally there is the already mentioned report on his happy *rêverie*. Attention is drawn to the fact that this perfectly natural garden demands complete control to achieve its perfection. "Saint-Preux" is surprised nowhere to see "the slightest trace of cultivation," not even a "human footstep" – and the baron explains that "it is because we have taken great pains to efface them" (p. 479). Julie asserts that "nature has done everything, but under my direction, and there is nothing there that I have not administered."[11] The garden is her *Elysée,* a female paradise that accepts some help from men – thus the baron sometimes gives a hand as *garçon jardinier.* And, above all, he contributes with the water. The luxuriant green foliage is due to the excellent watering system, to which "Saint-Preux" devotes an enthusiastic page (p. 474). The water, Julie informs him modestly, has been led to the garden from the big fountain on the terrace of the estate. This fountain was built by Julie's stern father and has been devotedly preserved by the baron. But it is of no use, according to Julie: "the fountain plays for strangers"; when the water has been led to her garden, on the other hand, it is made useful: there "it flows for us" (p. 474). The source of the water that is the precondition of the female paradise is, in other words, male: the water has been derived from the husband and ultimately from the father.

10 "Je m'étais promis une rêverie agréable; j'ai rêvé plus agréablement que je ne m'y étais attendu. J'ai passé dans l'Elysée deux heures auxquelles je ne préfère aucun temps de ma vie" (p. 487).

11 "Il est vrai ... que la nature a tout fait, mais sous ma direction, et il n'y a rien là que je n'aie ordonné" (p. 472).

Julie lets her ex-lover in on an occasional visit. The garden is locked and we are told that there are few keys – meaning that the garden must be bounded by some kind of wall, with the gate, which opens to Julie's key, and the canal from the fountain, i.e. the baron's water, as the only connections to the world. It remains an interesting riddle why the garden must be framed and protected in this way – if that was not the very condition of its paradisiac flourishing. When "Saint-Preux" makes his second and lonely visit, longing for his pleasant *rêverie*, he has to borrow Julie's key – and we must believe that the female key also opens his possibilities to *rêverie*. Yet "Saint-Preux" finds room in his letter to say that he rather would have borrowed the baron's key – perhaps he would prefer to penetrate the female garden in the name of the Law?

If the garden is locked and framed, then its text (i.e. the letter describing it) is framed by silence. When "Saint-Preux" first gets there he becomes, as already mentioned, "speechless" and "motionless" for a moment; in the end he falls into his silent, wordless and (therefore?) ravishing *rêverie*. This speechless framing of the garden, as well as its isolation and security, contribute to its allegorical or metaphorical character. (The difference between allegory and metaphor is the length of the allegory, according to some theories.[12] That should qualify this extensively described garden as an allegory, while it functions as a metaphor within the novel; just as for example the baron's fountain functions as a metaphor within the allegory of the garden.)

Julie's *Elysée* is an image, which "Saint-Preux" can take possession of with the help of her key, and indulge in through his own *rêverie*. But an image of what?

There is no lack of pre-texts in older allegorical literature on erotic gardens – Julie's *Elysée* is a worthy *locus amoenus*, a *hortus clausus* among many others.[13] They all signalize paradisiac abundance, and so does Julie's garden, mediating delicately between male and female, between nature and culture and between discipline and freedom. Apart from these allegorical signs, the garden functions metaphorically/allegorically *within* the novel: it is suggested that Julie built her garden as a replica of (or an answer to) a kind of orchard called "le

---

12 Heinrich Lausberg, *Handbuch der literarischen Rhetorik* (Munich, 1960), para. 895: "die Allegorie ist eine in einem ganzen Satz ... durchgeführte Metapher."

13 Paul de Man discusses this letter as an allegory first in "The Rhetoric of Temporality" then in "Allegory (Julie)," especially p. 205.

bosquet," which played its part as an erotic setting for her and for "Saint-Preux" in the first book of the novel, but which now, in the epoch of marriage, is wasted and deserted. Her garden is a metaphor that transports (metaphor meaning literally "transport" or "bringing over") the period of first love into marital love. The garden can, therefore, be read, depending on our preferences, as an allegory on a marriage in good order in contrast to the *bosquet* of wasting passion; or on Julie's way of caring for her past love as memory. The extreme flourishing of this memory/memorial is, as we remember, due to its watering sources: husband and father, marriage and patriarchy.

Julie's *Elysée* is an allegory; a riddle that "Saint-Preux" can appropriate only after having been provided with a guide and a key. "Saint-Preux" is, therefore, the ideal reader of Julie's flourishing "text," and the garden a metaphor or image of the "love" of the novel. This text and image demand a pre-text − "le bosquet" − just as the novel has as its condition for getting started that love is what has already happened. It is a nicely idealized image: the garden has solved all conflicts of the novelistic world, primarily Julie's precarious balance between lover, husband, father. On top of this, the *Elysée* solves the permanent problem of all novelistic worlds: time. The garden is separated not only from the world, but also from time. The garden shows no epic sequence, only a cyclical one; and there are no breaks within the garden, no interruptions, no voids and no death. Everything points to the garden as a moment in standstill, in permanent full flourish.

In his *Confessions*, Rousseau writes in the ninth book about some of the circumstances of writing *Julie* − as he remembers them or wants to remember them. "I plunged whole-heartedly into my reveries," he writes on one occasion, when he is describing how he was absorbed by the novelistic fantasies that he had a little earlier called "the land of chimeras, *le pays des chimères.*"[14] Both terms occur frequently in *Julie* and both are, as we have seen, associated with the lover "Saint-Preux", who plunges into his reveries and chimeras with the same ardor as Rousseau starting his novel-writing and getting absorbed in his fiction. Julie, the object of all dreams, is not allotted any fantasies,

14 I quote *Confessions* from the Pléiade edition of 1959, and will as far as possible give the page reference in my text. Here it is pp. 435 and 427. I will follow J. M. Cohen's translation in Penguin Classics with due modifications.

but on one occasion she actually uses the interesting term "le pays des chimères." Her use of the term in the novel develops into an ideological point of departure for a remarkable criticism of fantasies of proximity and presence, as they have been represented by the lover and by Rousseau himself.

This takes place in the eighth letter of the sixth book, the last that Julie sends to "Saint-Preux" before her drowning; afterwards, on her death-bed, she is given time for another letter, which also makes an end to the novel. In VI: 8 she surprises us, and probably "Saint-Preux" as well, with abundant intimations of the old fire not being extinguished, in spite of every effort to domesticate it in the utopian idyll of Clarens. This makes Julie capable of a sober summary of the dialectics of desire:

Unhappy the one who has nothing more to desire! He loses so to speak all that he owns. One enjoys less what one gets than what one hopes to get, and you are happy only before you are happy ... But all marvel disappears when confronted with the object itself, nothing embellishes the object in the eyes of its owner any longer; one does not imagine what one can see; fantasy no longer adorns what one owns, the illusion ceases when possession starts. The land of chimeras is the only one in this world worthy of being inhabited, and such is the nothingness of human affairs that, apart from the Being existing for itself, there is nothing beautiful except that which is not.[15]

In *Confessions*, the notions of "rêverie" and "le pays des chimères" looked much the same; both were identified with the fiction that Rousseau was elaborating in the novel *Julie*. "Fiction" was a concept that Rousseau later, in the fourth of *Les rêveries*, defined as lying without harm: "To lie without advantage or prejudice to oneself or to other people is not lying; it is not a lie, it is fiction."[16] Nothing of this accords very well with Julie's last message, because of its critical

15 *Julie*, p. 693: "Malheur à qui n'a plus rien à desirer! il perd pour ainsi dire tout ce qu'il possede. On jouït moins de ce qu'on obtient que de ce qu'on espère, et l'on n'est heureux, qu'avant d'être heureux ... Mais tout ce prestige disparoit devant l'objet même; rien n'embellit plus cet objet aux yeux du possesseur; on ne se figure point ce qu'on voit; l'imagination ne pare plus rien de ce qu'on possede, l'illusion cesse où commence la jouïssance. Le pays des chimères est en ce monde le seul digne d'être habité, et tel est le néant des choses humaines, qu'hors l'Etre existant par lui-même, il n'y a rien de beau que ce qui n'est pas."

16 *Les rêveries du promeneur solitaire* is quoted from the 1959 Pléiade edition with page references given in my text, here p. 1029: "Mentir sans profit ni préjudice de soi ni d'autrui n'est pas mentir: ce n'est pas mensonge, c'est fiction."

import. There *chimère* is unambiguously connected with desire: desire is what creates chimeras, and without chimeras desire will die. The death of desire is death itself — or so I read the exclamation that started my quotation.

There is a remarkable difference in tone between this letter and the love-letters at the beginning of the novel, where both Julie and her lover are full of desire and where "only" social and practical obstacles seem to delay or prevent the consummation of desire. The later Julie, summarizing her experience in the quotation above, also believes in desire as in life itself, but certainly not in its realization — "the illusion· ceases when possession starts." (Maybe she or Rousseau had Pascal in their minds, Pascal writing in *Pensée*, 168, that "we never live, we only hope to live.") The logic of this argument may remind us of the passage quoted earlier from I: 22, when "Saint-Preux" was pulled out of his *chimères* by the arriving mail; in both cases an imaginary world is contrasted to the real.

But again there are remarkable differences. "Saint-Preux" (I: 23) certainly does not write his letter to Julie in order to tell her that "possession" of her would in any way conflict with his "illusion" of her (to use Julie's terms in the letter quoted). On the contrary, his *chimère* consists of the "possession" of her; i.e. he writes to her not to say that he does not want her, but, that he wants to "get" her. The early letter presupposes that desire could be realized as proximity and presence — and only the postal reminder of social obstacles and narrative principles disturbs this fantasy. Julie's later letter expresses her trust in desire, but a radical mistrust of satisfying realization, and she actually develops a kind of negative dialectics of desire. Julie has, throughout the novel, been the very emblem of love, of love as presence, and of the reality of love, attracting and absorbing everyone around her. When this presence seems to be at hand she turns her back, declaring that presence could only kill the hope of presence, and that a less unauthentic presence is to be found only in the chimeric kingdom of hope. For such is the "nothingness of human affairs, *le néant des choses humaines.*"[17]

---

17 Paul de Man discusses this phrase on several occasions: *Allegories of Reading*, p. 198, *Blindness and Insight*, p. 131 and p. 17 — and there he writes that Julie "discovers desire as a fundamental pattern of being that discards any possibility of satisfaction." And Jan Rosiek considers the quotation to be "the hidden motto of de Man's collected works" (*Figures of Failure, Paul de Man's Criticism*

The fact that, after such a declaration, Julie throws herself into Lac Léman (in order to save her drowning child) and dies – leaves – her utopian congregation of love, the nest of presence, is perhaps a reasonable consequence of this pathos of distance. Furthermore, she leaves life attired in an allegorical emblem suggesting exactly the differentiating distance: a veil. That is, we learn from the baron's final account that Julie's friend Claire covers Julie's face with a veil dotted with pearls that "Saint-Preux" had brought home from his travels in India, i.e. from his exile. "Saint-Preux" has earlier (v: 9) reported a dream, in which he desperately and in vain tries to tear a veil off Julie's face. When the veil finally covers her dead face it ceases, to use Starobinski's words, "to be an episodic and fleeting metaphor and becomes a sustained allegory. The veil *is* the separation and the death."[18] The great project of the novel – love as a fact of presence, reality, utopia – culminates in separation, distance and death.

The rough conclusion I have arrived at has, however, its positive aspects; it involves, after all, a tribute to the kingdom of chimeras as the only one worth dwelling in. This kingdom is, if one is to believe the use of the term in *Confessions*, identical with fiction – and, therefore, with the novel where conclusion and tribute are found. Fiction could, on the other hand, *not* be called a harmless lie, as it was defined in *Les rêveries*. Instead, chimeric fiction is an irreconcilable opposite to the reality that infallibly kills it – "the illusion ceases when possession starts," according to Julie in her quoted letter. A chimeric fiction must, therefore, mean something radically different from the world of reality, something dissimilar, different and distant from reality; something that is differentiating, that *is* difference.

Fiction is what is not.

Such a "definition" of fiction is, I think, in harmony with Julie's, but less with Rousseau's, handling of the term in *Les rêveries*. On the other hand, it is surprisingly compatible with another famous text by Rousseau dealing with fiction: the letter to d'Alembert "sur les spectacles" – on theatre. To be sure, the tone and tenor of this long public letter do not pay any tribute to fiction. The letter to d'Alembert

1953–1970 (Århus University Press, 1992), p. 192. It also appears in the third of the recently published Gauss lectures of 1967 (*Romanticism and Contemporary Criticism. The Gauss Seminar and Other Papers* [Baltimore: Johns Hopkins University Press, 1993], p. 51).

18 Starobinski, *Transparency and Obstruction*, p. 119.

is by no means a love-letter, but rather a harsh attack on fiction in general and Parisian theatre in particular. (The letter is an imitation of key parts of Plato's criticism of *mimesis* in the *Republic*.) We learn from Rousseau here that the art of the actor is to dissimulate and "imitate" ("contrefaire"), to "attire" oneself with the character of someone else, to appear different from what one really is; and the citizen of Geneva (which is what Rousseau calls himself here) takes it for granted that honest people find something "servile et bas" in this "trade" with oneself.[19]

We can glimpse here a definition of fiction that is negative in several ways: theatrical fiction not only is morally "low," but is different from reality, since it does not allow the actor (and, after him, the spectator) to be "what one really is." The theatrical realm is certainly not worth living in, but, according to the letter to d'Alembert, it has the interesting correspondence with Julie's chimeric kingdom that it is something else and different from the realm of reality.

How are we to understand, then, that Rousseau here is condemning something that seems close to what he has Julie evoke and almost praise? In an attempt to answer this question I shall mention some interesting complications in the letter to d'Alembert (without questioning its highly moral intentions). One kind of contradiction, often commented upon, seems to surface at the end of the long letter, where Rousseau says in a note that he for his own part is charmed by Racine and "has never voluntarily missed a performance of Molière"[20] – the very same Molière who had just been strongly criticized for making fun of Alceste's chimeras! This is, however, contradictory only if we forget that Rousseau in Paris is not quite the same person as the Rousseau who in this letter calls himself "citizen of Geneva." The criticism came from the citizen – not from the enthusiastic theatre visitor or from the playwright! Nor is the "citizen" identical with Jean-Jacques, of whom Rousseau tells us, in *Confessions* (book VII) about his passion for Italian opera.

This leads, however, to a more serious complication: in order to be able to criticize theatre as fiction – the playing of rôles and difference – Rousseau must play the part of the "citizen from Geneva," use another voice than his own. He must, in other words, enter the

19 Rousseau, *Lettre à M. d'Alembert* (Geneva, 1948), p. 106.
20 Ibid. p. 176: "La vérité est que Racine me charme et que je n'ai jamais manqué volontairement une représentation de Molière."

kingdom of chimeras to be able to criticize the kingdom of chimeras – just as he can criticize modern culture only from the most developed cultural perspective, and can criticize language only with language.

Fiction is, to summarize, what is dissimilar and different. The chimeric kingdom of fiction is what is not. And, as we remember from Julie's negative dialectic as quoted above: beautiful is only that which is not ("il n'y a rien de beau que ce qui n'est pas").

The novel about Julie is a fantasy of love, and both dream and love aim for proximity, identity, presence. But the letters of the novel measure the distance between text and reality: they establish distance. Julie, the central character and the topic of the novel, Julie who is a personification of love – she is actually unattainable. She even preaches the pathos of distance and celebrates "le pays des chimères" at the expense of reality. The novel moves between presence and distance with a dialectical fervor that reminds us of, for example, the criticism of theatre by the theatre-lover Rousseau or the dreamer's criticism of dreaming or the writer's criticism of writing. And he wanted to be taken seriously, in criticism as well as in dream. "Should we smile," Starobinski asks us, when Rousseau "tells us that he was never more himself than on his days of reverie? Not at all. For Jean-Jacques, being himself means being free to *become someone else* in his imagination."[21] To that wise observation I can add only that Rousseau (as in the letter to d'Alembert) took advantage of his liberty to *become someone else* in order strongly to criticize such "trade" with one's self. (And we had already found the embryonic version of this "trade" in Rousseau's originator: Plato.)

This last criticism was pronounced by Rousseau acting as "citizen from Geneva." Neither that nor other rôles seem to give a complete coverage of himself – his "self" – and Rousseau often takes the liberty of disagreeing with himself. Nobody but Rousseau had full access to his "self" (or so he said) and, as is well enough known, he devoted a whole autobiographical project to describing this "self" – while starting the project by asserting that any written description could only cover or even *hide* the "self"![22] The position of the

21 I follow Arthur Goldhammer's translation of Starobinski's essays as they have been collected in *The Living Eye* (Cambridge, Mass.: Harvard University Press, 1989), here p. 37.

22 "Ebauches des Confessions," in *Confessions*, p. 1149: "Nul ne peut écrire la vie d'un homme que lui-même. Sa manière d'être intérieure, sa véritable vie n'est connue que de lui; mais en l'écrivant il la déguise."

"citizen" is certainly not a complete identity or "self." But what is a complete self? Rousseau's is a modern specimen, a split and divided self with a variety of contradictory parts and versions – as when the writing of the self is said to hide the self; or when Rousseau suggests that one's duties as a citizen are best taken care of when you are not a citizen, i.e. in exile! As we read in *Confessions*, book IX: "if one wishes to devote one's books to the benefit of one's country, one must absolutely not write them in their midst."[23] "Saint-Preux", many times exiled, was aware of this truth in spite of his longings for the home of Julie's bosom. And Julie, who was permanently domiciled, knew nevertheless that "le pays des chimères" was the only true homeland.

Confessions: memory and silence

Novel and autobiography are apparently *not* one and the same; yet, it is difficult, or perhaps impossible, to draw a firm line between them. Novels inevitably use biographical elements, while biographies inevitably use narrative devices, such as those we connect with novels or at least with fiction.

Take Rousseau's novel *Julie* in comparison with his autobiographical *Confessions*, which he finished about 10 years after the novel (in about 1770). Signature[24] and structures differ. In the novel, Rousseau presents himself as the editor collecting and publishing a large number of letters, which have been circulating for some undefined period of time between "two lovers" and some others. This change from olympic "editor" to pathetic author bears some resemblance to the relations between the nostalgic-elegiac author of *Confessions* – Rousseau – and his picaresque hero: Jean-Jacques. In *Confessions*,

---

23 *Confessions*, p. 406: "quand on veut consacrer des livres au bien de la patrie, il ne faut point les composer dans son sein." Something similar is said in the fifth book of *Emile*, where exile is more or less called a civil duty.

24 Although games with authorship(s) are striking in Rousseau, especially in *Confessions* – and apparently relevant for the dialectics of mimetic resemblance and difference that I am tracing – I have not been able fully to accommodate (or even understand) the investigations of names and signatures in Rousseau recently published by Peggy Kamuf (*Signature Pieces: On the Imitation of Authorship* [Cornell University Press, 1988]) and Geoffrey Bennington (*Dudding. Des noms de Rousseau* [Paris: Galilée, 1991]).

Rousseau makes himself the first person, presenting himself energetically on the first page as "moi seul," and then telling of his life as Jean-Jacques from birth in twelve books up to the very moment when he reads from the text we have just finished reading for some chosen listeners. (And the audience has shrunk from the grand perspective of the first page, where Rousseau expects to present his *Confessions* for "le souverain juge," i.e. God.)

The tools differ. In *Julie*, Rousseau enters the kingdom of chimeras, as sketched above: fantasy and dream are both means and ends. In *Confessions*, the *memory* governs the narration in combination with the ambition to tell all, as we learn at the end of the fourth book. There Rousseau tells us about his wish to make his soul "transparent to the reader's eye," to tell all and everything ("tous dire"), and to leave the interpretation and choice to the reader (p. 175). That is an ambition that could easily be called vain and unreasonable, and Rousseau was himself (as always) the first to object: on the first page of the first book he tells us that "defect of memory" could easily create "voids" in his narration, which should mean that *all* will not be told, after all – and if *all* is not told the whole project could (or should) capsize. At the beginning of the seventh book, which could be called an introduction to part II (where Rousseau starts telling of his life as Jean-Jacques in Paris), Rousseau admits that the earlier part was "entirely written from memory" and that "many mistakes" must therefore have been made (p. 277). "Mistakes"! If one accepts this, an embarrassing light is shed backwards over the book; a critical doubt is sewn – where are the "mistakes" in everything told, which he has already assured us was absolutely true? – and the project could (or should) again capsize, so to speak, retrospectively. Memory is, according to one commentator, Rousseau's "only means to self-awareness and the memory is bottomless."[25]

These perhaps self-evident ingredients in Rousseau's autobiography invite some interesting complications. His project is to "tell all" and thereby make himself "transparent" to the reader. This could also be worded as follows: Rousseau's autobiographical self – Jean-Jacques – is created by words and the creation is endless – bottomless like his memory and inexhaustible like language. Yes, "language *is* the authentic self," to use Starobinski's observation: "yet at the same time

---

25   Ann Hartle, *The Modern Self in Rousseau's Confessions. A Reply to St. Augustine* (Notre Dame, 1983), p. 103.

language reveals that perfect authenticity has still not been achieved."
Rousseau was therefore the first to experience "the dangerous pact of
the self with language: the 'new alliance' in which man makes himself
into word."[26] (My reader will surely acknowledge that this "dangerous pact" is not new to Rousseau, and that *Don Quijote*, according to
my analysis in the previous chapter, represented an attempt, albeit
within fiction, to make oneself into literature and therefore "into
word.")

The autobiographical project, the self as established by memory
and in writing, is affiliated with language and troubled by the same
problems as all other linguistic constructions; this too is perhaps
evident (but still not without complications). Above I studied how
Rousseau developed a dialectic between presence and distance in the
novel *Julie*. This was a linguistic problem in the sense that it had to do
with the possibilities (or impossibilities) of language naming and
directly expressing feelings. Now, in *Confessions*, the issue is the self or
ego, the figure consequently named Jean-Jacques by Rousseau, his
reconstruction in memory and his construction in language. The
question now is not *if* memory could do without language, but *how*
language is used by memory, and if Jean-Jacques – the self – finally
becomes "transparent," which I take to mean something like
immediately present. How does Rousseau mediate, represent and
imitate, the presence of an unmediated Jean-Jacques?

My answer to this will consist of an effort to isolate some narrative
elements in Rousseau's *Confessions*, approaching, perhaps, something
like a narrative phenomenology somewhat analogous to the dialectics
of desire as established in *Julie*. As should be clear by now, the reason
for this strategy is *not* to ignore obvious differences between
autobiography and novel, but to explore the topography of the
borderland, bearing in mind that Rousseau seems always on the move
across borders. Starting with the idea of a "pact" between man and
language, it would not be unreasonable to imagine biographical man
as narratively constructed – and, as will presently be shown, Rousseau
actually insists that narrative in the mode of "novels" actually played
a decisive part in the construction of Jean-Jacques.

We will come to this through an observation concerning the overall
narrative structure, because I find it difficult to avoid the impression
that the organization of *Confessions* is patterned by revolution,

---

26 Starobinski, *Transparency and Obstruction*, p. 200.

metamorphosis, transformation, conversion. The Rousseau of reality becomes the Jean-Jacques of language through epoch-making narrative events; again and again something revolutionary determines the character and self of Jean-Jacques, once and for all — or at least until the next revolution. One of the most famous revolutions is reported in the eighth book: his "vision" on the way to Vincennes, when he suddenly realizes the dialectic of nature and culture that he was famously to develop in his works of social philosophy. According to the biographical memory, this insight comes over him when reading an advertisement in *Mercure de France*, in which the Academy of Dijon asks for answers to the burning question of the importance of culture for the development of manners. *Reading* is what makes Jean-Jacques into Jean-Jacques: "The moment I read this I beheld another universe and became another man" (p. 351).

He was "another man" from the beginning: on the first page of the first book he declares himself to be another, "je suis autre." In the course of the book this feeling seems to be strengthened into being *unique*, and the autobiographical project as being unparalleled, as it is already pronounced to be in the very first sentence of the book. From the beginning it is *reading* (and therefore language) that has made him become himself, i.e. uniquely another. Rousseau pinpoints the first "unbroken consciousness of my own existence" to his first experiences of reading (p. 8). And what he reads first is — novels. We get no titles, but some details: Jean-Jacques reads in bed the novels his dead mother left him, and these initiate him into "émotions confuses." This gives us the following setting: with the help of Rousseau's memory we learn that Jean-Jacques was established by reading and when reading "novels"; and when memory approaches this reading experience the newly established self is dissolved in "confused emotions." The common denominator between phenomena and self is called "novels."

These preliminary examples show that the affiliation of language with identity is by no means a recent idea that is now being squeezed into Rousseau's text; rather, Rousseau actually insists that Jean-Jacques is created by reading, therefore in language. That affiliations exist, even intentionally, has, however, little to say about *how* these relations are created and what they mediate — even if the examples chosen indicate that the establishment of the self is revolutionary and in one way or another connected with the self being, from the beginning, "another" and even "unique." Memory remembers in leaps or revolutionary cycles, it seems. And catastrophically: each revolutionary creation of another self paves the way for a catastrophic development. After the revolution on the way to Vincennes, when Jean-Jacques suddenly "became another man," Rousseau states curtly that all his "misfortunes followed inevitably as a result of that moment of confusion" (p. 351).

Similar statements function within a revolutionary and catastrophical setting as a kind of refrain all through *Confessions*, starting with the physical birth which, in one of Rousseau's famous phrases, was "the first of my misfortunes" (p. 7). When he immediately after that fatal event – his birth – tells us how novel-reading creates (the consciousness of) an "unbroken" Jean-Jacques, he adds that he was actually never "cured" of the "romantic notions" of life that his reading created as a kind of basis for himself; the biographical self, therefore, seems like a chronic disease, instituted by "novels." Starobinski is, as always, to the point when he writes that the reader of *Confessions* "discovers that the expulsion from paradise is repeated several times"[27] – Rousseau's memories of catastrophic revolutions in his life have all the character of paradise and innocence lost; and of a repeatedly lost innocence.

We have isolated a narrative element in Rousseau's *Confessions*, but have only started the exploration of the borderland of autobiography and novel. After all, conversion, transformation and revolution make up a topos that is as well known in the novel as in history and biography. Conversion is the very topic of one of Rousseau's obvious pretexts, Augustine's *Confessiones* (which, incidentally, also establishes a connection between language and reading and the new self: in the famous revelation under the fig-tree in book VIII, chapter 12, Augustine reports hearing a voice telling him "Take and read!" – and what he takes and reads, with revolutionary effect, happens to be a piece by Paul, another well-known convert). Rousseau, as it were, secularizes the depiction of conversion and combines it with the narration of fall, expulsion, loss of innocence – and the recovery by memory.

No doubt we can reach further in narrative analysis – although without domesticating the borderland between novel and autobiography (nor would that be an aim). Rousseau's biographical memory remembers not only in revolutionary sequences, but also in dramatic scenes. The narrative construction of these scenes probably has some elements in common with those "novels" that made up the

27 Starobinski, *The Living Eye*, p. 46.

first Jean-Jacques. Furthermore, the narratives have strong links with Rousseau's philosophical and sociological thought.

Remember Julie's *Elysée* in the novel *Julie* (IV: 11)! In the analysis of that passage sketched above, I emphasized the metaphorical situation of the erotic garden in the novel, and the lover "Saint-Preux" as the ideal reader of Julie's "text". His reading-description is started and finished in silence, and his silent and motionless astonishment is broken by his cry of "involuntary enthusiasm" (p. 471).

Then compare the scene in the second book of *Confessions*, where Rousseau tells of young Jean-Jacques in Turin meeting Mme. Basile, a brunette he remembers as "extrêmement piquante" (p. 73). As an introduction to the scene we get a description of Jean-Jacques' fascinated (and silent) worship of the sight of the lady, and his sighs when he watches "the lace on her bosom rise" (p. 74). After this preparation, giving us some mental and scenic essentials, the scene itself starts, classically, with a temporal signal: "un jour." One day, then, it happens that Jean-Jacques enters the lady's chamber while she is sitting at her embroidery with her back to the door. The sight overwhelms Jean-Jacques, who throws himself on his knees with his arms outstretched in "passion," believing himself to be unseen. But a mirror reveals him. Mme. Basile says nothing, only points with a finger to the mat at her feet. "I trembled, cried out and threw myself on the spot she had designated on the spur of the moment."[28] There lies Jean-Jacques – "motionless and dumb, but certainly not calm" – playing in what he remembers as a "lively dumb-show" until a noise breaks the spell and Mme. Basile makes him get up. When he does he presses two burning kisses on the hand that pointed out for him the spot at her feet and thereby gave Jean-Jacques what Rousseau remembers as the most delightful moment of his life.

The commentary in the philological Pléiade edition of *Confessions* tells us that Rousseau worked on this scene in several versions, and that the final version stresses Jean-Jacques' dumb passivity, giving extra weight to the two movements of the scene: Madame pointing with her finger and Jean-Jacques' immediate activity after that: trembling, etc. Rousseau's emphasis on the silence of the scene gives dramatic importance to its only sound: the cry uttered by Jean-Jacques when trembling and throwing himself at her feet.

---

28 "Tressaillir, pousser un cri, m'élancer à la place qu'elle m'avoit marquée ne fut pour moi qu'une même chose" (p. 75).

Starobinski discusses this scene thoroughly, giving its speech-lessness its due importance: Madame Basile pointing her finger is then the kernel, he writes, "around which the whole scene crystallizes"; it is feeling transformed into "sign," pointing to a kingdom of meaningful signs before or beyond language. In such a kingdom Rousseau can imagine a presence of feeling that language normally prevents, and for Jean-Jacques "the pleasure of love lies not in possession but in presence, in the intensity of presence."[29] Such a presence, or intensity of presence, is of decisive importance for the autobiographical self, although negatively (to use another felicitous choice of words from Starobinski): the glory of presence is "that state in which exaltation, by its very intensity, culminates in depersonalization."[30]

The moment of presence is also the moment of the revolutionary transformations of the self, its birth coinciding with its death.

These observations can, perhaps, be enlarged by some comparisons. Julie's *Elysée* again: the flourishing garden framed and fenced by silence. The immobility and silence created by the sight of the garden are broken by the lover crying out in an "enthousiasme involontaire" – while he reports on his final *rêverie*, in lonely silence, as being the most delightful hours of his life.

These scenes seem structurally alike, and the similarity has a phenomenological relevance: a dialectic of silence and language in which the frustrated lover – Jean-Jacques as well as "Saint-Preux" – is given the task of breaking the silence with a sound that still is not articulated speech (in *Julie* we learn that the cry of the lover sounds like the words "O Tinian!" Rousseau explains this pedantically in a note as referring to a desert island in the South Seas, i.e. to the pre-cultural state of nature). But, if the lover's sound is not articulated as language, but remains purely natural sound, it is also a formidable expression of passion. This makes these two scenes into summaries of the origin and history of languages, as developed by Rousseau in other writings: from silence into passionate sounds and from sounds into articulated speech. Rousseau stated philosophically that mankind was silent for ages before uttering the first sounds of passion that still later became metaphors and finally our language – but autobiographically he gave Jean-Jacques only seconds between silence and cry (but has to add the

29 Starobinski, *Transparency and Obstruction*, p. 154.
30 Starobinski, *The Living Eye*, p. 26.

transference to his own *writing* in order to record the scene). Furthermore these scenes develop a dialectic of movement and motionlessness: "Saint-Preux" becomes *immobile* when first looking at the garden, and the cry he utters comes out "involontairement," without his will or intention. Jean-Jacques "trembles" when he sees Mme. Basile's finger – and his trembling must also be interpreted as an involuntary movement.

Rousseau remembers Jean-Jacques as dumb and immobile at the feet of Mme. Basile. But he uttered a cry when he "trembled" and "threw himself" at her feet. Since he had already thrown himself on his knees when entering the room and seeing her, it would mean that both his movements, so to speak, point to the floor as figures of subjection; or, perhaps, as regressive movements, analogous to the cry, which is regressive in relation to speech, but, therefore, gives a more immediate expression of passion (according to Rousseau's philosophy of cultural development).

Or they are like erotic movements: the three verbs quoted above and describing Jean-Jacques' physical activity in Mme. Basile's chamber are apparently erotically charged and their being piled one upon the other and described as instantaneous – or, more exactly, as "une même chose" (one and the same) – gives his movement an intense acceleration in making a "phallic" gesture towards the female room, where the woman sits silently waiting, almost without moving – we are given the impression that only her pointing finger moves, although we know that she was sitting working with her embroidery. In the novelistic scene from Julie's *Elysée*, the lover's involuntary crying out when seeing the woman's intensely flourishing garden seems like a battle-cry for the holy knight – "Saint-Preux" – who then proceeds to penetrate this verdure, where he is finally absorbed in a *rêverie* more delightful than anything he can think of.

Jean-Jacques' "trembling" relates to controlled physical expression, just as the cry succeeding the trembling relates to speech: like expressions beyond control and, therefore, expressions of passion. "Tressaillir" – tremble, shiver, shake, shudder – can be observed on some other occasions in *Confessions*, always similarly charged. At the beginning of book II, Jean-Jacques meets Mme. Warens for the first time, and Rousseau recalls this meeting in a short scene with interesting parallels to the scenes discussed above. This scene is situated in the garden belonging to Mme. Warens, a garden apparently surrounded by water. There, young Jean-Jacques – "trembling" and apparently speechless at seeing the beautiful woman – delivers his letter of introduction. Her voice (i.e. the *sound* rather than the meaning of the words) pronouncing her first words, "Eh! mon enfant," makes him start, tremble or shudder, or however it should be translated: "me fit tressaillir" (p. 49). By that we are given premonitions of erotic presence related to Mme. Warens who is to be "Maman" to Jean-Jacques, and who will also (as described in book V) give him erotic lessons, always against a background of rural and flourishing nature.

A last trembling is remembered by Rousseau towards the end of *Confessions* (book XII). It has to do with good memories of a tiny island in a Swiss lake, Lac de Bienne, where Jean-Jacques has escaped the world for a while (Rousseau describes the same episode extensively in the fifth walk of his *Rêveries* and I will come back to that later). Here I want only to observe that Rousseau remembers trembling for joy – "une joye qui alloit jusqu'au tressaillement" (p. 643) – from meeting not women, though, but water: he trembles without reason or intention as soon as he sets out alone in a boat on the lake. The absence of women does not mean an erotic absence, however: water was floating, as mentioned above, around the garden of Mme. Warens and cascades everywhere in Julie's *Elysée*. I will soon try to show that water is an element that not only gives erotic signals, but is actually a constitutive element of the autobiographical self – not in itself but in combination with the voice talking in and through the supreme faculty of biography: memory. The trembling mediates between immobility and movement; just as the cry breaks the barrier between silence and speech and language. Water knows of no such boundaries, but floats freely between movement and motionlessness, sound and silence.

The examples I have sketched above from novel and autobiography suggest an interesting narratological affiliation, concerning not large-scale narrative structure, but the narrative constructions of scenes. This has given us some means of orientation in a borderland, and, perhaps, this borderland consists of nothing but narrative elements. In any case, these strategies can be related to Rousseau's thinking in general, and – what concerns us here – to the constitution of the autobiographical self. This self was, as we saw, from the beginning determined by the reading of "novels." Now we can add that the self cannot after all be completely constituted as language; before or beyond language it requires *silence*.

The scenes analysed above suggest that Jean-Jacques as well as "Saint-Preux" at decisive moments – moments that for both are described as highlights – fall into silence (and immobility) or, at least, silence appears to be a necessary precursor to the loving sounds of cry, speech, language (as immobility prepares for trembling and movement). This could also be expressed more paradoxically and perhaps on a more elevated level if we remember Starobinski's observation concerning the scene with Mme. Basile: Jean-Jacques' exaltation culminates in *depersonalization*. If we lastly compare this with "Saint-Preux" in his penetration of Julie's *Elysée*, we remember that this culminated in his lonely *rêverie* in which he, as it were, lost himself and disappeared silently from his text.

Silence not only frames important scenes in *Julie* and in *Confessions*; silence actually frames the autobiographical project, i.e. the self. Silence and darkness: Rousseau raises his voice and starts writing in order to break the silence he regards himself as surrounded by, and to make his unique voice heard: "je suis autre." Yet darkness keeps spreading. The seventh book (i.e. part II) starts, after "two years of patient silence," with Rousseau complaining that he is forced to speak again and that he would rather bury what he has to say in the "darkness of time" (p. 279). When we reach the last book we learn that here "begins the work of darkness," *l'œuvre de ténèbres*, in which Rousseau considers himself to have been buried for 8 years (p. 589). When the book finally ends it is in silence: Rousseau reads his work to an audience where only one Mme. d'Egmont shows her uncontrolled reaction with a kind of trembling by now well known to us: she "trembled visibly [tressaillit visiblement]." But this reminder of a happier past quickly disappears as she pulls herself together and joins the immobility and the silence of the rest of the audience (p. 656).

The autobiographical memory, the faculty instituting the self, is "bottomless," or, its bottom is darkness. The autobiographical voice is surrounded by silence; or, to use a word with more ominous connotations, nothingness. This word is used with confidence by Julie towards the end of her novel, where she exposes the dialectic of desire (VI: 8). The probably unanswerable question now is whether the "darkness" and the "silence" of the autobiography are the attempt made by memory to reach what Julie called "le néant des choses humaine." That would, then, be a "nothingness" at the limit of the autobiographical self, and also its necessary condition, all according to the, perhaps, elementary logic implying that both "something" and "everything" presupposes "nothing."

I have suggested that these observations could probably be related to the social philosophy that Rousseau developed as his famous dialectic of nature-culture; and similarly to his speculations on the origin and development of languages. Here the narratology we have observed in scenic concentration is applied to a full-scale history of civilization. It would probably also be possible to relate his linguistic speculations to the dialectic of presence and distance described above in *Julie*; Jacques Derrida has found that Rousseau, in his *Essay on the Origin of Languages*, "puts speech against writing as presence against absence," and in his hunt for origin (and for proximity and for presence) finds so many "supplements" that Derrida can critically discuss Rousseau's "faculté de supplémentarité."[31] Finally it would be possible to relate the dialectic of presence/absence to the narratologic phenomenology I found in the borderland of novel and auto-biography.

It is in vain that we ask what comes "first" in this "chain" of "supplements." But silence frames Rousseau's text. "The tremendous power of the negative," to allude to Hegel, works constantly while instituting both self and love and text. We have, in earlier chapters, glimpsed this negative dialectic in Plato (cf. the "blinding" insight of *Phaedrus*) and Cervantes (cf. Don Quijote's sudden inability to name Dulcinea). Still, we have touched on something novel with Rousseau, something more like *element* than supplement, and that is *water*. I am now referring to the simple observation that water had a striking importance in the novel *Julie* as well as in *Confessions* (as will be shown later, even in the speculations on the origin of languages) and most of all in his final text, *Les rêveries*. We have to proceed, then, from narratological relations in Rousseau's family of texts to the element they have in common.

"Il me fallait un lac"

This is what Rousseau writes in book IX of *Confessions*, where he remembers his tender endeavor to find the right setting for his loving couple in *Julie*: "But I needed a lake [Il me falloit cependent un lac]." The lake was needed to enable him to indulge in the novelistic and, therefore, imaginary happiness, "bonheur imaginaire" (p. 431). Lac Léman was an easy choice, yet no one could say that the lake offers

---

31 Jacques Derrida, *De la grammatologie* (Paris: Minuit, 1967), pp. 239 and 343.

happiness to the lovers. In the fourth book (letter 17), "Saint-Preux" relates how he manages to take ex-mistress Julie on an outing on the lake. But the wind starts blowing and they are dramatically forced to land at a place called Meillerie, which happens to be a spot for reminiscing about their love in the first book: here "Saint-Preux" once stood loving and longing among running brooks (which still make their feet wet), and here he carved the stones full of lines from Petrarch, as always a reminder of love's original language. But this unexpected repetition is not a success: real love has long since been exiled to the past by both partners (and, according to the analysis above, it originated in the past from the beginning). The storm on Lac Léman has mixed both times and feelings, and provoked a glimpse of the presence of the love that can exist only in absence. This makes both lovers melancholy, and "Saint-Preux", on his way home on the lake turned calm, to dream of death – death by drowning and together with Julie.

That death also comes to Julie, although only in the sixth book, and not together with "Saint-Preux," but as a consequence of her saving a drowning child. The lake that Rousseau needed to get the novel started is apparently also needed for its ending. Water ominously mediating between love and death is a well-known topos to which Rousseau gives an original twist only when combining it with a more idyllic version of water, for instance the pastoral brooks at Meillerie, the place of yearning love. The most elaborated version of the running water is Julie's *Elysée*. An important part of the enthusiastic description given by "Saint-Preux" has to do with the water-supply of the garden (VI: 11, especially p. 474). As we remember from above, the erotic garden is criss-crossed by channels, originating from the fountain of the estate, built by the father and administered by Julie's husband, the baron. The channels from this patriarchal – but no longer useful! – source are used to provide the extraordinary verdure of the garden and are arranged in a style that immediately appeals to the ex-lover: he observes not only calmly running water and a mirroring pond, but also water that mysteriously "bubbles" and "cascades" out of the earth. The water is here giving life, as well as offering obvious erotic associations; yet we have to look to other places to find the common denominator between water in deadly immobility and life-giving movement.

We have, as usual, to look to *Confessions*, to find Rousseau where Jean-Jacques is hiding. My first example comes from the third book, where Jean-Jacques is working as a servant in a noble house and becomes interested in a young lady, Mlle. de Breil. I will not go into the scene that Rousseau remembers, merely state that it could easily be read according to the narratological dialectic of silence and speech, immobility and movement, that I found above in the scene with Mme. Basile. Here water is added. At the decisive moment Jean-Jacques spills water over the lady. He has distinguished himself at the dinner-table by crossing the line beween silence and speech and thereby caught the attention of the girl. Then the step to take is from immobility to movement, as always accompanied by trembling; Mlle. de Breil asks for water, Jean-Jacques rushes to her chair with a glass of water, but "when I came to her I was seized with such a trembling and since the glass was overfilled I spilled some water on her plate and even over her." Mlle. blushes, the scene is finished and the romance is over: "Ici finit le roman" (p. 96).

Starobinski has given this scene a thorough analysis underlining its allegorical and literary character; he has not failed to point out that the "trembling, the spilled water, the blush, all point to the realm of the body and are tumid with erotic significance." The climax of the scene seems based on (male) orgasm, although the overfilled container and the spilled water may have had a special fascination for an author well known for his permanent urinary troubles.[32] If we relate this scene with the enthusiasm shown by the lover when confronted with the bubbling and cascading water in Julie's garden, it would seem that Rousseau uses water to develop an erotic phenomenology.

But even this has complications; at least I would expect to find quite different dimensions in a happy episode from the sixth book of *Confessions*, where water — or, rather, its conduit or even the lack of it — is given bizarre importance in the erotic education of Jean-Jacques.

This time we meet Mme. Larnage, an experienced woman who runs into Jean-Jacques on his trip to the south of France, where he has gone to be cured of various ailments. Mme. takes care of him with erotic expertise, and for a while it is "good-bye to poor Jean-Jacques, or rather to his fever, his *vapeurs* and his polypus," as Rousseau puts it with unusual self-irony (p. 249). The background to this singular incident must be sketched. The sixth book starts with Rousseau remembering the "short period of his life's happiness" (p. 225); that is, the rural idyll in which Jean-Jacques lives with his Maman, who has

---

32 Starobinski, *The Living Eye*, pp. 205f.

recently initiated him into bodily love. Happiness looks like a homecoming or a return to the womb that expelled him at birth — Maman is, of course, a new mother, ideally combined with mistress. Fall and rejection are what created Jean-Jacques and motivate his story; but the "short happiness" of homecoming is not creative: it does not allow for narration and it corrupts his body.

This sounds odd, but that is what Rousseau remembers. He remembers this happy period, he writes, "tout entier," as if it were one single moment (p. 226). The problem is only that the moment cannot be recounted according to the narrative rules of memory; the happy feeling itself can hardly be described or named, but keeps dissolving in boring repetitions. Rousseau immediately provides an example of this impossibility by trying to narrate the memory of a happy day: "I rose with the sun, and I was happy; I went for walks and I was happy; I saw Maman, and I was happy; I left her, and I was happy," etc. (p. 225).

Memory makes the happy moment repetitive and, therefore, boring. The presence of happiness can, perhaps, be contemplated at a distance, but not described. Furthermore it was physically unbearable. As soon as happiness is established, Rousseau remembers that the happy Jean-Jacques was "languid, and became more so." Milk he cannot drink any longer, wine is not to be thought of. He tries a "water cure" and drinks so much water that he can no longer digest his food and gives up all hope (p. 227). (Some pages later Rousseau remembers differently, describing Jean-Jacques' appetite as huge — p. 239.) Jean-Jacques prepares for an imminent death and Rousseau remembers this as advantageous: "I can well say that I did not begin to live until I looked upon myself as a dead man" (p. 228).

Perhaps we should remind ourselves that this misery befalls Jean-Jacques in the middle of his short happiness, meaning that it strikes a young man in rural circumstances living with his first mistress. No matter: the water cure only makes things worse. Only Mme. Larnage can provide the famous remedy called sex. Mme. Larnage also means a change in the unpleasant combination of momentary repetition that characterized happiness and made it impossible to name and boring to describe. She is related to the journey Jean-Jacques is making and, therefore, to movement, transport and adventure; this is only mentioned as a new illustration of the affiliations between narrative logic and Jean-Jacques himself — or as a nice example of Starobinski's idea that Rousseau's autobiographical style is a mixture of elegy and the picaresque,[33] and that elegy (here represented by the memory of a short happinesss) alone cannot make up a narration.

Such is his story. Jean-Jacques leaves his happy state for picaresque adventures, and is cured of his devastating happiness. Soon he can think only of Mme. Larnage and "even Maman was forgotten" (p. 255). But not even this successful misery lasts for long: an aqueduct gets in the way!

This is how. Jean-Jacques takes a rest from his new mistress in order to look at a Roman remain near Nîmes, Pont-du-Gard. His meeting with this "so-called bridge," which is really an aqueduct, is described in half a page (p. 256) containing several ingredients that should be well known by now: dumb immobility and fantasy. Jean-Jacques is overwhelmed and speechless at the sight of this huge bridge/aqueduct and he walks reverently, dreaming on it and around it for hours — "I was lost like an insect in that immensity." When he returns he is still "distrait et rêveur" and this *rêverie*, writes Rousseau, "was not to the advantage of Mme. de Larnage." She is forgotten as well — and the erotic divertissement with her. An aqueduct conveys water, and the element (water), both in its running movement and in its mediating function, seems vital to the fantasies that this aqueduct inspires in Jean-Jacques. Yes, water seems like the very element of mediation — although this aqueduct was probably, and long since, dry. This, together with its size and its grand Roman history, patriarchal to Jean-Jacques' imagination, was arguably important for its "sublimating" effect. We can observe that Jean-Jacques, in this case, first becomes overwhelmed and speechless, then walks around and finally falls into *rêverie*. He is therefore following the pattern that is familiar from "Saint-Preux" in Julie's *Elysée* or from Jean-Jacques himself in the waterless, but more dramatic, episode with Mme. Basile. In all these cases, silence grows out of the situation (or are water and aqueduct mediating between sound and silence?); they all have an exalted character that develops into a *rêverie*. In this *rêverie* the regressive subjection we have noticed before (when Jean-Jacques falls at the feet of Madame Basile) quickly comes close to impersonality or loss of self. Jean-Jacques becomes, after all, an "insect" in the aqueduct, and that cannot be far from the "depersonalization" that Starobinski used to describe the turning-point of Rousseau's exaltation of presence.

Forgetfulness. Let us call it forgetfulness; but remembering that this

---

33 Ibid., pp. 179f.

forgetfulness occurs at the moment when the exalted self turns into a lost self, that this kind of dialectic seems analogous to what we have already discussed as presence and distance, as speech and silence – and, in earlier chapters, as the dialectics of Plato's "mimesis" and Cervantes' "imitación." And this dialectic can be worded more generally if we use the terms given to Julie in her summary, already much quoted, of the dialectic of desire: "Being" and "Nothingness" (with the reservation that Julie in vi: 8 does not use *l'Etre* in a general sense, but is referring to God; still in immediate contrast with *le néant*). The loss, absence and silence of forgetfulness are a terrible negative power (Hegel again), but my examples suggest that forgetfulness, etc. is necessary and therefore desirable: the self must, to put it biblically, lose itself in order to gain itself.

Water, for Rousseau, seems to be the element that mediates the powers of silence, oblivion, nothingness.

That is perhaps saying a lot, but still not very much about the erotic connotations of water: water had, as we could see in Julie's *Elysée* and in the episode with Mme. Breil, a distinctly erotic significance; whereas the water conduit of the episode with Mme. de Larnage made an end of such associations. But the associations, if any, could, perhaps, be illuminated by another episode – and this will be my last from *Confessions* – that includes aqueducts, this time at the beginning of *Confessions*, book I, where Jean-Jacques as a child is boarded with pastor Lambercier.

We have in a few pages been through a series of catastrophic downfalls: not only has Jean-Jacques been born ("the first of my misfortunes"), he has also been initiated into some negative erotic possibilities by Mlle. Lambercier, and he has been unjustly accused of breaking a comb (Rousseau now takes the opportunity to "declare before Heaven that I was not guilty" – p. 19). Still, he regards the innocence of his childhood as having come to a definite end (p. 20). As we remember, Jean-Jacques keeps losing his innocence all the way through his story; but it is only here that Rousseau remembers that Jean-Jacques, while falling, was building an aqueduct.

This enterprise is undertaken in imitation of the pastor, who has ceremonially planted a walnut tree with a kind of trench around it for watering it. Jean-Jacques, together with his playmate, instead plants a willow at some distance, and to water it they make a secret tunnel from the trench round the walnut tree. When the connection is established and water comes running Jean-Jacques cannot help (following a by now well-known pattern) crying out in joy; but his uncontrolled sound draws the attention of the pastor to the watering arrangement that threatens his own tree. He, in his turn, cries out in surprise before fetching a mattock and furiously destroying the laboriously built conduit while crying "an aqueduct"! The word is repeated five times in half a page, and Rousseau finds it so memorable that he italicizes it in order to stress his point (p. 24).

But what is the point? The water conduit seems here to be related to subjected silence and involuntary sound or cry; and to the planting of a green tree. If this planting is perhaps a "phallic" project (even patriarchal when associated with the pastor), in order to be successful it calls for control over the "femininity" represented by water and earth; in short, it calls for a water conduit. Therefore this scene is a kind of parallel to – or a commentary on – Julie's *Elysée*, where the verdure was due to the water benevolently provided by the paternal source that was situated outside the garden. Perhaps it would be a good idea, as has been suggested, to read these two scenes as allegories of the dialectic of male and female in Rousseau's *text*. The text would then be called "a closed maternal haven separable from, but dependent on, an open-ended paternal source outside its boundaries."[34]

That seems reasonable; yet we should not forget that the point of the aqueduct (also) is that Jean-Jacques *failed* in his effort to build an aqueduct and plant his tree (or to control the relations of source and haven) – although some pages later he is planting again, this time at a safe distance while comically, but discreetly, repeating the word "aqueduct!" cried out by the pastor. No wonder that Jean-Jacques, five books later, is overwhelmed by such a monumental edifice as the Roman aqueduct of Pont-du-Gard! Still, the successful connection of male and female is distant for Jean-Jacques, and the short moments of happiness that are reported are closer to the water suddenly spilled all over Mlle. de Breil than to the style of the pastor Lambercier and his well-planned plantation.

The failures of Jean-Jacques are, however, the condition of the success of Rousseau, the author. Still there is a gulf separating Rousseau's irregular text as well as Jean-Jacques' disorderly life from the grand – but dry – Roman aqueduct! The gulf is remarkably similar to the one separating literary classicism from the Romanticism of

---

34 Huntington Williams, *Rousseau and Romantic Autobiography* (Oxford, 1983), p. 100.

"novels" or *rêveries*. Rousseau "needed a lake" in order to dream and write. And to get further into Rousseau – text, life, dreams – we have to go for the impossible and determine the indeterminable: the water that should have been flowing in the destroyed aqueduct of Jean-Jacques the boy, the water as it once was under full Roman control and as it ideally flows only in the kingdom of chimeras.

Rêverie

"I have always been passionately fond of water and the sight of it throws me into a delicious *rêverie*," writes Rousseau in the twelfth and last book of *Confessions*, where he remembers living peacefully for some months on a tiny island in Lac de Bienne (p. 642). The same period is remembered in an even more elegiac tone in the fifth walk of his last work, *Les rêveries du promeneur solitaire*, where he calls it the happiest time of his life (p. 1042). (This should perhaps be compared with the second book of *Confessions* where he calls the episode with Mme. Basile the most delightful moment of his life; or the fourth book, where he declares a picnic with two girls to be the most pleasant event of his life; not to talk of his life's "short happiness" as it is remembered at the beginning of the sixth book, as mentioned above.) *Rêverie* is, in any case, a phenomenon that Rousseau mentions and handles with obvious delight (e.g. as a pleasant conclusion when "Saint-Preux" visits Julie's *Elysée*) and often connects to water.

I have chosen not to translate the term in order to keep the special meaning that Rousseau gives it. Nor is it easy to translate, and no less an authority than John Locke supports me on this point, to judge from this passage from *An Essay Concerning Human Understanding*:

The same *idea*, when it again recurs without the operation on the external sensory, is *remembrance*; If it be sought after by the mind, and with pain and endeavour found, and brought again in view, 'tis *recollection*: If it be held there long under attentive consideration, 'tis *contemplation*: when *ideas* float in our mind, without any reflexion or regard of the understanding, it is that, which the *French* call *reverie*: our language has scarce a name for it.[35]

This shows, at least, that with Locke (1690) the term was already associated with what was "floating" and not easily supported by

---

35 The Locke quotation is provided in the excellent analysis of *rêverie* in Morrissey, *La rêverie jusqu'à Rousseau*, here pp. 68ff.

reason or understanding. Apparently the term goes back to the "reexvagare" of medieval Latin, meaning vagabondizing, while a modern meaning was created by Montaigne, who related it to "deliratio," to "folie" and to daydreaming.[36] I find it edifying that the creator of the non-genre *essai* could not keep his fingers away from the floating concept "rêverie."

Writing about a *rêverie* is not the same thing as having one; and reading about it is something else. Rousseau tries to mix the cards, however. In the first walk he writes that he expects his future reading of *Les rêveries* to "recall the pleasure I have in writing them," thus reviving "le temps passé" and "duplicating" his existence (p. 1001). Only a couple of pages later, in the second walk, he admits the obvious, which is difference: "As I try to recall all these sweet *rêveries* I fall back into them instead of describing them" (p. 1003). The fifth walk is the one that extensively describes one of these sweet states in musical prose, apparently in an effort both to relive and to re-create those movements of water that once, according to memory, lulled Rousseau into a *rêverie*. He finishes the fifth walk by asking himself and us if the dream about the dream does not extinguish these (and all) differences: "Is it not the same thing to dream that I am there [on Isle de St. Pierre in Lac de Bienne]?" (p. 1049); i.e. he asks himself if, when writing, he actually dreams the same dream that he remembers once having dreamed and now writes about.

The question is rhetorical, but, if one had to answer, the answer would have to be "no": the difference is still there and it is unavoidably difference and distance that give a nostalgic beauty to *Les Rêveries* and make them important for the development of temporal and differential aspects of *mimesis*. Starobinski, with his usual accuracy, made this point when writing that "the author of the *Rêveries* stands in relation to the ecstatic contemplator of the Saint-Pierre Island as Orpheus, estranged yet full of desire, when he looks back to see Eurydice who follows him and disappears forever."[37]

The perspective controlling *Les Rêveries* is, therefore, the same as in *Confessions*: Rousseau looks back and remembers what Jean-Jacques

---

36 The history and idea of *rêverie* is found in Morrissey, *La rêverie jusqu'à Rousseau*; for the relation to Montaigne see p. 42; also in Arnaud Tripet, *La rêverie littéraire* (Geneva, 1979) and several works by Marcel Raymond, for example *Jean-Jacques Rousseau. La quête de soi et la rêverie* (Paris, 1962), and the introduction and commentaries of the Pléiade edition of Rousseau's *Les rêveries*.

37 Starobinski, *Transparency and Obstruction*, p. 363.

once was doing – and in the first walk he duly calls "these pages" an "appendix" to *Confessions* (p. 1000) providing, in the first few lines, an echo from the opening of the earlier autobiographical text. In *Confessions* he stressed his being unique – "moi seul" – and now he starts in absolute loneliness: "Me voici donc seul sur la terre ['Thus I am now alone in the world']" (p. 995). He admits the relation of his project to Montaigne's, while emphasizing the important difference that Montaigne "wrote his essays only for others and I am writing down my *rêveries* for myself alone" (p. 1001). The little "donc" from the first line, however, reveals the audience that was already implied when Rousseau started writing, not satisfied with only dreaming. Who or what else but an audience would agree in a "thus"? The question from the fifth walk quoted above may be rhetorical and call for no answer; but it does call for an audience.

These distinctions may be obvious; still it must be admitted that *Les Rêveries* is in many senses imbued with loneliness, written as if from the perspective of the already dead Rousseau on the still living Jean-Jacques. Borderlands – between times, feelings, genres – are explored; as in the second walk, where Rousseau describes an accident making him unconscious and, on waking up, not being able to separate himself from surrounding things and phenomena; or the fourth walk, where he sophistically tries to dissolve the difference between true and false in concepts of *fiction* and, above all, *sentiment*; and then the fifth walk, touching on the limits of time and self in the element of water.

There, Rousseau looks back on a couple of months of botanical excursions and boat trips on the lake, a period of self-centred indolence – "je m'etois enlacé de moi-même" (p. 1042) – without "boring paper-work" and demands to think. Several times and in several ways Rousseau tells us that *rêverie* is *not* a way of thinking, but a way of escaping thinking – in the seventh walk, for instance, in an incisive wording: "*rêverie* amuses and distracts me, reflection wearies and depresses me; thinking has always been for me a disagreeable occupation *sans charme*" (p. 1062). We should remember that *rêverie* also, and still, is a tool of the autobiographical project that was supposed to make the self, under the name Jean-Jacques, "transparent" to the world. The visual metaphors of transparency might suggest that "enlightenment" was in charge of the project, but Rousseau's contrasting of *rêverie* with thinking shows that "enlightenment" in the sense of "reason" is not enough to illuminate Jean-Jacques, and even gets in the way. Georges Poulet has, among others, found a kind of affinity between Rousseau's autobiographical assertion of "moi seul" and Descartes' epistemological basis "ergo sum" — but with the interesting difference that Descartes' famous "cogito" is not enough for Rousseau; his maxim should instead be something like "I am since I hardly think" or, even, "since I do not think."[38]

In the fifth walk, water is the element for this dreaming (non)activity, creating the self by dissolving its thoughts or by admitting only a "brief and insubstantial reflection concerning the instability of worldly things" (p. 1046). Water is what invites this relaxed or weakened reflection; the surface of the water gives Jean-Jacques an "image" of instability. But the image of water is in its turn effaced by its movement: "soon these fragile impressions gave way [s'effaçoient] before the unchanging and ceaseless movement which lulled me," etc. (ibid.).

Rousseau remembers here with delight how the last remnants of his thinking "gave way" when he was standing on the shore watching and listening to the movements of the water. The giving way or effacement ("s'effacer") was a little earlier remembered as his "absorption" into the element of water. First, Jean-Jacques takes off in a flat little boat, stretched out on his back with his eyes looking skywards. There he drifts for hours "wherever the water took me [au gré de l'eau]", plunged ("plongé") "in a host of vague yet delightful rêveries" (p. 1044). And then, towards the evening, when he walks back to the shore the movement of the water again "plunges" him into a "delicious rêverie" (p. 1045).

Plunged, effaced; delivered from thought and from will — the rêverie induced by water comes a long way along a *via negativa* approaching the "depersonalization" we could observe in some scenes from *Confessions* as analysed above. In all these scenes we noticed that dumb immobility was an important stage in the negative dialectics of the self, if that is the correct term for Rousseau's recurrent phenomenology. Here the sound of water in movement seems to create the self by extinguishing its thought:

The ebb and flow of the water, its continuous yet undulating noise lapping against my ears and my eyes compensated for the inner movements that the

---

38 Georges Poulet, "Le Sentiment de l'existence chez Rousseau," *Studi Francesi* 64 (1978), 36–50. The comparison with Descartes was first made by Jean Wahl in *Tableau de la philosophie française* (Paris, 1946), pp. 94ff.

rêverie had extinguished within me and sufficed to make me feel my existence with pleasure, without troubling myself with thought.[39]

The water of the lake could not have any ebb and flow ("flux et reflux") in any ordinary sense, but Rousseau's reason for using the term comes out a bit further on in the text when he develops a substantial deliberation (in spite of his declaration that deliberations disappear in a *rêverie* and that the text of a *rêverie* provides the same effect as, once, did the *rêverie* itself). Inspired by the water, Rousseau now gives us a sketch of nothing less than a philosophy of movement. First we learn that everything on earth is in constant movement, *flux*: "Tout est dans un flux continuel sur la terre" (p. 1046). This means that nothing is constant or "arrêtée." It applies, not least, to our feelings and desires ("nos affectations") which lack "solid" points of attachment owing to the permanent movement of the real world. At this point in the argument it may seem as if Rousseau, seduced by his own memory of the gently moving water, is fast approaching an embarrassing relativism; embarrassing, that is, for his declaration that this watery *rêverie* was singularly happy. Presently, however, he makes a hardly noticeable turn (remember that turning-around was a decisive move for this "orphic" project) and comes up with a definition of happiness as a resting-place similar to his own rest at the lake. Happiness is a state in which we rest from needs, desires and feelings; a state without change, i.e. without time, a state "where the present always lasts [ou le présent dure toujours]."

Such was his happiness on Isle de Saint Pierre in Lac de Bienne, Rousseau assures us. He goes on in his description of happiness coming into relevance for the autobiographical self: the effacement of thought and the erasure of desires have miraculously "plunged" the self into a state of complete fullness; in a *rêverie* of such a standard the self is all, and as long as the *rêverie* lasts "one is self-sufficient like God" (p. 1047). (Remember Julie's discussion of the dialectic of desire in VI: 8: only the "Being existing for itself" is exempted from the "nothingness" of human affairs.) Here, the effaced, and at the same time god-like, self has come as close as one could come to nothing less than "le sentiment de l'existence." Rousseau points out that *neither*

---

39 "Le flux et reflux de cette eau, son bruit continu mais renflé par intervalles frappant sans relache mon oreille et mes yeux suppléoient aux mouvements internes que la rêverie éteignoit en moi et suffisoient pour me faire sentir avec plaisir mon existence, sans prendre la peine de penser" (p. 1045).

movement nor rest, *neither* silence nor sound nor speech are enough to guarantee this fragile happiness of pure *sentiment*: "There must be neither a total calm nor too much movement but a steady and moderate motion that is neither jolting nor recurrent." We need, in other words, a movement that is no movement. Perhaps a little trembling? Because movement is needed (perhaps Rousseau was thinking of his Pascal, who points out in *Pensée* 198 that "our nature is movement; complete rest is death").

We need a sound that is no sound; but sound is needed since complete silence "induces melancholy as an image of death."

I have made this longish summary of the fifth walk because it is probably the text in which Rousseau most extensively and para-doxically tries to co-ordinate the autobiographical project with the *positive* fantasy he associates with *rêverie* and the *negative* movement towards effacement that seems provoked by water. We recognize the effect from similar scenes mentioned above: "Saint-Preux" on his visit to the *Elysée* already finding "the accents of the fifth *Rêverie*",[40] and Jean-Jacques at the feet of Mme. Basile or lost at the Pont-du-Gard, seem to prepare the way. If memory was the faculty governing the autobiographical project, forgetfulness must be called the faculty of *rêverie*; and water is the element of dreams and forgetfulness. *Mnemosyne* is the mother of Muses, but *Lethe* is her Grace.

The most remarkable aspect of Rousseau's handling of these normally opposing faculties is that he keeps them opposite, but still entwined or mediated in compulsory co-operation. The task given to memory – to create the autobiographical self – is accomplished by forgetfulness. Or, more precisely, the negative components of a *rêverie* (efface, forget, escape thinking) positively create a self that is self-sufficient in making its own world. The self gains itself by losing itself. "In this little death, then," writes Michel Beaujour, referring to the passage from the fifth walk summarized above, "Rousseau has gained the nothingness that he needed, the negativity that was necessary for a description of the divine state."[41]

It is also remarkable, in the fifth walk, that Rousseau frames the

40 Jean-Louis Lecercle, *Rousseau et l'art du roman*, p. 223.
41 Michel Beaujour, *Miroirs d'encre. Rhétorique de l'autoportrait* (Paris: Seuil, 1980), p. 69: "Dans cette petite mort Rousseau a donc gagné le néant qui lui faisait défaut, la négativité nécessaire à la description de l'état divin."

conditions for his trick – loss of self as gain – in words that cannot be but incisively paradoxical. The conditions are: movement that is no movement; sound that is no sound; time that is no time.

Movement that is no movement. Above we have come across some examples of Rousseau's attempt to determine the idea of movement dialectically. In *Julie* he falls into one of the most common novelistic patterns for this: making men mobile and women stationary. A similar pattern turns up in *Confessions*, although with complications: Jean-Jacques has been in hectic movement since his birth, it seems, always looking for the permanent coming to rest that Rousseau associates with his "Maman" also with every place that is not Paris (where Rousseau actually was more settled than anywhere else). At least in some phrases, he develops something like an enthusiastic philosophy of movement, walk and travel. In the third book he declares himself incapable of writing at a desk and on paper: "it is on my walks ... that I write in my head" (p. 114). In the fourth book: "When I stay still I can hardly think at all, my body has to be on the move to set my mind going" (p. 162). And again in the ninth book: "I can only meditate when I am walking, as soon as I stop I cease to think and my mind only moves with my feet" (p. 410).

But we have also seen some scenes in *Confessions* becoming magically tense in a stillness that means silence as well as immobility. It is stillness that Rousseau associates with the strong feeling of presence in the scene with Mme. Basile in the second book discussed above. "I was motionless and dumb," Rousseau remembers; adding, "but certainly not calm" (p. 75).

In the fifth walk of *Les Rêveries* it would seem that opposite circumstances create a similar strong feeling of presence: the incessant movement of the water is said to compensate for his "inner movements" having been "calmed" by his ecstatic *rêverie* (p. 1045).

Still, in both cases it is the balance or dialectic or mediation that counts, and when Rousseau gives voice to this balance towards the end of the fifth walk it comes out as paradox: he wishes for movement that is no movement, sound that is no sound.

And time that is no time. He defines happiness as a moment of presence. But the presence that happily fills the self, effacing its boundaries with the world, is a momentary state that is miracuously permanent: "où le présent dure toujours" (p. 1046).

Rêverie is not a concept and can, therefore, hardly be defined; but at least we have now approached a characterization of the state of *rêverie* as a frozen movement or an instant outside time. Such outrages (from the point of view of normal logic) could best be handled as floating, that is, in water. Rousseau remembers in the fifth walk how Jean-Jacques stretches out in a boat that floats on its own, calmly, but still moving, "plunged" into a state in which he forgets the timetables of his dinner and his work, i.e. he is floating outside time.

In the fifth walk this graceful moment is temptingly described, and the reader is invited to forget the difference between Rousseau, plunged into remembering while writing, and Jean-Jacques, plunged into his floating dreams – the difference that Starobinski recalled as the relation between the yearning and singing Orpheus and his forever lost Eurydice. But still, it is easy to find similar situations in Rousseau's writings. Julie's *Elysée* again, where "Saint-Preux" finally loses himself in a silent and exquisite *rêverie*, is described as a little kingdom separated not only from the world, but also from time. Rousseau himself, in the eighth book of *Confessions*, remembers how – when following the "reform" after the revolutionary insight on the road to Vincennes – he not only changes habits and clothes, but also puts away his watch in order to live permanently in the present: "I shall not need to know the time any more" (p. 363). And Emile, in the epistolary continuation of the educational tract that Rousseau just started, is allowed to write the following remarkable sentences:

I have taken a great step towards stillness ... I decided to put myself entirely in the situation of a man starting to live. I said to myself that we really do nothing but start, and that there is no other connection in our life but a succession of present moments, of which the first is always the one that counts. We die and we are born every moment of our lives and what interest could death then leave us?[42]

This "succession of present moments" is, again, a tempting paradox: according to normal logic the moment excludes the succession and the succession excludes the moment. But Rousseau apparently wants us to imagine his *rêverie* as potentially neither-nor, and the water as the element privileged to this unknown, but

42 Rousseau, *Emile et Sophie ou les Solitaires*, in Œuvres Complètes (Paris, 1969), vol. 4, pp. 905ff.: "J'avais fait un grand pas vers le repos ... Je me tâchais de me mettre tout à fait dans l'état d'un homme qui commence à vivre. Je me disais qu'en effet nous ne faisions jamais que commencer, et qu'il n'y a point d'autre liaison dans nôtre existence qu'une succession de momens présens, dont le premier est toujours celui qui est en acte. Nous mourons et nous naissons chaque instant de nôtre vie, et quel intérêt la mort peut elle nous laisser?"

tempting, logic. This should be apparent – but only when taken with some other observations. *Rêverie* may well be the state for the negative to accomplish its terrible work – using forgetfulness, effacement and speechlessness – but this negative work gives positive results. Jean-Jacques may be effaced, and Rousseau goes on living. Jean-Jacques may (like Emile above) be able to live permanently in the moment; and Rousseau imagines to be already dead. Jean-Jacques quits thinking, and Rousseau never stops thinking about, and writing, the auto-biographical project. In this project he returns, again and again, to the tempting moment when he would not have to create himself, but would take Emile's step towards stillness and put away language to become pure existence and *sentiment*. Apparently these two figures need each other; after all, they were one and the same person, separated by time. Mnemosyne needs Lethe. This should also mean that the autobiographical project – and the name for that was "transparence" – needs its negativity, its bottomless darkness, in order even to get started. Language, and not least language, needs its measure of the negative, i.e. difference and forgetfulness, in order to become language; and presence needs distance, just as similarity needs difference. Rousseau had two ambitions with his autobiographical project: one was to show himself; the other was to hide himself. This is not necessarily more contradictory (or paradoxical in similar ways) than Heidegger, a long time later, insisting that *difference* and *forgetfulness* hang together like Being itself does with what is existing ("*Sein und das seiende*").[43] Heidegger also used to imagine "truth" as "aletheia," which is most often translated (by Heidegger) as "showing" or "opening," while, in a late text, he poses the question whether or not the place for truth – the "opening" – would be the place for hiding, a place, that is, for hiding the self; and whether Lethe, therefore, relates to *A-Letheia* not as an "addition" or as "shadow to light," but, on the contrary, as the very heart of truth, as "das Herz der Aletheia."[44]

Rousseau actually hinted, in allegorical ways, at a necessary relation between language and the negative – the negative as associated with the element of water – in his (nowadays) famous speculation on the origins of languages: *Essai sur l'origine des langues ou il est parlé de la mélodie et de l'imitation musicale* (from the 1750s). Among many other

---

43 Heidegger, *Identität und Differenz* (Pfullingen: Neske, 1957), pp. 46ff.
44 Heidegger, *Zur Sache des Denkens* (Tübingen: Niemeyer, 1969), p. 75.

remarkable things stated here, Rousseau claims to have found two original phrases that are eminently creative for all society. One is "aidez-moi" (help me), which is the passionate cry issuing from northern people in their need to gather around the fire to get heat, food, protection and community in "those frightful climates where everything is dead for nine months of the year, where the sun heats the air for a few weeks only to give the habitants a taste of the goods they are deprived of and to prolong their misery" – to quote from Rousseau's conception of *Ultima Thule*.[45]

The other phrase is "aimez-moi" (love me). These fatefully sociable words were, according to Rousseau, pronounced for the first time by *water* or, more precisely, by the sources and wells of southern countries. That is, first, he imagines, comes the need for water, and after that wells are dug in co-operation. To these wells come, first, the girls to get the water needed for the homes. Then come the boys in order to get water for the cattle. Girl meets boy and passion arises. Original man breaks his profound silence and takes a step over the great threshold of civilization: the step into language. Original man breaks into song. And out of the song – which is the language of passions and close to the involuntary cries we have heard from "Saint-Preux" and Jean-Jacques – are wrought the first and most important of words: "aimez-moi." "There, at last, was the true cradle of the people," writes Rousseau, "and from the pure crystal of the springs emerged the first flames of love."[46]

Without water, no language.

When this connection is established it is, again, as a paradox: how flames can emerge from water no one can understand. It is quite as incomprehensible as the connection between Mnemosyne and Lethe that Rousseau establishes in his autobiographical project; or as the relations of distance and presence that he sought and found in Julie; or as the similarity and difference that I found in concepts like "mimesis" and "imitación."

45 Rousseau, *Essai sur l'origine des langues* (Paris, 1990), p. 110: "Dans ces affreux climats où tout est mort durant neuf mois de l'année, où le soleil n'échauffe l'air quelques semaines que pour apprendre aux habitants de quels biens ils sont privés et prolonger leur misère."

46 Ibid., p. 107: "La fût enfin le vrai berçeau des peuples, et du pur cristal des fontaines sortirent les prémiers feux de l'amour."

Kierkegaard's "Gjentagelse"

The text

Kierkegaard published *Repetition* in 1843; his pseudonym this time was Constantin Constantius. The Danish title is *Gjentagelsen*, meaning literally "the taking back." It is not easy – it is never easy with Kierkegaard – to decide what sort of text this is: a narration or a philosophical essay or perhaps an ironic mixture of both. Kierkegaard has Constantin make fun of this problematic in a sort of appendix, where he turns to "the real reader of this book," called "Mr X, Esq."[1] This real and ideal reader is apparently not a critic or an "ordinary reviewer," since such a specimen would have taken the opportunity to:

elucidate that it is not a comedy, tragedy, novel, epic, epigram, story and to find it inexcusable that one tries in vain to say 1.2.3. Its ways he will hardly understand since they are inverse: nor will the effort of the book appeal to him, for as a rule reviewers explain existence in such a way that both the universal and the particular are annihilated. (190/226)

This is said in the final pages, retrospectively, like a "repetition" to remind the reader – "Mr X" – in what manner and genre he has *not* read and, perhaps, to hint at a failed dialectic ("tries in vain to say 1.2.3."); and that the "ways" of the text are "inverse."

"Inverse"?

This odd statement at the end of the text may persuade reader X to "repeat" the very beginning of the text, or to read backwards to

---

1 I will quote from Kierkegaard's *Repetition* in Kierkegaard's *Samlede Værker* (Copenhagen: Gyldendal, 1962), vol. 5, here p. 187. Page references will be given in the text. Translations will be taken from Howard Hong and Edna Hong, *Kierkegaard's Writings* (New Haven: Princetown University Press, 1983), vol. 6, here p. 223. The English page reference will be given after the Danish. The translations are often modified.

where Constantin discusses "movement" in relation to the concepts of "repetition" and "recollection" and comes up with this first definition:

Repetition and recollection are the same movement, only in opposite directions, for what is recollected has been, is repeated backward; whereas the real repetition is recollected forward. (115/131)

As a conceptual introduction to this text, at the end of which the "ways" are called "inverse," we are invited to think of "repetition" and "recollection" as the same movement – only in opposite directions. The same, but opposite. "Repetition" as a movement "forward".

"Forward"?

The beginning and the end of the text give us two directions, both quite surprising. The beginning tells us to repeat in order to go forward; and the end tells us that the repetition made was "inverse." The beginning I quoted is, furthermore, prefaced by a little anecdote about directions and movement: there Diogenes is said to have "refuted" the Eleatics, who "denied movement" not by saying anything at all, but by pacing "back and forth a few times" (115/131).

"Back and forth"?

Turning back and forth is a first point of turning in this text.

If we then regard the Diogenes of the anecdote ("back and forth") as a rubric for the text *Repetition* and keep diverging directions in mind ("forward", "inverse"), it could, perhaps, be said in a preliminary way that *Repetition* is a text on an "inverse" movement back and forth. This movement takes place in several ways in the text, including its own temporality: I will show later how the text changes its narrative mode between past and present time. Philosophically the text discusses the *past* of recollection and the *now* of repetition. The text paces back and forth between temporal modes as it shifts between narrative and philosophical discourses. The conditions for the movement of the text are defined in its framework, in the "back-and-forth," "same-but-opposite," "backward-forward" of the beginning, and in the "inverse" of the end. Opposite directions: a restless text.

Kierkegaard wrote this restless text under a pseudonym suggesting permanence and immobility, apart from its associations with the Emperor Constantin, famous promoter of Christianity and of the dialectical unity of Father-Son-Holy Spirit (Nicaea in the year 325). The text was published together with *Fear and Trembling* – this under another pseudonym, Johannes de Silentio – which concludes with a Heraclitean anecdote: Heraclitus is said to have had a disciple who "developed" the master's notion that you cannot enter the same river twice by saying that one "cannot do it even once. Poor Heraclitus, to have a disciple like that! By this improvement, the Heraclitean thesis was amended into an Eleatic thesis that denies motion" (111/123).

Repetition starts with Heraclitus, Diogenes and the Eleatics, thereby alluding to the classical logical problem of motion and movement. First, Constantin praises "repetition" for a couple of pages: repetition "is reality and the earnestness of existence" (116/133). "Repetition" is called the "new" philosophical idea of the same phenomenon that "the Greeks" called "recollection" (anamnesis) – although "repetition" moves "forward", as we remember, while "recollection" moves "backward."

Constantin then starts a narration. "About a year ago," he writes and remembers, "I became very much aware of a young man" (117/133). This young man – the Danish word is actually "menneske": "human being" – is melancholically in love; Constantin's diagnosis is (or was) that the young man as a poet lives in memory and that the beloved girl lacked reality (for him). "The young girl was not his beloved, she was the occasion that awakened the poetic in him ... and precisely thereby she had signed her own death sentence" (121/138), implying that the word, and especially the poetic word, establishes a distance called "death." Constantin suggested a treatment: the young man should fake love for another girl – meaning that Constantin wanted the young man to say one thing and mean another; that is, become ironic. That is, however, impossible since the young man is everything but ironic, and the relation and the narration are broken. The suspicious reader (but not the ideal reader, Mr X) has to wonder if this possibly was what Constantin intended? Constantin asserts that the young man was lacking in the "elasticity of irony" (127/145). As a poet – romantic poet? elegiac poet? – he has only one language, whereas the ironist has two: the ironist "discovers an alphabet that has as many letters as the ordinary one, thus he can express everything in his thieves' language so that no sigh is so deep that he does not have the laughter that corresponds to it in thieves' language" (127/145).

Constantin makes some further philosophical reflections on the concept of "repetition" in relation to the Greek "kinesis" (to be discussed below), then changes to a new narration – about the "exploring expedition I made to test the possibility and meaning of repetition" (132/150). (It is the same Constantin who has already several times made a case for the necessity of "repetition.") The expedition heads for Berlin, where Constantin has once been and where he now wants to "repeat" what has happened already. Extensively and enthusiastically Berlin is remembered as it once was, while the "exploring expedition" is dismissed as ridiculous and impossible. The longest description is given to a *Posse*, a popular farce, which Constantin once saw and loved, but now finds unbearable – "The only repetition was the impossibility of repetition" (149/170). The exception comes at a restaurant where everything is the same: "the same in the same." And that is even worse: "Horrible thought, here a repetition was possible" (149/170).

This part of the text, the philosophical journey, seems to me difficult to handle. Why this bizarre farce after the romantic love-story? Why this enthusiasm about (a) memory (when memory earlier was called the source of melancholy)? Why this sudden and extreme refutation of "repetition"? *If* it is a refutation – could it perhaps be a demonstration that "repetition" of *something*, whatever it is, is doomed to failure, although "repetition" as such – as movement, as strategy – is necessary?

The text gives no answers, but moves on to its second part, also called *Gjentagelsen* ("the taking back," *Repetition*). The part has the name of the whole. Or does this mean that the second part "repeats" the whole as a "repetition" of *Repetition*? That the second part is the *secunda philosophia*, which Kierkegaard in other contexts calls "repetition"?[2] If, then, the second part is a real "repetition" – "repetition" in all earnestness, whereas the first part only toyed with the concept (and both parts, making the whole of the text, must in that case be

2 The *secunda philosophia* is discussed in *Begrebet Angest* ("The Concept of Agony") (*Samlede Værker* vol. 6, p. 119). "Repetition" is discussed there (especially in the long note on pp. 116f.), and also in *Philosophiske Smuler* ("Philosophical Trifles") (ibid.) and extensively in Kierkegaard's *Papirer* ("Papers") of 1844, especially when he makes Constantin polemical against Heiberg, but also the first part of Johannes Climacus' *De omnibus dubitandum est*. I will not examine those passages, whatever their importance to an understanding of Kierkegaard, but will stick to the text *Repetition*. Nor will I go into the philosophical and theological literature discussing Kierkegaard, although I should mention Kjell Eyvind Johansen's thorough investigation in *Begrebet Gjentagelse hos Sören Kierkegaard* (Oslo: Solum, 1988). Danish commentaries on the text have traditionally a biographical bias, although some recent efforts come close to the textual analysis.

both in play and in earnest) – it must be due to the fact that the second part concludes the love-story from the first part. And the name of this conclusion is "separation."

"Repetition" moving forward and being made real as the final separation of the young man from his beloved? This may sound like poor dialectics, but is, at least, a summary telling us what is happening. The young man turns up again writing letters to Constantin, in which we can follow his romantic outbursts up to the point where the beloved girl turns out to be already married! This the young man in his last letter pronounces to be a "thunderstorm" and a real, a veritable, "repetition".

The tone has changed in this second part of the text. Gone are the ironies of the first part, and we meet instead the favored form of romantic self-expression: the sentimental letter. Gone, too, is the temporal distance of the first part: Constantin the narrator moves into the present tense, and his few comments remain in the same vague *now* as the letters he is commenting on. Narratologically Kierkegaard and Constantin move from retold *diegesis* into the scenic representation of *mimesis*, to use the Platonic terms (cf. chapter 1). In the shape of *mimesis*, the duplicating repetition or reversal, the moving forward that Kierkegaard calls "repetition," is made acute.

The text is kept in this temporally vague present tense until the young man has produced his last letter. Then Constantin writes his own letter, separated from part II (the "repetition" of *Repetition*) by a page visualizing the envelope of a letter addressed to Mr X, "the real reader of this book." We meet, in other words, a very literal and drastic separation directly after we have been separated from the young man, and the young man has been separated from his girl. We meet, again, irony in an extended and highly romantic form – making a contrast with the romantic pathos of the young man. Constantin uses this ironic moment to inform his reader of what has happened and of what kind of text he has *not* read. He repeats his diagnosis of the first part, calling the young man a "poet," and contrasts him with himself: "I myself cannot become a poet, and in any case my interest lies elsewhere" (192/228). He also calls himself a "vanishing person" – and in relation to the young man he has been like "a woman giving birth" (194/230).

Constantin steps parabasically forward to call himself "vanishing" and promising to "serve" his reader by being "another" (192/228); and by calling the "ways" of his text "inverse" (190/226). It seems that the only way to come to terms with his "repetition" would be to read the text again, spelling out that other alphabet and stealing the "thieves' language" that Constantin ascribed to the ironist.

The concept

What is "repetition"?

It is the title of the text *Repetition*, and the title of the second part of the text *Repetition*. It is a concept referring to a kind of movement back and forth that seems to be going on between the different parts of the text, between its irony and its pathos, between the two characters of the narration – the narrator (an ironic Constantin) and his object (a pathetic young man) – between the two parts of the text and its appendix, between the text and the reader, between the ideal reader Mr X and all other readers, between the two or even three or four temporal levels of the text (the first part has two retold stories, the second part is held in an undetermined present, while the appendix letter is given a date).

"Repetition" is all this, but it is also a philosophical concept, promoted by Kierkegaard through Constantin as a reply to the Greek (i.e. Platonic) recollection (anamnesis) and the "mediation" ("Aufhebung") of newer (i.e. Hegelian) philosophy.

Let me now, after the introductory summary above, try philosophy. There are two passages in the first part in which Constantin develops the concept "repetition." The first is in the opening pages, where Constantin situates the concept in relation to "recollection": they are, as we remember, "the same movement, only in opposite directions," "repetition" moving "forward" (115/131). The second comes in the transition between the narration about the young man and that about the expedition to Berlin. Here, in a couple of pages, Constantin develops his criticism of "what has mistakenly been called mediation" (130/148), i.e. Hegelian dialectics. Against Hegel he asks us to remember the "Greek development of the teaching of being and nothingness, the development of 'the instant,' of 'non-being,'" etc. (131/148). This is apparently different Greek theory from the one connecting knowledge and reality with recollection; i.e. we have another Plato here: we find concepts like "Being" and "Nothingness" in Plato's dialogue *Parmenides*, which is also Plato's most rigorous analysis of the "Eleatics," who became famous for "denying motion" according to the first pages of *Repetition*.

Constantin's discussion makes it apparent that he has found more in
Plato's *Parmenides* than Platonic anamnesis and Eleatic immobility. He
has even found a term that sounds more like Kierkegaard than Plato:
"øieblikket," literally meaning "the glance of the eye" and here
translated as the "instant." The term probably derives from a
suggestive passage of *Parmenides* that I will take up later. Here the
"instant" is associated with "repetition" before Constantin continues
his discussion of the relation of the concept to Hegelian "mediation"
(dialectics):

(1) It is in our days not explained how mediation comes about, if it is a result
of the movement of the two elements, and in what way it already from the
start is contained in these, or if something new is added, and in that case how.
(2) In this regard the Greek ideas about the concept *kinesis*, which corresponds
to the modern category "transition," should be considered seriously. (3) The
dialectic of repetition is easy; because what is repeated, has been, otherwise
it could not be repeated, but the fact that it has been, makes repetition into
the new. (4) When the Greeks said that all knowledge is recollection, then
they said that all of existence, which is, has been, when you say that life is a
repetition, you say: the existence, that has been, now becomes. (5) When you
haven't got the category of recollection or repetition, all life dissolves into an
empty noise devoid of content. (131/149)

First, Constantin discusses dialectics: is the *Aufhebung* of synthesis
("mediation") the result of movement in or between thesis and
antithesis ("the two elements") or is it a new movement? The question
may seem narrow, but is interesting since it indicates Constantin's
interest: to make dialectics into a form of movement. The association
with "repetition" makes it clear that the movement is a movement in
time: a temporal figure. The second sentence prepares for this
temporality of "repetition" by way of terms like "kinesis" (movement)
and "transition"; the latter may be Kierkegaard's version of *metabállon*,
and both these terms are extensively used in *Parmenides*. (The Danish
term is "overgang," literally meaning "move over.") The sentence
seems unclear to me, but could be expanded by a comparison with
Kierkegaard's *Papers* from the period, in which he has long discussions
on *kinesis*; in any case the sentence underlines Constantin's fascination:
movement.

Then (3) the "dialectics of repetition" is established – in contrast,
we may assume, to Hegelian dialectics, and in conflict with the Eleatics
(who "denied movement"), but in affiliation with kinesis. "Repetition"
is here a movement in time: re-take, re-peat, re-turn, re-verse, mean

going back in time to what "has been." But still, in spite of this movement backward, "repetition" makes it new and is, therefore, a movement forward: it "makes" new and *is*, therefore, "the new." The reason this movement backward is actually a movement forward is temporal: you cannot re-peat/re-take what has been, since what has been, has been. The moment or instant of "repetition" is always an *after*. But not only an after. Since the movement of "repetition" also makes it new, makes "the new" (simultaneously with being a repeating reduplication), "repetition" suspends the temporal order of before-after in or by that *now* previously called "the instant." The temporal dialectics of "repetition" suspends temporal sequence: the *now* that is always an *after* actually comes *before* – it is the *now* of "the instant," the sudden intervention in sequential time, the cesura that defines what has been, makes it possible to tell its story and makes way for the "new."

Two things should be added to this formula of "repetition." First, as a "definition" it may appear empty and formalistic, demanding quite a hermeneutical effort in order to give meaning. Secondly, it is constructed as a regular chiasmus:

what is repeated, has been, otherwise ... the fact that it has been, makes repetition into the new.

A chiasmus is the very opposite of a transitory *metaballon* (and another name for the chiasmus is also antimetabole), but according to my quotation it is the chiastic definition and not the transition that is the renovating repetition. What appears to be a closed and perhaps empty formula is – ironically? – said to result in "the new."

Next (4) Constantin contrasts "repetition" with Platonic anamnesis. The philosophy of recollection gives priority or even absolute value to what has already been, according to Constantin, and thereby excludes the movement forward, "the new." Recollected life is elegiac or posthumous life, whereas "repetition" transcends recollection and reduplication by its "taking back" and making new. "Repetition" installs *now* as the impetus of existence and *becoming* as its movement: with "repetition" existence *now becomes*.

Both these sentences (3–4) work to give a temporal priority to the *now*; not just any *now*, but a paradoxical *now* that could be approached only by "repetition." Before my quotation, Constantin pointed out that "instant" and "non-being" had something to do with "rep-etition" (but not with Hegelian "mediation"). Kierkegaard is probably thinking of a sequence in Plato's *Parmenides* (156DE) that discusses the relations among movement (kinesis), standstill (*stasis*) and change or transition (*metaballon*). Plato has Parmenides ask himself and us what strange position time is taking when change-movement-transition occurs. He answers: "the instant [to *exaiphnes*]").[3] Further discussion emphasizes that this concept is a non-concept, since it refers to a phenomenon that exists yet does not exist – or exists only in the state of what Constantin would call "non-being." Which probably is his word for, or summary of, what Plato has Parmenides put like this: "this strange instantaneous nature, this something that is patched between movement and standstill and that does not exist in any time; but into this instant and out of this instant that which is movement changes into standstill and that which is at a standstill changes into movement."

Remember from my first chapter that, in another dialogue, Plato (*Timaeus* 37D) called time itself a "moving image of eternity." I imagine that Kierkegaard felt inspired and provoked by such Platonic dialogues from *Timaeus* and *Parmenides* (and surely other dialogues as well) when he developed his own dialectic of instant and eternity (in *The Concept of Agony*). Here I stick to *Repetition* and am now prepared for the conclusion that the temporal concept of "repetition" is connected with the paradoxical "instant" of Plato's *Parmenides*; together they give temporal priority to an instantaneous *now*, interrupting any temporal sequence on behalf of the movement of becoming.

The final sentence of my quotation (5) takes a step backward in the dialectic by suggesting that the contrast between "repetition" and "recollection" is not as absolute as it seemed to be in the previous sentence (and at the beginning of *Repetition*, where the concepts seem opposite). Now Constantin asserts that both "repetition" and "recollection" are concepts of order bringing some sort of structure to a life that without this order would be a "noise" without meaning. It is worth noting that, when he imagines the world of non-meaning, Constantin leaves his prominent temporal or spatial metaphors to evoke an auditory horror: pure noise.

3 The classical translation of the term is "momentum." It is of overall importance in Kierkegaard's writings being discussed, for example in his *The Concept of Agony*, and giving a name to Kierkegaard's later theological-political journal.

The non-concept

In the passage quoted above[4] we can look for a first answer to the question: what is "repetition"? But only a preliminary answer: the passage is a part of the text *Repetition* and this text starts and ends, as already mentioned, in confusing directions ("forward," "inverse"). Furthermore, the passage is found in the first part of the text, while it is the other part that carries the title *Repetition*, which may be a suggestion to read the first part as preliminary or tentative. Finally the passage comes from Constantin Constantius, who calls himself ironic – being able to "express everything in his thieves' language so that no sigh is so deep that he does not have the laughter that corresponds to it in thieves' language" (127/145).

These reservations, given directly in the text, underline the fact that the answer to the question about "repetition" that we might extract from the passage quoted tends to paradox. "Repetition" is, as we found, a figure of movement giving priority to an instantaneous, interruptive and paradoxical *now* in a temporal dialectics. Constantin, therefore, comes close to – and I have to use words that are not to be found in the text and actually in no text of Kierkegaard's, as far as I know – something that perhaps could be called a fascination with *presence*. What Constantin (and Kierkegaard in many other places) calls "Øieblikket" and what I hint at with the italicized *now* is the point in time (or perhaps break in time) when the essence of eternal existence becomes manifestly present. "Øieblikket" is a "metaphorical expression and therefore not very easy to follow," as Kierkegaard has Vigilius Haufniensis conclude his analysis in *The Concept of Agony*: "Still it is a beautiful word to handle. Nothing is as quick as the glance of the eye and still the glance is compatible with the substance of eternity."[5]

This fascination with presence and with essence comes close to metaphysics in the sense that the privileged instant of *now* is declared to be transcendental – and Kierkegaard insists that "repetition" is a

---

4 A good discussion of the same passage is found in Aage Henriksen's *Kierkegaards romaner* (Copenhagen, 1954), pp. 101ff. – although Henriksen takes the remarkable stand that an "extensive discussion of the system of thought that gives meaning to these detached remarks takes us away from the text and real problems of *Repetition*." Henriksen does not discuss *to exaiphnes*.

5 Kierkegaard, *Samlede Værker*, vol. 6, p. 175.

category of transcendence[6] – and not something that we just come across in this "noise devoid of content" that makes up our unstructured world of phenomena. The instant of presence established by repetition as it unveils a truth that exceeds normal temporal order is transcendental in a metaphysical sense. A new epistemological regime is established that, however, must stay in hiding or paradoxically coexist with normal and sequential human time. And I guess that we are close, here, to Kierkegaard's interest in the absurd and the paradoxical, and in the "indirect communication" that is demonstrated in Constantin's ironic "thieves' language" as well as generally in Kierkegaard's consequently pseudonymous writings.

The temporal dialectics of "repetition" is, however, not a metaphysics of presence of the sort that Jacques Derrida has recently criticized and deconstructed as the stigma of "Western thinking" since Plato. On the contrary, Kierkegaard is actually a fierce critic of the "metaphysics" he identified as the "system" of, especially, Hegel and is in this respect a precursor of both Heideggerian "destruction" and Derridian "deconstruction." As I will try to show below, Kierke-gaardian "repetition" repeats itself as a necessary ingredient in Derrida's own vocabulary, and even a Kierkegaardian *Øieblikk* is actualized in his deconstructions. Also, "repetition" ("Wiederho-lung") and *Øieblikk* ("Augenblick") are decisive terms for Heidegger in his criticism ("destruction") of the "vulgar" temporal concept of normality (although Heidegger makes an effort to dissociate himself from Kierkegaard). And for Paul de Man, lastly, *repetition* seems to be the closest he can imagine an "authentic" temporality. These thinkers will be given their due treatment in the final sections of this chapter, and, had I but time and capacity, I could have treated many more important moderns – Nietzsche! Freud! – who in one way or another have contributed to the dialectics of "repetition."

But first I have to get closer to the conceptual and narrative dimensions of Kierkegaard's "repetition." I have already introduced some impressive recent critics of all kinds of metaphysics in order to suggest some consequences of his and Constantin's effort to conceptualize "repetition." The reason "repetition" attracts thinkers who are normally critical of the idea of "presence" (Derrida), "das Jetzt" (Heidegger) or any connection with *mimesis* (de Man) must be

---

6 Constantin writes that "repetition" "is and remains a transcendence" (161/186) and Vigilius Haufniensis agrees in *The Concept of Agony* (p. 117n).

that "repetition" may suggest a fascinating presence by its instantaneous *now*, while *excluding* this presence.

The device of "repetition," which Kierkegaard uses to invoke the *now* of presence, is a paradoxical strategy making *now* of what has already been. What has already been is the necessary prerequisite of the *now* — and, as a consequence, what has already been can be found, understood and retold only through this instantaneous *now*! The instant is never pure presence: it always carries a past. This intricate relation between past and present actually introduces an imperative of recovering and renovating interpretation, starting from the present and creating the past that was already there. This is what Constantin called "easy" in his precise (and forbiddingly chiastic) formula of the "dialectic of repetition" as quoted above: "what is repeated, has been, otherwise it could not be repeated, but the fact that it has been, makes repetition into the new."

The temporal device of "repetition" is a paradoxical movement between past and present; between time as instantaneous point or break or interruption; and time as process of past into present. Kierkegaardian "repetition" tries to keep these divergent dimensions of time together in one movement — making "repetition" into a non-concept or a paradoxical concept negating the presence it suggests; or a non-concept related to Plato's *to exaiphnes* in *Parmenides* — "this strange instantaneous nature, this something patched between movement and standstill and that does not exist in any time" (156DE) — but also related to Plato's *mimesis* as I read that concept in my first chapter, and to the renovating sense of Cervantes' *imitación* in the second, and to floating as the non-concept of Rousseau's *rêverie* in the third.

The story

The philosophical parts of *Repetition* are narratively framed, and the question is now how concept and narrative combine: do they support each other or are there tensions? The text is confusingly rich in possibilities, and I will discuss just two: its pathos, concentrated in the young man's sublime wishes, and its ironic and allegorical dimensions, exemplified by the textual reversals or inversions that I will call "ordo inversus."

Sublime silence

Repetition as told by Constantin Constantius tells us primarily about the nameless young man in love with a nameless young girl. In the second part, which is also called *Repetition*, the young man is given the word through the letters he sends to Constantin reporting on his feelings up to the point he learns that the girl has married. The girl does not get either name or word; her "presence" in the text is entirely created out of her absence.

Constantin reacts to the young man's letters by stating that "he has now come to the border of the marvellous and if it [i.e. repetition] is to take place at all it must take place by virtue of the absurd" (160/185). The young man uses different words, but he is just as obsessed by "repetition," connecting it with the ordeal of Job of the Old Testament and the "thunderstorm" he thinks that Job had to live through. "How beneficent is a thunderstorm!" he exclaims in one of the last letters (180/212), having reached the conclusion that the finally happy outcome for Job — "Job is blessed and has had everything *double"* — is a real "repetition." The thunderstorm and the ordeal are apparently "marvellous" preliminaries to the "absurd" instant of "repetition." For the young man, the ordeal consists apparently of his pains as an unfortunate lover; "repetition" should be the happy outcome of the affair. When the outcome happens to be the opposite — i.e. when he is reached by news of the girl being married — he is still prepared in his last letter to interpret this as a "thunderstorm" and a "repetition" together: "Is there not, then, a repetition? Did I not get everything double? Did I not get myself back and precisely in such a way that I might have a double sense of its meaning?" (185f./220f.).

The young man's thoughts on "repetition" apparently mean a displacement from Constantin's irony into pathos. But the question just quoted suggests, at least in its form, that the young man is not quite confident that he has got it all right. His lack of confidence turns up in several commentaries, where problems of interpretation are solved by the idea that Kierkegaard may have corrupted an original version, in which the young man was to commit suicide.[7] Our young

---

7 I agree with Henriksen (*Kierkegaard's romaner*, p. 131, in his comparison of the existing end with the earlier one (which, it should be said, is purely hypothetical): "The result of it all should be negative and negative it is, and in that respect the new ending goes well with the old plan, but it is rough and sparkling, permeated

man welcomes his liberation. My "yawl is afloat," he exclaims (186/221), looking forward to sailing (again?) on the sea where "ideas spume with elemental fury, where thoughts arise noisily ... where at other times there is a stillness like the deep silence of the South Sea," etc. He compares his new position to a "beaker of inebriation" and praises the "cresting waves, that hide me in the abyss" and "fling me up above the stars."

The young man's passage from poetical expectation into the "thunderstorm" of repetition and final deliverance is actually a *mysterium tremendum*, a mystery-play of upsetting conversion of the kind that is well known in the religious tradition, starting with St. Paul and highly problematized in the story of Abraham, as Kierkegaard presents it in the volume that accompanies *Repetition: Fear and Trembling*. Most commentators seem to have taken this pathos as expressed by the young man as Kierkegaard's own, neglecting the ironies involved in the narrative as well as the concept of "repetition." (Not to mention that the habit of reading *Fear and Trembling* as pure pathos ignores the heading of the main part of the text: *Problemata*.) I will here try to demystify the *mysterium* of *Repetition* with the help of its ironies and starting with the nautical metaphors as expressed enthusiastically by the young man in his last letter — because these are both familiar and disturbing. The prospects for a "yawl" on a spumy sea do not seem very promising. And if the young man is the "yawl," who, then, is the helmsman?

His sailing fantasies possibly have a connection with some similar observations made by Constantin. The first time is at the beginning of the book, when he writes that if "you haven't circumnavigated life before beginning to live you will never come to live" (116/132). Yes, Constantin could express himself with such confidence and in such a brilliant paradox while in charge of the first part of the text. In the present tense of the second part he sounds less confident: "I have abandoned my theory," he writes, "I am adrift" (161/186), and he has nothing to give: "I can circumnavigate myself, but I cannot come out of myself," etc.

Constantin "is adrift." That should mean that he cannot give advice, and that no one gives him advice: no one steers his yawl. Constantin seems to stay in this irresolute mood (and in his present

with a deep and remorseless hilarity, in which private mishap and theatrical suicide are turned into comedy."

tense) – at least until the final letter to the ideal reader Mr X, in which Constantin has suddenly regained his old ironical spirit. In the young man, the present tense creates a crisis that finally explodes in enthusiasm.

This surprising enthusiasm – after all, his project has failed and the girl has married someone else – is expressed in terms that only a little earlier were the norm in aesthetic theory when describing the *sublime*: "spume with elemental fury," "waves that hide me in the abyss ... that fling me up above the stars." We recognize the vocabulary from one of the young man's nearest predecessors, that nameless, unfortunate and sublime lover in Rousseau's *Julie*: "Saint-Preux." When he learns that his beloved Julie has actually married, he does not exactly welcome this, but he bids farewell to everything for the sea. And in his farewell-letter (III: 26), which is also the last in the third book of the novel and its very turning-point, he listens to the signal from the departing boat and welcomes the "vast sea, the immense sea, which perhaps will engulf me."[8]

Immanuel Kant, too, who was an avid reader of Rousseau, but certainly not excessive in his vocabulary, comes up with sea and stars when discussing the sublime ("das Erhabene") in paragraph 29 of *Kritik der Urteilskraft* (1790). The sea is not in itself sublime, but it can be experienced as sublime, according to Kant, if we manage to purge the experience of purpose and meaning. In order to experience the sea as sublime, writes Kant, we must not see it as we represent it in thought, not as, for example, an element uniting people and separating continents, because "such are only teleological judgements." To find the sea sublime "we must regard it as the poets do, according to what is revealed to the sight of the eye, as, let us say, when it is calm, a clear mirror of water bounded only by the heavens, or, when it is agitated, as an abyss threatening to engulf all," etc.[9]

---

8 Rousseau, *Julie, ou la nouvelle Héloïse* (Pléiade, 1961), p. 397: "Il faut monter à bord, il faut partir. Mer vaste, mer immense, qui dois peut-être m'engloutir dans ton sein; puissai-je retrouver sur tes flots le calm qui fuit mon coeur agité!"

9 Immanuel Kant, *Kritik der Urteilskraft* (Reclam, 1963), p. 175f.: "denn das gibt lauter teleologische Urteile; sondern man muß den Ozean bloß, wie die Dichter es tun, nach dem, was der Augenschein zeigt, etwa, wenn er in Ruhe betrachtet wird, als einen klaren Wasserspiegel, der bloß vom Himmel begrenzt ist, aber ist er unruhig, wie einen alles zu verschlingen drohenden Abgrund, dennoch erhaben finden können." The passage is thoroughly commented on by Paul de Man in "Phenomenality and Materiality in Kant," in G. Shapiro and A. Sica (ed.)

Even the "thunderstorm," which Kierkegaard's young man in his last letters is looking forward to as an upsetting preparation for the instant of "repetition," has its counterpart in Kant: in paragraph 27 he writes that the experience of the sublime is mobile ("bewegt") in contrast to the beautiful, which is experienced calmly, in "ruhiger Kontemplation." The movement is more precisely called an agitation ("Erschütterung"), that is, a "rapidly changing repression and attraction of the very same object."[10] (Constantin would – ironically? – have reminded us of the usefulness of the Greek notion of *kinesis* when it comes to the paradoxes of "repetition.")

The sense of the upsetting agitation could perhaps also be expressed by Constantin's words of resignation in the second part of the text – "I am adrift" – as well as with the young man's enthusiastic final words: "my yawl is afloat." Both cases indicate a movement or a sort of transport with no direction or purpose. The young man expects that his risky transport will lead him into the sublime or, to copy Kant, to both abyss and heaven. What is remarkable is that the young man describes his expected experiences in auditory terms: ideas are about to "spume," thoughts to "arise noisily"; and he also expects a "stillness like the deep silence of the South Sea" (186/221). Noise as well as silence indicate that the young man's expectations of the sublime point to the non-verbal or to pure sound: i.e. to language without purpose or direction or meaning. Or to deep silence. The desire expressed in this text for a privileged *now* of presence can be realized only beyond a language that carries meaning.

Such is the young man's pathos. Which is contradicted, or at least ironically commented on, by what follows. After the young man has had his last word expressing his spuming desires to leave language, comes neither silence nor void – but the text transformed into a visual object. What follows on the page after the young man's last word is the picture of an envelope addressed to the anonymous Mr X and "containing" (rather than communicating) Constantin's letter to "the real reader of this book." This could actually be regarded as an ironical

---

Hermeneutics. Questions and Prospects (Amherst: University of Massachusetts Press, 1984).

10 Ibid., p. 155: "Das Gemüt fühlt sich in der Vorstellung des Erhabenen in der Natur *bewegt*: da es in dem ästhetischen Urteile über das Schöne derselben in *ruhiger* Kontemplation ist. Diese Bewegung kann … mit einer Erschütterung verglichen werden, d.i. mit einer schnellwechselnden Abstoßen und Anziehen ebendesselben Objekts."

realization of the young man's wish for a language beyond communication: what we get is language as anonymous and as pure materiality.

But the whole text carries another expectation that is *not* realized in any way (and certainly not ironically) when the young man heads for his sublime noise. I am thinking of the conceptual analysis quoted above, in which Constantin stated that both "repetition" and "recollection" are concepts of order, and without these "all life" would dissolve in "an empty noise devoid of content" (131/149). It was apparent in this passage that "recollection" and "repetition" were not opposites in this respect, and that both organized (in different directions?) the "noise" of the phenomenal world or of life into meaning – we may guess from the circumstances that "repetition" would offer a paradoxical meaning, but still a contrast to pure noise. Our text may create the expectation that "repetition" should be realized in the presence of its story: paradoxically, but definitely not as any "empty noise devoid of content."

Perhaps we should now remember that the text *Repetition* was published together with *Fear and Trembling*, which was presented under another pseudonym (Johannes de Silentio). These two texts are close in the aspect of "repetition" that has to do with test, ordeal, agitation, with virtually everything that the young man associates with Job and with himself – everything that here has been called pathos (in contrast to irony); the pathos of a *mysterium tremendum*. In *Fear and Trembling* it is the ordeal of Abraham that is both pathetic and sublime in the sense of devoid of meaning and purpose, or, in Kierkegaard's term: absurd.

In *Repetition* the young man is tested by the agitating (and sublime) "thunderstorm," which he associates with Job and with "repetition." His ordeal is a "psychological experiment" if one is to believe the subtitle of the text: "A Venture in Experimental Psychology." The result of his ordeal is, however, hardly comparable to the "repetition" including bonus – repetition as not only taking back, but also giving back – that is finally given to Kierkegaard's absurd heroes Abraham and Job – "Job is blessed and has received everything *double*" (180/212). Instead the young man's new life is suggested in terms that seem suspiciously close to the "noise" that made a negative contrast to "repetition" in the conceptual investigation. He certainly seems to imagine something more heroic than an "empty noise devoid of content," but his metaphors show that he is heading for void and for noise. Or not even noise: for stillness.

Something has gone wrong here in the relation between concept and narration – or between Constantin and the young man. Perhaps we should judge the young man's final letter with its expectations of a sublime noise simply as a mistake or as an indication of Kierkegaard's problems with getting his story finished. The letter should have been amended in accordance with the conceptual analysis, and we should have been given the possibility of the young man, for instance, starting to write poems, i.e. living in his recollection. Or Constantin could have made it clear that the young man had simply misunderstood "repetition" and was acting in Kierkegaardian "agony."

Nothing in the text, however, prevents us from seeing the young man's desperately enthusiastic last letter as a narrative correction of Constantin's irony and his conceptual analysis – nothing, at least, until Constantin's own last letter concluding the text. The correction would situate "repetition" in the "abyss" or among the "stars" or in "noise" or in "silence" – in any case beyond language, as a hint that the privileged *now* of the "instant" can be found only outside the time of human communication and existence.

Ordo inversus

Constantin informs us repeatedly that the young man is a poet. This is in contrast to himself: "I myself cannot become a poet" (192/228), he says, and calls himself a "prose writer" (184/218) – the Danish "prosaist" can also be understood as "prosaic writer." Developed full scale in Hegel's aesthetics in Kierkegaard's time, this well-known opposition of prose versus poetry coincided with something like Romanticism versus prosaic reality, and the romantic-poetic pole of the opposition was associated with subjectivity, imagination and visions of Orphic dignity. This opposition coincides with the romantic notion we met in the chapter on Cervantes: "prose as the idea of poetry." We may actually regard Constantin as the "idea" of the young man and the young man as poet: not that he is writing poems, but he enjoys a romantically poetical imagination.

Other ingredients of the text contribute to making Constantin and the young man into opposites: the name and the eye. While Constantin is a telling pseudonym, the young man is nameless; he even points it out himself by signing two of his letters in the second part as "nameless friend."[11] And he has trouble using his eyes to *see* the girl he loves and goes as far as leaving the country in order to escape the sight of her — "Think of me spotting her," he writes in his first letter to Constantin, "I believe I would have gone mad" (166/192). Only at a distance can he freely imagine her.

Constantin has a less problematic eye. In the first part of the text he tells of two instances when he used a seductive regard, and the second occasion in particular — a memory of watching a show in Berlin — emphasizes the importance of the regard: "my eyes were upon her," he writes of the girl he remembers having watched, "my eyes sought her, and the sight of her refreshed my whole being" (146f./167). The glance of the eye — *Øieblikket* — has a decisive importance for Constantin's development of the philosophy of "repetition."

It is different with the young man, our Orphic poet: he escapes seeing his nameless Eurydice, and his final fantasy of presence — including the absence of the girl — is beyond the eye and its glance in the sense that it is auditory.

The eye and the glance were problems also for the mythical Orpheus, whose tale may well be *one* allegorical pattern behind or before Constantin's young poet and his sad love-story; another could be Psyche, who was blinded by meeting Eros or could face the God only in darkness. Mythical Orpheus famously sang himself alive through the underworld and induced its powers to let him bring his Eurydice back to the living world on condition that he did not turn to see her. The myth of Orpheus has to do with glance, with retrieval and with turning around — and with inspiration, song, poetry. The ambiguity of the myth has been beautifully analysed by Maurice Blanchot, who writes that the turning of Orpheus towards Eurydice "ruins" his project or task, sending Eurydice back to "the shades." "To his eyes, the essence of the night proves to be inessential" and that is why he turns towards Eurydice, betraying her:

But not turning to Eurydice would not be less of a betrayal, to be unfaithful to the excessive and unreasonable power of his movement, which does not want Eurydice in her daylight truth and everyday appeal, but which wants

11 Interesting views on the young man's namelessness are found in Louis Mackey, "Once more with feeling: Kierkegaard's Repetition," in R. Schleifer and R. Markley (eds.), *Kierkegaard and Literature* (Oklahoma University Press, 1984), p. 98: "The decisive event in the letter of August 15 is the young man's loss of his name."

her in her nocturnal obscurity, in her distance, with her body closed and face sealed, which wants to see her, not when she is visible but when she is invisible.[12]

This remarkable passage, which happens to be the turning-point of Blanchot's own Orphic work, tells us something about our feeble Orpheus, Constantin's young man and poet, who wants to see his girl, but yet not see her; perhaps he is so unenterprising in relation to the girl because his alternatives are deceptive? Perhaps her absence in the text means that she "exists" only as the young man's poetical fantasy? Or that he can "meet" her only in darkness, i.e. absence, wants to see her only "when she is invisible"?

An allegorical reading allows for conjectures in this vein that the text, however, is slow in answering. The young man's project seems to be marriage: making himself real to the girl and making her real and visible to him. "Repetition" is what was to accomplish this happy turning (or "repetition" *is* this turning that resulted in separation). But why, then, escape her presence? Could it be because the Orphic pre-text makes it obvious that "repetition" in the sense of turning-around "destroys his work," to use Blanchot's words? "Repetition" as turning-around destroys the work and the project by repatriating the girl to the shadows (of marriage), which is still in accordance with the allegorical pattern. Perhaps – and that was Blanchot's version – this *was* the project: seeing her not as real, but as shadow. And poetical "work," according to Orpheus, has this distance as its first condition.

The young man worships his girl at a distance. Early in the text, Constantin points out that the young man's love is poetical: the girl "awakened the poetic in him and made him a poet" (121/138) – allegorically speaking, Orpheus creates his Eurydice in order to sing. Constantin adds, in the same sentence, that "precisely thereby she had signed her own death sentence": the Orphic-poetic love demands the absence of the woman; situates her at a distance as shadow or death.

12 Maurice Blanchot, *L'Espace littéraire* (Paris 1955), p. 228: "en se tournant vers Eurydice, Orphée ruine l'œuvre, l'œuvre immédiatement se défait, et Eurydice se retourne dans l'ombre; l'essence de la nuit, sous son regard, se révèle comme l'inessentiel. Ainsi trahit-il l'œuvre et Eurydice et la nuit. Mais ne pas se tourner vers Eurydice, ce ne serait pas moins trahir, être infidèle à la force sans mesure et sans prudence de son mouvement, qui ne veut pas Eurydice dans sa vérité diurne et dans son agrément quotidien, qui la veut dans son obscurité nocturne, dans son éloignement, avec son corps fermé et son visage scellé, qui veut la voir, non quand elle est visible, mais quand elle est invisible," etc. There is an English translation by Ann Smock (Nebraska University Press, 1982).

149

On only one occasion does the girl stop being the silent shadow of the text: by her suddenly getting married. This — her first and last sign of life — makes her finally dead to the young man. The allegorical reading according to Orpheus would indicate that this is a result of the young man's turning-around, his reversal in order to see. But at this point the allegorical reading does not work. If there is any reversal leading to "repetition" it is her action: fatal repetition is the result of *her* turning her back on him and walking into the Hades of marriage. Here an allegorical reading according to Psyche/Eros may be closer: at the decisive moment the loving eye turns away or is blinded.

No allegorical expectations, however, according either to Orpheus or to Psyche, fit the young man's final fantasies after the girl has turned around and disappeared. His *auditory* enthusiasm is a striking contrast to the *visual* fantasies on the conditions of love, language, poetry and knowledge that found mythical expression in the tales of Orpheus and of Psyche/Eros.

It is at this decisive point in the text — when voice threatens glance and when sound threatens meaning — that Constantin makes his visual coup: the picture of a letter, framing his final message to the "real reader," Mr X. It is an ironic or even parabasical intervention, a punctuation of the pathetic letters of the young man and comparable to Diogenes' visual demonstration of mobility in face of the Eleatic motionlessness (according to the anecdote that starts our *Repetition*). The irony is thematized by Constantin in the letter when he addresses the type of writer who knows how to write "in such a way that the heretics could not understand it" (194/225) — that is, the writer who writes with double meaning, or, as Constantin put it in the first part of the text, who "can express all in his thieves' language so that no sigh is so deep that he does not have the laughter that corresponds to it in thieves' language" (127/145). Irony is finally underscored when Constantin gives himself a Socratic position: he is the one who has "created" the young man, but he is himself "a vanishing person, just like a woman giving birth in relation to the child" (194/230).

Constantin's ironic position puts an end to the allegories according to Orpheus or Psyche/Eros, and also to the young man's auditory fantasies. Constantin is a man of the eye and a philosopher of the glance of the eye. There is, nevertheless, a connection between his ironic eye and the allegory, between irony and the principle of allegory, and this connection is the same as the concept, the story and the text: "repetition."

In his well-known analysis of allegory, Paul de Man writes that the "meaning constituted by the allegorical sign can then consist only in the *repetition* (in the Kierkegaardian sense of the term) of a previous sign with which it can never coincide, since it is of the essence of this previous sign to be pure anteriority."[13] De Man connects this formal definition of allegory with irony, and argues that allegory and irony are "linked in their common discovery of a truly temporal predicament" (p. 222). We will find this "predicament" at the point where time as sequence coincides with time as event, i.e. in the discovery of an instantaneous *now*, or, rather, the presence of an instantaneous *now* that must have a precedence in time.

The Kierkegaardian "repetition" that de Man had in mind can only be the text *Repetition*, including the "dialectic of repetition" in its chiastic formula as analysed above, and the "taking back" that tells us that "the existence, that has been, now becomes" (131/149). This is a "temporal predicament," to use de Man's judgment, because the *now* that is privileged by "repetition" is also an *after*, meaning that the presence of the *now* presupposes an absence – an ironic position reminding us of the absence of the girl who is needed to serve the young man's Orphic pathos; or the pathos of distance, which we found, in the chapter on Rousseau, at the very moment of presence.

How can such a temporal dialectic be recounted?

Kierkegaard's answer was the "indirect message." Kierkegaard communicated indirectly through pseudonyms, and by letting a pseudonym like Constantin communicate ironically, in "thieves' language." Indirectly Constantin tells the reader how to read the text *Repetition*, by telling him, in the concluding letter, how *not* to read: not as a "comedy, tragedy, novel, short story, epic, or epigram"; and not straight, since its "ways" are "inverse" (190/226).

Such is the indirect way Constantin tells us about the ideas of the text and its temporal movement. To begin with I pointed out that this created a kind of restless text, and I have also pointed to possible tensions between the concept of "repetition" and the story *Repetition*. Now I should be prepared to conclude that this restlessness and tension still make up a kind of almost stabilizing mutuality: an exchange between the levels of the text, its first part and its second,

---

13 Paul de Man, "The Rhetoric of Temporality," in *Blindness and Insight* (London: Methuen, 1983), p. 207. This essay will be quoted with page references in the text.

between Constantin and the young man, between philosophy and love-story, between irony and allegory.

The connection of irony to allegory is called "repetition"; according to de Man: *"repetition* (in the Kierkegaardian sense of the term)." "Repetition" is the allegory of irony and the irony of allegory, it is the coincidence of story and concept, sequence and instant.

The connection may become more obvious if "repetition" is related to the *inverse*, which is the final word used by Constantin to describe the "ways" of the text. This word hardly exists in Danish, and, therefore, calls for attention. It seems to be derived from the Latin *inversio*, which, in classical rhetoric, was a term with both a syntactical and a semantical meaning. Syntactically the term meant a reversed order of the sentence or sentences; semantically the term meant "to say in another way," that is, it (more or less) translated the Greek *allegory*. Both these senses of an *ordo inversus* (a reversed order) combine in *Repetition*: the young man's allegory according to Orpheus or Psyche/Eros is semantical by repeating a myth. Constantin's ironic intervention with his final letter is syntactical, making a reversal of text. Constantin thereby ironically underlines what his letter indirectly communicates: that the "ways" of the text *Repetition* are "inverse," making the text into an ironic allegory of movement; moving, like Diogenes, back and forth between eye and ear, between irony and pathos, between past and present time, between concept and story.

Whether all this mobile mutuality between the levels of the text functions to organize or to disorganize the text – and whether irony and allegory are united or separated in the concept of "repetition" – may have to do with our reading of the relation between the young man and Constantin, that is, between pathos and irony, between "repetition" as an "existential" and as a textual possibility. Constantin's irony has the first and the last word of the text, but the pathos of the young man creates its tensions. The young man's project may be read as making "repetition" into the movement of life, while Constantin's ironic interventions can be seen as the cold glance of textual death on the nameless life of poetical passion (as represented by the young man).

But the young man's project of giving life to shadows and turning absence into presence may also be read with suspicion. It presupposes the absence or even death of the girl, and it culminates in nothing like presence at all, but in a fantasy on noise and silence. The young man's last words prepare for a leap out of language into the "noise" that

Constantin in the conceptual analysis of the first part condemned as "devoid of content" (131/149). The young man's *inversio* seeks life in order to leave the text. Constantin's *inversio* is a back-and-forth in the wake of Diogenes, who, according to anecdote, took a walk to refute those Eleatics who "denied motion" (115/131). But Constantin differs from Diogenes in using words. Language is his field. The indirect and ironic message seems to be that his mobile text keeps language alive — and keeps life within linguistic order.

Ordo inversus, the reversed and repeated order, means standing things on their head: putting them right. The philosophy of the subject inaugurated by Kant is radicalized by Kierkegaard, who (ironically) proclaims subjectivity as the truth. That is an *inversio* working ironically in the text *Repetition* against the pathos of presence. But this irony hardly lacks its own pathos, and it even has some sublime touches. A romantic poet of Orphic dignity, Hölderlin, had an eye for the possibilities of *inversio* when he wrote in a fragment: "One has inversions of the words in the sentence. But greater and more efficient must be the inversion of the sentences themselves. The logical position of sentences ... is only rarely useful to the poet."[14] A recent follower of his, Paul Celan, also had a sense of this sublime reversal; as he once pointed out, "whoever walks on his head, ladies and gentlemen — whoever walks on his head, he has the heavens as an abyss underneath him."[15]

Heidegger's "Wiederholung"

With his central terms "Augenblick" (instant) and "Wiederholung" (repetition), Heidegger is concerned with a Kierkegaardian *Øieblikk* and the recuperating, renovating version of "repetition." He is not concerned with Kierkegaard, though, who is mentioned only in some

---

14 Friedrich Hölderlin, "Reflexion", in *Gesammelte Schriften*, 4: 1 (Stuttgart, 1961), p. 233: "Man hat Inversionen der Worte in der Periode. Größer und wirksamer muß aber dann auch die Inversion der Perioden selbst sein. Die logische Stellung der Perioden ... ist den Dichter gewiss nur höchst selten brauchbar."

15 Paul Celan, *Der Meridian und andere Prosa* (Frankfurt-on-Main: Suhrkamp, 1983), p. 51: "Wer auf dem Kopf geht, meine Damen und Herren, – wer auf dem Kopf geht, der hat den Himmel als Abgrund unter sich." There is a reminder here of the fragment just quoted by Hölderlin, where he says: "Man kann auch in die Höhe fallen, so wie in der Tiefe."

dismissive notes in *Sein und Zeit* (1926). The main objection seems to be that Kierkegaard "clings to the vulgar concept of time" when he, as demonstrated above, defines his *Øieblikk* "with the help of now and eternity."[16] I will not discuss here whether or not Heidegger handles his relations to Kierkegaard correctly;[17] nor will I comment further on the provocative arrogance involved in Heidegger's labeling of various conceptions of time as "vulgar." Instead I will sketch the relations between time and "Wiederholung" in *Sein und Zeit*, and then the relations between time and language, poetry and "Wiederholung" as they may appear in the later Heidegger – with everything considered as an "Auslegung" (to use one of Heidegger's favorite terms), meaning interpretation, commentary and "stretching out" – of Kierkegaard's allegorical, rhetorical and paradoxical "repetition."

Wiederholung

The importance of "time" for Heidegger in *Sein und Zeit* comes out in the title. On the first page he announces the provisional aim of the book to be an "interpretation of *time* as horizon for an understanding of Being" (p. 1). In the programmatical introduction Heidegger says that "the fundamental ontological task of interpreting Being as such includes working out the *temporality of Being*" (p. 40). The question that Heidegger states is philosophically fundamental in *Sein und Zeit*, i.e. "the question of Being," can be answered only in terms of time.

But the question is not answered, and the task remains provisional. The book ends when Heidegger has worked his way through two of the three sections that were to make up part I, according to the introduction; the remaining section – called "Zeit und Sein" – would have analysed Being as time and time as Being. The likewise foreboded second part would have accomplished a "phenomenological destruction" of the philosophical history of ontology. What we have is provisional – according to the plan for the book – not leading us

16 Martin Heidegger, *Sein und Zeit* (Tübingen: Niemeyer, 1986, first published 1926), p. 338n: "Kierkegaard ... bleibt am vulgären Zeitbegriff haften und bestimmt den Augenblick mit Hilfe von Jetzt und Ewigkeit." Cf. p. 235n. When possible I will cite page references in the text when quoting from *Sein und Zeit*. I follow the English translation by John Macquarrie and Edward Robinson with due modifications.
17 It is a leading idea in John D. Caputo, *Radical Hermeneutics* (Indiana, 1987), that paragraphs 64, 65 and 74 in *Sein und Zeit* "are directly drawn from Kierkegaard's writings" (p. 82).

much further than to the point where we started: the enigmatic Being. And what is enigmatic about Being, writes Heidegger towards the end, has to do with *movement*: *movement* combines the obscurities of Being with the questioning of Being into an *enigma* of Being.[18]

Movement is movement in time: Heidegger calls the various states of time "ec-stasies" – which could mean "outside stillness" (stasis) or what is not still; or being "beside oneself." He insists that this ec-static "beside" should be thought of not as some temporary diversion from normality, but as an "authentic" and "real" condition: the motion or movement is the real being-in-time that is concealed only by an everyday normality making the individual falsely at home in the stillness of a repetitive *now*.

That was my attempt to paraphrase Heidegger in his polemics against the commonplace and everyday in their being out of tune, in "fahlen Ungestimmtheit" (p. 345), or against "das Man," being the commonplace "subject" where real subjectivity is "spread out" (p. 129). Being in the world in "calm" and "confidence" could never mean being in a stasis, but always in something outside of stillness (*ec-stasis*); also "calm" and "stillness" are versions of the "Unheimlichkeit" of existence, its not-feeling-at-home, Heidegger assures; and *not* feeling at home ("das Un-zuhause") is a more original state of existence and ontology than feeling at home (p. 189).

The point of departure, as well as the final point in Heidegger's great work, is, then, Being in its enigmatic movements in time. And most enigmatic is the movement that makes Being present in time while withdrawing (in the same movement): Being is always as present as it is concealed, always appearing and always in the act of withdrawing. In the introduction to the book, Heidegger defines Being in Greek inspiration as "*ousia*, which signifies, in ontologico-temporal terms, 'presence' [Anwesenheit]. What is being is grasped in its Being as 'presence', i.e. is understood in relation to a definite mode of time, the 'Present'" (p. 25). Present time and the presence of time ("die Gegenwart") in their relations to the presence of Being are, then, the central topics of Heidegger's recurrent meditation in *Sein und Zeit* and throughout his writings.

The second section of the first part of *Sein und Zeit* – the passage

---

18 "Die Dunkelheiten lassen sich um so weniger abstreifen, als schon die möglichen Dimensionen des angemessenen Fragens nicht entwirrt sind und in allen das *Rätsel* des *Seins* und ... der *Bewegung* sein Wesen treibt" (p. 392).

that was not intended to become the last that it nevertheless became
– is headed "Dasein und Zeitlichkeit" ("Dasein[19] and temporality").
There the "ec-stasies" of "temporality" are named (simply enough)
future, past time ("Gewesenheit") and present time ("Gegenwart"),
with the qualification that the "primary phenomenon" of "primordial"
and "authentic" temporality is the future, "die Zukunft" (p. 329).
What Adorno abused as "Jargon der Eigentlichkeit" is abundant in my
quotation ("primary," "primordial" and "authentic" in one sentence)
and, for that matter, in the whole of paragraph 65: Heidegger is
apparently raising his voice in order to establish the thesis that the
future has the key to the enigma of time, which was also the enigma
of existence and Being and of the presence of Being.

My guess is that Heidegger, with this dramatic gesture and his
mobilizing of terms for authenticity, wants to stress that the enigmatic
movement of Being – between presence and absence, or, better still,
between making present and withdrawing – should *not* be misunderstood as some kind of archaic or sentimentally mythical or
historical sense of tradition. The withdrawal of Being is not a myth of
a golden age and does *not* mean that its meaning, which once, in
mythical time, was present and obvious, is only waiting to be "drawn"
back by an understanding or interpreting activity. Heideggerian
movement is more radical than that – because the movement is
permanent. The fact that Being could be defined only in terms of time
has to do with its permanent movement and the forward direction –
into "nothingness" – of the movement. This direction towards
"nothingness" is named, by Heidegger, care, ("Sorge"), and he does
not hesitate to call this *Sorge* the Being of existence.[20]

In this movement forward towards "nothingness" we approach
Heidegger's version of repetition: "Wiederholung." In the movement
forward, i.e. in the presence that is determined by future, movement
moves towards "nothingness", "death" and "fate" ("das Schicksal").
It is primarily the fateful movement forward that Heidegger names
repetition: "Wiederholung."

Heidegger's *Wiederholung* is related to two other terms indicating
movement in time: resoluteness ("Entschlossenheit") and instant

19 It seems that English translations keep the German for *Dasein*, "existence" being
    too vague, and "to-being" or "being-there" too elaborate.
20 "Das Sein des Daseins ist die Sorge" (p. 284); "*Die Sorge selbst ist in ihrem Wesen
    durch und durch von Nichtigkeit durchsetzt*" (p. 285).

("Augenblick"). To paraphrase it: in "resoluteness" the floating or sequential and, in any case, "vulgar" commonplace time is concentrated into an "instant" that reformulates or repeats the possibilities of the past and transports them into future. In Heidegger's words: "In resoluteness, the present is not only brought back from diversion in what is close and cared for, but will be held in the future and in having been."[21] One can observe that Heidegger already in the verbal form (future tense: "will be held," *wird ... gehalten*) wants to demonstrate that this holding of time points forward or *is* a futural gesture. What Heidegger here suggests in the odd expression of "holding" time (in time) he also calls, in the same passage, instant ("Augenblick") and real presence or present time ("eigentliche Gegenwart").

This "real" and instantaneous time must – and Heidegger insists on this point – be separated from something completely unreal or inauthentic: that is the *now* that Heidegger calls "das Jetzt." This base phenomenon, "das Jetzt," is derived from the "within-timeness" ("Innerzeitigkeit") that makes way for the "vulgar" and "traditional" concept of time (arguments are found on p. 333). The "instant" has nothing to do with "das Jetzt." The "instant" dislocates or interrupts traditional time: in the "instant," "nothing can occur; but as an authentic present time it allows a *first encounter* with what can be 'in a time' as ready-to-hand or present-at-hand."[22] Heidegger hyphenates what was here translated as "present time" ("Gegen-wart"), perhaps to stress its authenticity, perhaps also in order to imply that the "instant" is something to "encounter" or to come up "against" ("gegen").

It is in connection with this argument that in a note Heidegger dismisses Kierkegaard's *Øieblikk* as stuck in the "vulgar concept of time," i.e. in "das Jetzt" and in "Innerzeitigkeit" (p. 338). It should be apparent from my discussion of Kierkegaard's *Repetition* above that Kierkegaard was just as interested as Heidegger in conceptualizing the paradoxical *now* that lifts time out of time to make movement into the basic category of Being. "In this connection, the Greek discussion of

21 "In der Entschlossenheit ist die Gegenwart aus der Zerstreuung in das nächst Besorgte nicht nur zurückgeholt, sondern wird in der Zukunft and Gewesenheit gehalten" (p. 338).
22 "Das Phänomen des Augenblicks kann *grundsätzlich nicht* aus dem Jetzt aufgeklärt werden ... 'Im Augenblick' kann nichts vorkommen, sondern als eigentliches Gegen-wart läßt er *erst begegnen*, was als Zuhandenes oder Vorhandenes 'in einer Zeit' sein kann" (p. 338).

the concept of *kinesis* ... should be given close attention," as Constantin puts it in *Repetition* (131/149). Such close attention will show that Heidegger's *Wiederholung* and Kierkegaard's *repetition* have kinesis in common; and other relations too. *Wiederholung* is perhaps not only an act of fateful resoluteness, but could also be – like Kierkegaard's "repetition" – a movement of the text, an *ordo inversus* of syntactical as well as semantic effect.

So far, however, *Wiederholung* is resolutely connected to resoluteness, *Entschlossenheit*. The term actually has several possible meanings, and Heidegger seems sometimes to be close to a more literal sense of "locking up" or "dissolving," thus giving some relaxed overtones to his basically activistic tone. Still, he seems to insist on the possibility of establishing authentic Being here and now – and we may pause to think that he is not far removed from Don Quijote's mission, as described in chapter 2: to re-establish and renovate an authentic golden age of authenticity. Heidegger's *Entschlossenheit* indicates an active intervention in time, and his breakneck language, his seemingly logical and paragraphical account and his insistent italicizings all point to such a "resoluteness" in making new, in making everything new – emphasized in the heading of the first paragraph: "The Necessity of an Explicit Repetition of the Question of Being."

The "explicit repetition" turns up again in paragraph 74, which is devoted extensively and intensively to *Wiederholung*. There we learn that the *Wiederholung* of repetition is an "explicit handing-over" (p. 385) – the term is "Überlieferung", meaning "handing-over" or "handing-down" as well as "tradition" (which, again, literally means "handing-over" – and I will return to the metaphorical sense). The possibilities of the past are thus handed-over or transported, not, however, in a repetition meaning reduplication, but enlarged and "resolutely" improved: made new. "The rejoinder of the possibility in resolution is, however, also *as instantaneous* a *calling back* of what today is working itself out as 'past.' Repetition does not abandon itself to that which is past, nor does it aim at progress. Both are indifferent to the authentic existence of the instant."[23]

23 "Die Erwiderung der Möglichkeit im Entschluß ist aber zugleich *als augenblickliche* der *Widerruf* dessen, was im Heute sich als 'Vergangenheit' auswirkt. Die Wiederholung überläßt sich weder dem Vergangenen, noch zielt sie auf einen Fortschritt. Beides ist der eigentlichen Existenz im Augenblick gleichgültig" (p. 386). I have translated *Widerruf* by "calling back"; it could also be, for instance, "disavowal."

It could be said that, with words like "the authentic existence of the instant," Heidegger expresses an "existential" pathos close to Kierkegaard's different versions of *Øieblikket*. But he differs in tone: here we find not a trace of Kierkegaardian irony or of the "indirect communication" that Kierkegaard took to be the only way to communicate. Heidegger is, at least here, caught in his own "resoluteness" concerning the possibility of the immediate expression of Being. On the other hand, he rids himself of this possibility. (And there was, as mentioned above, no third section, in which *Sein und Zeit* was to have been "resolutely" repeated as *Zeit und Sein*.)[24] He has already rid himself of this possibility in his fascination with time as movement, with Being as present only in its withdrawal, with the "resoluteness" derived from the figure of "repetition."

One could imagine that Constantin Constantius, the philosopher of "repetition," might have commented acidly on Heidegger's "resolute" ambition to express Being immediately. The dialectic of "repetition" was easy, according to Constantin: "that which is repeated has been, otherwise it could not be repeated, but the very fact that it has been makes the repetition into the new" (131/149). No "resoluteness" could embarrass this forbiddingly chiastic dialectic, and nothing could make what was into what is (although time could be dislocated in that magical "instant"). Nor could any expression or wording make Being immediately and fully present, since sign and phenomenon are simply not the same. Presence escapes the word and the eye – as our allegorical pre-text on Eros and Psyche has already incomparably stated when allowing the full visual meeting to take place only in darkness.

But back to "resolute" Heidegger, who in *Sein und Zeit*, paragraph 74, describes the *Wiederholung* of repetition as the "mode of the resoluteness that hands itself over, the mode by which Dasein exists explicitly as fate" (p. 386). With "fate" he suggests the future as the basic category of time, with "handing-over" he gives direction and motion, and with instantaneous "resoluteness" all is made present. Such is the program. But the program includes some problems. One has to do with the ambiguity of the central term "Entschlossenheit." Another problem arises from describing the decisive "resoluteness" as "handing-over" ("überliefernde Entschlossenheit"). Through this we

---

24 A sort of repeating and renewing commentary came, at last, in a lecture in 1962 entitled "Zeit und Sein."

also get a kind of movement (or hesitation) in the instant of "resoluteness" and even in the futural "fate." "Handing-over" suggests a movement between past and present time with a distinct similarity to Constantin's dialectics of "repetition" that I just repeated by quoting. And Constantin's "repetition" was, according to my analysis, after all a movement back and forth of *text*, a transport or a "handing-over" of Diogenes' famous demonstration into movement of text or, to put it in textual terms, into a kind of ironic allegory.

Heidegger's transporting and handing-over "Überlieferung" is closer to metaphor than to allegory. Not only is *Überlieferung* a metaphorical expression suggesting the resolute movement of thought in time; *Überlieferung* also *means* metaphor — just as metaphor literally means exactly handing-over. The tone certainly separates our philosophers of "repetition" — Kierkegaard (as Constantin) and Heidegger (as Heidegger) — just as irony differs from pathos and allegory from metaphor. But still they seem to be related by the temporal maneuver suggested by Heidegger's explicit *Überlieferung* and his *überliefernde* resoluteness. "Allegory is," as pointed out by the rhetorician Heinrich Lausberg, "to thought what metaphor is to the single word: allegory stands in a relation of similarity to the intended serious thought ... Allegory is a metaphor extended throughout the whole sentence."[25]

My observation is simply that Heidegger operates with a metaphorical element at a vital point in his argument when asssociating his *Wiederholung* with *Überlieferung* — and no "resoluteness" can wrench time out of this (metaphorical) movement. No matter how "explicit" his repetition, Heidegger cannot escape a metaphorical transport.

This observation is made in spite of Heidegger's well-known suspicion of metaphor (he seems to regard "metaphor" as "metaphysical").[26] It is not original: Derrida has recently pointed out

25 Heinrich Lausberg, *Handbuch der literarischen Rhetorik* (Munich, 1960), para. 895: "Die Allegorie ist für den Gedanken, was die Metapher für das Einzelwort ist: die Allegorie steht also zum gemeinten Ernstgedanken in einem Vergleichnis-verhältnis ... die Allegorie ist eine in einem ganzen Satz ... durchgeführte Metapher."
26 For instance in Heidegger's "Das Wesen der Sprache", in *Unterwegs zur Sprache* (Pfullingen: Niemeyer, 1959), p. 207: "Wir blieben in der Metaphysik hängen, wollten wir dieses Nennen Hölderlins in der Wendung 'Worte, wie Blumen' für eine Metapher halten."

Heidegger's use of metaphors in his effort to find words for Being. Derrida observes that Heidegger's description of Being as withdrawal – essential presence as a kind of absence – is a metaphorical "detour" that is remarkably similar to the essential retreat characterizing Being in Heidegger's staging: "Being cannot be named except in a metaphorical – metonymical deviation."[27]

Derrida goes on to associate metaphor with metaphysics and both with the notion of similarity that we recognize from the tradition of *mimesis*. Although close to Heidegger in this procedure, Derrida finds "detour" and "deviation" when Heidegger is naming essential Being in terms of time and movement. The next step in this "detour" must be the repetition of *Wiederholung* as it is inscribed in the "handing-over," i.e. the temporal dialectics of past, present and future. Only in handed-over (and handing-over) "repetition" can we, according to Heidegger, reach the privileged instant of Being – which is "instant" itself. There is no direct path. There are several good philosophical reasons why Being cannot be immediately present or why we cannot directly name what we cannot directly be present in. Time and language are two good reasons. With his *Wiederholung* Heidegger named a reason of time – Constantin would have agreed and perhaps added a word or two on the relevance of *kinesis*. When *Wiederholung* is described as handing-over and handed-over we get another good reason, this time of language: names and words (like Time and Being) are handed over and down from presence into absence and from absence into presence, becoming metaphors in the transport.

Nach-sagen

Some time after *Sein und Zeit* Heidegger makes his famous "turning": "die Kehre." Whatever that may be – and I am far from capable of saying anything distinguished on that – it is in any event not a turning away from the question that Heidegger discussed (but never answered) in *Sein und Zeit*, the question of Being. Perhaps it could simply be said that Heidegger now approaches the question – and

27 Jacques Derrida, "Le retrait de la métaphore," in *Psyché* (Paris: Galilée, 1987), p. 79: "Cette métaphysique *comme* tropique, et singulièrement comme détour métaphorique, correspondrait à un *retrait* essentiel de l'être ... l'être ne se laisserait nommer que dans un écart métaphorico – métonymique."

Being — differently. Gone, or so it seems, is the "resoluteness" dominating the text of *Sein und Zeit*. It has given way to its alternative meaning — *Entschlossenheit* as a dissolving or locking up — and become *Gelassenheit*: the relaxed equanimity characterizing the later Heidegger's relation to Being. Gone is the "resolute" determination to transport and unite the ec-stasies of time in an ecstatic instant, "handed-over" by repetition.

Has, perhaps, the *Wiederholung* of repetition turned into a more modest *Kehre*? Turning was an important device in Kierkegaard's "repetition" too, as I tried to show in my discussion of its allegorical pre-text: Orpheus. Such Orphic relations to Heidegger's *Kehre* cannot be more than a hypothesis here, but could perhaps function as a reminder that an important part of Heidegger's *Kehre* is his turning to art and literature and, not least, Orphic poetry.

In *Sein und Zeit* we find none of the quotations, allusions and references to poetry, from Hölderlin to Stefan George, that the later Heidegger uses so frequently. On the contrary. In the programmatic introduction to *Sein und Zeit* we read: "If we are to understand the problem of Being, our first philosophical step consists in not *mython tina diegeisthai*" (p. 6) — Heidegger uses a (slightly corrupted) quotation from Plato's *The Sophist* (242c), which he translates as "tell a story." The philosophical consequence is a ban on stories: "keine Geschichte erzählen." He goes on to explain what story-telling is and why it must be avoided: it is "defining entities [Seiendes] as entities by tracing them back in their origin to some other entities, as if Being had the character of some possible entity."

It may be as a result of translation that Heidegger's contribution to narratology sounds enigmatic. I will, however, permit myself a simplifying interpretation: telling a story is, according to Heidegger, saying one thing by another; or, naming what is real by what is possible, i.e. fictitious. Since his ambition at this stage of *Sein und Zeit* is to name, as they are, the things themselves — "die Sachen selbst" (cf. para. 7) — he must discard story-telling. In fact, he must put a ban on fiction.

It should be obvious after my brief investigation of *Sein und Zeit* that it was not all that easy for Heidegger to name the things themselves. Time and language came in the way. Linguistic transport as "handing-over" became necessary even — and not least — at the very moment when he resolutely and in *Wiederholung* went directly to the thing — Being — itself. "Handing-over" opens a metaphorical index that Heidegger seems to have anticipated in his discarding definition of story-telling; because story-telling is also handing one thing over to another: transporting, repeating and making different. Returning to that early passage after having made one's way all through (the far from finished) *Sein und Zeit* one is tempted to read *language* where Heidegger writes story-telling. Heidegger's own language, and, to some degree, his analysis, has shown, by then, that language (and not just story-telling language) names reality in a figure of transport, naming one thing by another: "handing over," repeating and making different. Something in language and time – exactly this figure of "handing-over" in transport – is what bars us from the full presence of Being or, at least, from spelling out "die Sachen selbst." When Heidegger begins *Sein und Zeit* by banning story-telling he is in practice expressing a scepticism of language, i.e. of the possibility of naming Being and *Dasein* directly in language, and not (just) indirectly, metaphorically or in fiction.

Heidegger's *Kehre* is, among other things, a linguistic turning that is involved in a turning to poetry. This is emphatically stressed in *Der Ursprung des Kunstwerkes* of 1935/36. Art is there granted a privileged access to Being or the truth of Being: Art "is truth that makes itself into work";[28] and *all* art is "essentially poetry" (*Dichtung*) – yes, language itself is essentially "Dichtung." The truth concerning Being that art reveals or establishes or makes into work – i.e. art as *Dichtung*, *Dichtung* as language and language as *Dichtung* – is no simple presence. Heidegger was perhaps a philosopher of metaphysical presence in *Sein und Zeit*, at least if intentions count, but his *Kehre* complicates all presence. Instead, in *Der Ursprung*, Heidegger uses words like "Streit" and "Riß" in order to name what in principle seems unnameable (or what only language as *Dichtung* can suggest): strife and split. Being is not to be found as a harmonious whole, but is always already split, divided; no stillness, always already movement – a movement between presence and absence that constitutes some of Heidegger's most striking metaphors. These may be visual, as when Heidegger uses "Lichtung" to indicate the truth of Being, meaning a glade (in the forest of existence), and also lighting or even enlightenment. But "light" is also related to darkness in a movement that is never stable: already in *Der Ursprung des Kunstwerkes* Heidegger

---

28 Heidegger, *Der Ursprung des Kunstwerkes* (Reclam, 1960), p. 34: "Die Kunst ist das Sich-ins-Werk-Setzen der Wahrheit."

Theories of mimesis

writes that the truth established by *Dichtung* is the "Lichtung und Verbergung" of existence;[29] the unveiling enlightenment and the concealing endarkening in one and the same movement. In a later phase Heidegger seems more oriented to sound than to light, showing remarkable interest in, and insight into, the auditory and rhythmical qualities of language and poetry. In any case, and starting with *Der Ursprung des Kunstwerkes*, he gives *Dichtung* privileged access to Being while saying that language itself is "essentially" *Dichtung* – and defining *dichten/dictare* as "saying something that has not been said before", i.e. making new.[30] His examples suggest that a small group of German poets is successful in making language come true in poetry. Special attention is given to the poet of poets, i.e. Hölderlin, as in Heidegger's "interpretation" of Hölderlin's hymn *Andenken* with the famous final lines "Was bleibet aber / stiften die Dichter," read by Heidegger as proof of the poet's priority in instituting ("stiften") truth and language.

"For Heidegger," writes Paul de Man in one of his early essays, "Hölderlin is the greatest of poets ... because he states the essence (*Wesen*) of poetry. The essence of poetry consists in stating the parousia, the absolute presence of Being."[31] De Man then criticizes Heidegger's way of reading Hölderlin, meaning that "*it is the fact that Hölderlin says exactly the opposite of what Heidegger makes him say.*"[32] Hölderlin expresses not parousia, but a split of Being, according to de Man, primarily a split between language and Being, furthermore a "lived philosophy of repeated reversal, that is nothing more than the notion of becoming."[33]

I will not pursue the discussion of Heidegger's idiosyncratic readings of Hölderlin, but will mention only that "split" and "strife" are qualities that Heidegger (at least starting from *Der Ursprung des Kunstwerkes*) declares to be of the very essence of Being, named *Streit*

29 Ibid. p. 73f.: "Wahrheit als die Lichtung und Verbergung des Seienden geschieht, indem sie gedichtet wird".
30 Heidegger, *Hölderlins Hymne 'Der Ister'*, Gesamtausgabe (Frankfurt-on-Main: Klostermann, 1984), vol. 53, p. 8: "Dichten – *dictare*. Etwas sagen, was vordem noch nicht gesagt worden."
31 Paul de Man, "Heidegger's Exegesis of Hölderlin," in *Blindness and Insight*, p. 250.   32 Ibid., 254f.
33 Ibid., p. 265. The French original of 1955 has: "Il n'y a donc pas, dans Hölderlin, un retournement ontologique unique, mais une philosophie vécue du retournement répété, qui n'est autre que la notion du devenir."

and *Riß*; what de Man calls for in his criticism is already there. Moreover, the "repeated reversal" is to be found in his metaphorical "retreats" of Being (according to Derrida) or the exchange within truth of absence and presence, darkness and light(ing). In at least one late reading of poetry, a reading that is in itself a poetical reading, Heidegger links the word of the poet with Being itself, and also with something like the "repeated reversal" wanted by de Man – this something seems related to the concept of *Wiederholung* of *Sein und Zeit* and has now taken the name of "nach-sagen" (saying after).

I am thinking of the dense and difficult reading of Georg Trakl in "The Language in the Poem" (*"Die Sprache im Gedicht, Eine Erörterung von Georg Trakls Gedicht"*) of 1953. In this essay, Heidegger does not use solemn words like *ousía*, presence, Being or even truth in order to "investigate" Trakl's poetry. Instead he declares that "apartness" ("Abgeschiedenheit") and the "stranger" are the basic ingredients making up the "site" for the poetical work of Trakl.[34] What is strange or foreign about the "stranger" has to do with time: the "stranger" comes from what is "early" or from Early-ness itself ("die Frühe"), and this Earlyness is the site of the "still veiled," but nevertheless "primordial nature of time."[35] As we remember from *Sein und Zeit*, the nature of time is also the nature of Being (and perhaps we should also remember from *Sein und Zeit* that it was then a futural *Zukunft* that counted as the privileged measure of time – and not any archaic or early *Frühe*). Whether or not all this has anything at all to do with Trakl's poetry is difficult to say and I will not venture an answer; but it is interesting that Heidegger here declares the poet (Trakl) to be fundamentally "strange." Owing to his being "strange," he is given direct knowledge of what is otherwise veiled: the nature of time and Being. The stranger-poet becomes authentic and real because of his being "strange" and "apart."

Would that mean that the poet is now free to name Being and Time? That the language of poetry differs from all other language by naming directly – without any handing-over, without transporting metaphors, without saying one thing by another?

---

34 Heidegger, *Unterwegs zur Sprache*, p. 52: "Alles Sagen der Dichtungen Georg Trakls bleibt auf den wandernden Fremdling versammelt ... nennen wir den Ort seines Gedichtes *die Abgeschiedenheit*." I am using an English translation by Peter D. Hertz with due modifications.

35 "Diese Frühe verwahrt das immer noch verhüllte ursprüngliche Wesen der Zeit" (p. 57).

Still not; because poetry is the language of saying after: "nach-sagen." And, when Heidegger says that, it is no longer possible to decide if he is referring to the few fragments he quotes from Trakl or if he is referring to *Dichtung* in general. Or perhaps language in general, since language was essentially *Dichtung*? In any case, he now asserts that what the poetical word is saying after – or what the poetical word "turns" by "repetition" into *Dichtung* – is *sound*: "The poet's work means: saying-after – to say again the harmonies [*Wohllaut*] that were spoken to him by the spirit of apartness." This means that the poetical work is a "listening" ("ein Hören") for the "harmonies" that Heidegger describes like this:

The lunar coolness of the holy blue of the spiritual night rings through and shines through all gazing and saying. Its language becomes then a saying-after, becomes *Dichtung*. What it speaks shelters the poem as the essentially unspoken.[36]

Visual metaphors are here embedded in sound, and *Dichtung* is called "listening" to harmonious sounds. Such sounds are heard in "apartness," and this "apartness," we learned earlier in the essay, is to be found in "early-ness": "die Frühe." But the privileged site of the poet is, according to the quotation, not only filled with harmonious sounds; there is also the "holy blue" of the night, indicating that "apartness" is situated in darkness (the night) although slightly illuminated by a moon. Other senses too are involved: the moon is associated with coolness ("mondene Kühle"). The senses are mixed, as if Heidegger was attempting symbolistic synaesthetics: coolness, night and moonlight both sound and shine ("durchtönt und durchscheint").

If it is a primordial scene of *Dichtung* (and in that case also of language) that Heidegger is suggesting through "apartness" and "early-ness," it is primarily made of sound but also of darkness (and some light), coolness. Earlier in his investigation into Trakl, Heidegger had insisted that the "spirit" ("Geist") of "apartness" is fire ("Flamme"), shining "glowingly."[37] The primordial scene or the

---

36 "Die mondene Kühle der heiligen Bläue der geistlichen Nacht durchtönt and durchscheint alles Schauen und Sagen. Dessen Sprache wird so zur nachsagenden, wird: Dichtung. Ihr Gesprochenes hütet das Gedicht als das wesenhaft Ungesprochene" (p. 70). Heidegger's syntax, especially in the last sentence of the quotation, make an unambiguous rendering (or reading) impossible.
37 "Der Geist ist Flamme. Glühend leuchtet sie" (p. 62).

privileged site is, in short, physical. It is made up of sensual perception (but apparently no smells). The perceptions are unstructured or mixed, but dominated by sound, harmonious sound ("Wohllaut").

The sound being unstructured should mean that it is pre-linguistic, coming before words. The site of origin and lost presence, what is "early," is pre-linguistic. That would mean that this site could not be named; it is and remains "essentially unspoken." Language may be the "house" or "foundation" of Being, to use less poetical metaphors from other of Heidegger's essays on language; yet language cannot name Being. Even the poet, who has privileged access to Being owing to his being a "stranger" in "apartness," cannot do better than become Echo by saying after ("nach-sagen"), since what he has to say in poetical language always comes *after*, sounds after: after the sound.

In a way, Heidegger has gone full circle: in *Sein und Zeit* story-telling was discarded in order to make room for the philosophical word on Being, but metaphors entered the argument in the "resoluteness" of "handing-over" ("überliefernde Entschlossenheit") in which the *Wiederholung* of repetition gathered time in the instantaneous *now*. His "Kehre" means turning attention to art, and seems to allow *Dichtung* a privileged possibility of naming Being. But the investigation into Trakl gives Heidegger's thinking another turn: even the privileged poetical word hands over or transports the sound of Being into language. This language may be close to Being — for instance in the instant of repetition, turning or *Dichtung* — but it nevertheless always comes *after*. "Dichten heißt: nach-sagen." Sound is poetry. Poetry is sound. Language is poetry. Poetry is language. These chiastic formulas indicate that Heideggerian *Wiederholung* finally becomes as "easy" as Kierkegaardian "repetition," according to Constantin Constantius's formula: "for that which is repeated has been, otherwise it could not be repeated, but the very fact that it has been makes the repetition into the new" (131/149).

Derrida's "répétition"

Heidegger's never accomplished intention with *Sein und Zeit* was, as mentioned above, to outline "basic features of a phenomenological destruction of the history of ontology" (p. 39) and in that way to fulfill the philosophical criticism of philosophy started by Nietzsche (if not earlier). It may seem as if Jacques Derrida has started anew on this task — with the watchword adjusted to "deconstruction," and also including his own phenomenological basis. Here I have neither reason nor capacity even to sketch this great work in progress, so I shall restrict myself to a short summary of possible connections between Derrida's *répétition*, Heidegger's *Wiederholung* and *Augenblick* and also, directly or indirectly, Kierkegaard's "repetition" and *Øieblikk*.

In the full attack on the "metaphysics of presence," i.e. the history of ontology, that Derrida launched with his first major works in the 1960s, the concept of "répétition" plays a decisive part. It is primarily found in his investigation of Husserl's epistemology – which, in its turn, was an attempt to make a phenomenological end to metaphysics and gave Heidegger the starting-point for his "destructive" project in *Sein und Zeit*. In the fourth chapter of *La voix et le phénomène* of 1967, called "Meaning and Representation" ("Le vouloir-dire et la représentation"), Derrida "deconstructs" Husserl – or turns Husserl against Husserl – by showing how Husserl's concept of immediately presented ideas (unmediated sense-perception) presupposes mediation, repetition and re-presentation. Derrida comes to the remarkable conclusion: "The presence-of-the-present is derived from repetition, and not the reverse."[38]

Derrida seems to be doing something like Marx turning Hegel upside down in the name of revolution; or Nietzsche turning "Platonism" upside down in the name of eternal return. Derrida is turning ontological tradition on its head by giving priority to repetition and deriving presence as secondary. His argument leading to this conclusion should be followed before we discuss the consequences.

Derrida starts with the observation that language in Husserl can be thought of as an idea ("Vorstellung") as well as a re-presentation making present ("Vergegenwärtigung"), which is to say that language is both presentation and re-presentation. The presented idea gives, or is given, the impression of immediate presence, while re-presentation presupposes the already presented; and in re-presentation Derrida glimpses re-petition and re-production. Language in Husserl's phenomenology is split or divided, and its division is organized in a hierarchy separating immediate idea from re-presentation as primary

---

38 Jacques Derrida, *La voix et le phénomène* (Paris: Presses Universitaires de France, 1967), p. 58: "On dérive la présence-du-present de la répétition en non l'inverse." I am using an English translation by David B. Allison (*Speech and Phenomena* [Northwestern University Press, 1973]) with some modifications.

from secondary and presence from absence. The same or similar hierarchy is to be found, before that, in all "metaphysics," where the linguistic sign is derived from some presence: from the presence of reality and the reality of presence.

The metaphysical maneuver has, in Derrida's analysis, as its basis a real and fundamental split of the sign – the possibility of its repetition – meaning that language is always re-presentable, repeatable. Metaphysics, however, wants to conceal or extinguish this split to promote "presence." The "presence" that is the target of Derrida's polemics is exactly the "presence" that Heidegger, at the beginning of *Sein und Zeit*, derived from Greek *ousia*, "signifying in ontologico-temporal terms 'presence' [Anwesenheit]. Entities [Seiendes] are grasped in their Being as 'presence'; this means that they are understood with regard to a definite mode of time, the *'present'* [die Gegenwart]" (p. 25).

Against what Derrida repeatedly calls "the metaphysics of presence," as well as against any "idealized" permanence giving privilege to the presence of a *now* at the expense of an absence, Derrida argues from the point of view of the linguistic sign. A "sign is never an event"[39] because it is never uniquely and irreversibly present, but its character as sign is due to the possibility of its repetition. "The sign in general" has its origin in repetition, in a "primordial structure of repetition,"[40] meaning that it could not be derived from something else – and certainly not from an immediate presence. On the contrary, presence must be derived, and that was the thesis, from repetition, or more precisely: from the "structure of repetition" of the sign. As Derrida (at this stage) has been summarized by a commentator: "There is no general law but a repetition, and there is no repetition that is submitted to a law."[41]

The history of philosophy as it has dominated the Western world – and Derrida is definite on this – is the "metaphysics of presence," which is built as a hierarchy of presence and absence having to set aside the sign/language as repetitive absence in order to keep the idea of present reality as presence. That is, what must be set aside or neglected is the repeatability of the linguistic sign, since this "structure

---

39 Ibid., p. 55: "Un signe n'est jamais un événement si événement veut dire unicité empirique irremplaçable et irréversible."
40 Ibid., p. 56: "la structure originairement répétitive."
41 Geoffrey Bennington, "Derridabase," in *Jacques Derrida* (Paris: Seuil, 1991), p. 222: "*Il n'y a de loi en général que d'une répétition, et il n'y a de répétition que soumise à une loi.*"

of repetition" does not maintain the difference of what philosophy (ontology, metaphysics) must keep apart as different – the idea of reality from the re-presentation of reality.

Derrida therefore introduces – to relate to our earlier terminology – a Kierkegaardian *ordo inversus* when reading metaphysics against metaphysics. The first consequence of this is remarkable enough: if the sign is of an "originally repetitive structure," he writes, "the general distinction between the fictitious usage and effective usage of a sign is threatened. *The sign is originally wrought by fiction.*"[42] The other consequence has to do with the phenomenological attempt to get out of the logic of time, sign and repetition with the help of an instantaneous presence that "would be as indivisible as the *blink of an eye.*"[43]

I will first discuss the consequence that has to do with fiction. The repeatability of the sign is apparently not only a characteristic of the sign providing Derrida with arguments against "the metaphysics of presence"; repeatability also introduces an element of fiction in language – in any event, Derrida associates the "originally repetitive structure" of signs with "fiction." This association is not elaborated in his criticism of Husserl, but should mean that the reality of the present was to be derived from fiction, and not the other way around. This is analogous to the thesis that the "presence-of-the-present is derived from repetition and not the reverse." Furthermore, the association or identification of "repetition" with "fiction" could possibly be developed into a temporal definition of "fiction" as, precisely, "repetition," or at least as a version of "repetition."

We have, then, come a long way from Heidegger, at least from the programmatic Heidegger of the beginning of *Sein und Zeit* who made no-story-telling ("keine Geschichte erzählen") into his first philosophical rule, and in that way discarded "fiction" from Being as Plato once rejected the poets from the ideal state. We have also come far from the Heidegger who in a "resolute" *Wiederholung* imagined, one would think, getting away from "fiction" as a state of inauthenticity. But perhaps we have come closer to a Heidegger beyond his early

---

42 Derrida, *La Voix et le Phénomène*, p. 63: "la distinction générale entre usage fictif et usage effectif d'un signe est menacée. *Le signe est originairement travaillé par la fiction.*"

43 Ibid., p. 66: "Le présent de la présence à soi [Husserl's *Augenblick*] serait aussi indivisible qu'un *clin d'œil.*"

program? To the metaphorical Heidegger of "handing-over"? To Heidegger repeating "saying-after," when the Word is finally about to be said? We have, perhaps, come closer to a Heidegger mixed with a Nietzsche, that is to the Nietzschean fascination with "fiction," with mask and with *Schein,* and to the well-known metaphor of language as an "army" of metaphors. We have, in any event, come to a decisive point in what is called "deconstruction."

The idea of the repeatability of the linguistic sign that Derrida uses in his criticism of Husserl could perhaps be read as his incisive version of Saussure's famous idea of the arbitrariness of the linguistic sign and the system of language as a system of differences. Derrida is incisive by introducing an element of fiction in language, meaning that fiction is (no longer) a version of text, but that all text becomes versions of fiction. It should be obvious that this has drastic consequences for the system of genres, the levels of style and other conventions of text. Some possible consequences have been demonstrated not least in Derrida's own writing, which has become as difficult to situate in established genres (for instance, "philosophy") as Kierkegaard's writings; or Plato's.

Would that mean that Derrida in Nietzschean inspiration imagines language as a rhetorical machinery? And would that be a necessary consequence of his criticism of the "metaphysics of presence"? Derrida does not offer us any ready answers to such questions, and he evades easy and reliable classification. On the one hand he actually declares deconstruction to be "foreign to rhetoricism ... To take an interest in a certain fictionality ... does not in the slightest signify reducing, leveling, assimilating. On the contrary, it is to endeavor to refine the differences."[44] On the other hand, he maintains (as far as I can follow him) the idea of an element of fiction basic to language, although he does actually complain about the shortcomings of the notion of "fiction," wishing for a word beyond fiction[45] – perhaps indicating a wish for a language beyond language.

The basic argument in the criticism of Husserl – the "primordial structure of repetition" concerning signs – has, to my impression, been sharpened and developed by new concepts that reveal the similarity to Kierkegaardian "repetition" of being non-conceptual.

---

44 Derrida, "Afterword," in *Limited Inc* (Evanston, Ill., 1988), p. 156.
45 In the interview that starts *Acts of Literature* (ed. Derek Attridge; New York: Routledge, 1992), p. 49: "We should find a word other than 'fiction'."

That goes for his famous neologism "différance" and for the later developed (non-)concept of iteration or iterability.

"Iterability" may seem close to "repeatability," but was, nevertheless, introduced to replace "repetition" or at least those aspects of "repetition" that mean duplication: doing the same. "Iterability" derives, according to Derrida's etymological speculation, not only from the Latin *iter* (again) but also from *itara*: Sanskrit for "other." "Iterability" is, in any case, the name of "the logic that connects repetition with difference [altérité]";[46] "iterability" does not "signify simply ... repeatability of the same, but rather alterability of this same idealized in the singularity of the event."[47] Yes, "iterability" seems close to the "dialectics of repetition" that I have already quoted several times from Constantin Constantius: "that which is repeated has been, otherwise it could not be repeated, but the very fact that it has been makes the repetition into the new" (131/149).

But Derrida differs from Constantin by deriving "iterability" from language, sign and writing. He can write about "the iterability of the *mark* beyond all human speech acts"[48] and about "iterability" as what "structures the mark of writing itself."[49] That makes this (non) concept similar not only to Kierkegaardian "repetition," but also, to Derrida's own *différance*: a (non-)word uniting the spatial difference and the temporal displacement that characterizes all writing (according to Derrida).

Both these Derridean key terms, iterability and *différance*, could be viewed as developments of the *répétition* with which he started his "deconstruction" of the history of ontology and the "metaphysics of presence." None of these "concepts" is quite a concept in an ordinary philosophical sense. Iterability is, according to Derrida, "an aconceptual concept or another kind of concept, heterogeneous to the philosophical concept of the concept, a 'concept' that marks both the possibility and the limit of all idealization and hence of all conceptualization."[50] In this context, i.e. in the shadow of Kierkegaardian "repetition," it is important to observe that Derridean repetition is connected with fiction, fiction is connected to language as system and to the "repetitive structure" of the linguistic sign. That

---

46 Derrida, "Signature, événement, contexte," in *Marges de la philosophie* (Paris: Minuit, 1972), p. 375: "cette logique qui lie la répétition à l'altérité."

47 Derrida, "Afterword," p. 119.   48 Ibid., p. 134.

49 Derrida, "Signature, événement, contexte", p. 375: "Cette itérabilité ... structure la marque d'écriture elle-même."   50 Derrida, "Afterword," p. 118.

would also mean a stress on language as a (non-human) system of signs at the expense of language as (human) communication. Derrida's *ordo inversus* has a semiotic profile compared with Kierkegaard, who is certain to communicate, albeit indirectly, always indirectly.

To characterize Derrida's "deconstruction" it would perhaps suffice with the formula: repeatability of the sign / singularity of the event. The intersection of the two parts of this formula is important: repeatability always coincides with a singularity that Derrida can approach with terms like "signature" and "event." In Kierkegaard a similar intersection is made by the coupling "repetition/instant," and in Heidegger we remember the coupling "*Wiederholung /Augenblick.*" Derrida gets involved in this discussion as a part of his criticism of phenomenology. He touches on the "instant" in his criticism of Husserl in *La voix et le phénomène* directly after having "deconstructed" the phenomenological concepts of "Meaning and Representation," with the "repetitive structure" of the linguistic sign as the major argument. Concepts of meaning and representation need, according to Derrida, "the instant as a point, the identity of experience instantaneously present to itself."[51] Derrida seems to mean that phenomenology in Husserl's version invites movement and temporality into ontology; while demanding, like all philosophy, "presence" in order to keep the presented idea separate from its representation; i.e. in order to co-ordinate the *before/after* of temporality into the *absence/presence* of ontology. And that is a dilemma: movement and/or not-movement. The solution to this dilemma seems to be a point: the point in time where time is not time; or the point of time that miraculously annuls time.

We recognize this from Plato's *to exaiphnes* in *Parmenides*, Kierkegaard's *Øieblikk* and Heidegger's *Augenblick*; Derrida finds and discusses a similar *Augenblick* in Husserl and himself tries, we should add, something related with all his combinations of repeatability/ singularity, notably with his *différance*, constructing a word that spells both difference in time and difference in space. Still, Derrida's *différance* is obviously separated from the notions of an "instant" as mentioned above; because *différance* "is neither a *word* nor a *concept*," to use

51 Derrida, *La voix et le phénomène*, p. 67: "La pointe de l'instant, l'identité du vécu présent à soi dans le même instant porte donc toute charge de cette démonstration."

Derrida's own wording.[52] Even if Kierkegaard related the "instant" to the paradoxical and the absurd, he tried, with his *Øieblikk*, to conceptualize and thereby make absolute (Derrida would say, idealize) the point of time outside time. *Différance*, instead, is a construction that draws attention to its being a sign and to its double meaning. This double meaning includes *différer*, the activity of displacement that contains or conceals what is not present and not the same: the "other."

This "other" is always present in the presence of the present as a "trace" of the "movement of repetition," according to Derrida.[53] What is "other" or absent or outside is also present at or in the "instant," even if the phenomenological "instant" is presented and criticized by Derrida as an attempt to set aside from experience what is "other." But this "other" *must* be included in the "instant," Derrida argues; because the "instant" also has some (if only little) extension in time, making place for a temporality or a "continuity of the now and the not-now." With this temporality "we admit the other into the self-identity of the *Augenblick*; nonpresence and nonevidence into the *blink of the instant*. There is a duration to the blink, and it closes the eye. This *altérité* is in fact the condition for presence," etc.[54]

The "instant" is not an alternative to the ban of temporality, because it is in itself temporal – such is, in short, Derrida's criticism. But – or so I would like to imagine an objection to Derrida from Constantin Constantius, the philosopher of constancy and of *kinesis* and of the *Øieblikk* of "repetition" – what is actually happening at the very moment that the "instant" lasts? At the moment of the blink of the eye? Could it be possible to imagine the "instant" not as annulment of time, not as a singular point or break, but as a special form of movement in time?

Derrida's many different efforts to approach the singularity of the event could perhaps be seen as answers to that fictive question. And in a couple of later essays he actually discusses a Kierkegaardian *Øieblikk*; in one case with epistemological as well as university-political relevance. The title of the essay – "The Pupils of the

---

52 Derrida, "Differance," in *Speech and Phenomena* (Evanston, Ill., 1973), p. 130.
53 Cf. Derrida, *La voix et le phénomène*, p. 76.
54 Ibid., p. 73: "Dès lors qu'on admet cette continuité de maintenant et du non-maintenant ... on accueille l'autre dans l'identité à soi de l'*Augenblick*: la non-présence et l'inévidence dans le *clin d'œil de l'instant*. Il y a une durée du clin d'œil; et elle ferme l'œil. Cette altérité est même la condition de la présence" etc.

University" – has a double meaning. It includes a rare salute to Kierkegaard, the thinker of the "instant," called upon to force us to reflect on the conditions of reflection.[55] "Reflection" is the topic here, meaning both mirroring and thinking, and the "time" for reflection is described by Derrida as "the chance to look back on the very conditions of reflection, in all senses of this word, as if with the help of a new optical device one could finally see sight," etc.[56]

Reflection as thinking is the mirroring of thought – its repetition. But Derrida does not make the same mistake that he has criticized so many other thinkers for making: reflection is no immediate presence, but makes room for the "other." "The time of reflection is also another time, it is heterogeneous to what it reflects and perhaps allows time for what calls for and is called thought."[57]

Reflection, then, is the duration of time or the sequence in which thought thinks its thought. As time it could be a Kierkegaardian "instant," which "tears" time in a "brief" and "paradoxical" moment.[58] But reflection as the heterogeneous repetition of thought could also upset thinking and shake its basis. In this essay Derrida discusses – and upsets – nothing less than the "principle of reason" ("la raison d'être"). He wants (inspired by Heidegger) to show that the principle of reason has no reason of its own – and "the impossibility for a grounding principle to ground itself" opens, he argues, an "abyss" under the "ground."[59] This is shown by reflection: reflection opens the eye to the "abyss" of thought and makes thought mobile – on condition that the reflected thought is reflected not as identical, but as different. Reflection follows iteration, and both are submitted to the logic of repetition: the same but different, old but still "the new."

55 Derrida, "Les pupilles de l'université. Le principe de raison et l'idée de l'université," in *Du droit à la philosophie* (Paris: Galilée, 1990), p. 497. I have used an English translation by Catherine Porter and Edward P. Morris (*diacritics, autumn, 1983*) with some modifications.

56 Ibid., p. 497: "Le temps de la réflexion, c'est aussi la chance d'un retour sur les conditions mêmes de la réflexion, à tous les sens de ce mot, comme si à l'aide d'un nouvel appareil optique on pouvait voir enfin la vue," etc.

57 Ibid., p. 497: "Alors le temps de la réflexion est aussi un autre temps, il est hétérogène à ce qu'il réfléchit et donne peut-être le temps de ce qui appelle et s'appelle la pensée."

58 Ibid., p. 497: "Il peut être aussi bref et paradoxal, il peut déchirer le temps, comme l'instant dont parle Kierkegaard," etc.

59 Ibid., p. 473: "L'abîme ... ce serait l'impossibilité pour un principe de fondement de se fonder lui-même." On this point Derrida follows Heidegger's argument in *Der Satz vom Grund* from 1957.

It is a paradoxical logic showing some affinity to the discussions of repetition and temporality in both Kierkegaard and Heidegger (and, before them, in early German Romantics like Friedrich Schlegel, who, in his famous *Athenäum Fragment* No. 116, calls for the poetics of "reflection" as the highest form of thinking and writing). Derrida develops this logic with non-concepts, with changing forms of writing and with incessant "deconstruction." The logic is the logic of movement: *kinesis*. Reflection, which was Derrida's object in the essay quoted, is the movement of thought, and the movement of thought is its active form: the activity of thinking.

In a still later essay, "Donner la mort," Derrida discusses Kierkegaard's *Fear and Trembling* as an example of "the temporality of the instant."[60] This instant ("l'instant même") gives time for the contradictions of the *mysterium tremendum* that Derrida analyses here, referring to the tradition of upsetting conversions going back to St. Paul and nicely converging with his own philosophical practice of making tremble – because a thought or a way of thinking that is always on the move must become agitated and inverse and function agitating – "deconstructing" – in the world of thought. Such is Derrida's intention, anyway, if one is to believe his appreciation of the *mysterium tremendum* involved in the latin verb "sollicitare," a word that should mean "agitate" or "make all tremble." [61] He is, as has been said, the "thunderstorm" of hermeneutics[62] in exactly the sense that the young man of Kierkegaard's *Repetition* was fascinated by a metaphorical thunderstorm as a transport to the decisive "instant" of "repetition." Rousseau, in his fascination with *tressaillir*, would have followed suit. And even Kant, who associated the experience of the sublime with an agitating *Erschütterung*, would have liked the idea even if he would not have accepted the ideology. That is, if the ideology is best expressed by the young man from Kierkegaard's *Gjentagelse* and his exclamatory pathos: "How beneficent is a thunderstorm!" (180/212).

60 Derrida, "Donner la mort," in J.-M. Rabaté and Michael Wetzel (eds.), *L'éthique du don* (Paris: Métailié-Transition, 1992), p. 66.
61 Derrida, "Différance," in *Marges de la philosophie*, p. 22: "Partout, c'est la dominance de l'étant que la différance vient solliciter, au sens où *sollicitare* signifie, en vieux latin, ébranler comme tout, faire trembler en totalité."
62 Caputo, *Radical Hermeneutics*, p. 123.

Paul de Man's Repetition

Paul de Man has some images, notions, ideas, concepts that recur throughout his writings in a repeated attempt to say more or less the same thing. These include the *fall*, as has been observed[63] — and "in all senses of the term, including the theological Fall," as he puts it in one of his last essays, where he furthermore, taking help from the German plural of "fall" (*Fälle*), finds new and unexpected senses of the term: grammatical declension plus "trap."[64] This combination of grammatical and more or less "existential" categories also recurs in de Man's writings. And so does the "trap," sometimes in relation to "mirroring" and "reflection." These categories, like the "fall," indicate spatial motions but with an interesting difference: the motion of fall is extended and has no logical limits, while the motion of mirroring is limited to a kind of back and forth. Movement in time is another recurrent idea, and, with concepts like *irony* and *allegory*, de Man tried to identify the major ways that literary language handles temporality. Between the textual concepts irony/allegory and the spatial metaphors fall/mirroring there is the correspondence that allegory and fall both require sequence or extension; while irony and mirroring and reflection deal with the sudden, punctual or instantaneous — the last terms also used because of their frequence in de Man's writings.

Mimesis is the classical concept used in my earlier chapters to discuss phenomena like those de Man terms mirroring, reflection and irony. *Mimesis* is, however, not a concept used by de Man — or only condescendingly. In "The Rhetoric of Temporality" we read that mimetic representation belongs to nineteenth-century realism as a "mystification" pretending that "fiction and reality could coincide." Against such an obvious fraud, irony and allegory function as critical distance, reflection and insight.[65]

One wonders what the reason could be for such a dramatic

63 Cf. Deborah Esch, "A Defence of Rhetoric/The Triumph of Reading," in Lindsay Waters and Wlad Godzich (eds.), *Reading de Man Reading* (Minnesota University Press, 1989); and Cathy Caruth "The Claims of Reference," *Yale Journal of Criticism*, October 1990.

64 De Man, "Aesthetic Formalization in Kleist," in *The Rhetoric of Romanticism* (Columbia University Press, 1984).

65 De Man, "The Rhetoric of Temporality," in *Blindness and Insight* (London: Methuen, 1983), p. 222. Whenever possible I will quote from this essay with page references in my text.

deprecation – and in an essay that concludes with a novel from nineteenth-century realism, Stendhal's *Chartreuse de Parme*, as the prime example of an "allegory of irony," a text that beautifully combines its allegorical extension as narrative with the instantaneous *staccato* of its irony (p. 228). The ambiguity of this deprecation is not diminished by its being incorporated in a book with the title *Blindness and Insight*, and at least one idea in this title must come from the mythical encounter between Eros and Psyche, which I have had reason to evoke as an allegorical pre-text to Kierkegaard's *Repetition* (and which de Man evokes as a pre-text to Stendhal). It is, furthermore, a pre-text that already had its classical form in Socrates' second speech in Plato's *Phaedrus*, which must be called a basic text for all later speculation on *mimesis* as similarity/difference and as presence/absence – including de Man's speculation – and for the importance of memory and repetition in such dialectics.

De Man evokes no *mimesis*. On the contrary, he always opposes similarity and stresses the disjunctive, negative relation of works of art to "reality"; always literature as language and literature as difference. Such are the well-known axioms of his "deconstruction," and I will not pursue here the basis of this "negative," or at least differential, aesthetics as it develops the idea of language as "machine" and literature as the (relative) telling of the truth about the unorganic and unnatural machinery of language, its "radical figurality."[66] I want to follow another *line* and make another *point* by looking into some elements in de Man's writings having to do with mirroring, reflection and, not least, *repetition*. My idea is that these now emphasized terms – line, point, repetition – are derived from the mimetic tradition, as it has been discussed in this book, but a *mimesis* just as split as Plato's and an irony just as paradoxical as Kierkegaard's.

The already mentioned essay "The Rhetoric of Temporality" of 1969 is a good starting-point for my discussion. It has been declared to be de Man's "most fully achieved essay,"[67] but has also been judged as the turning-point leading from an earlier, existential-

---

66 In De Man's *Allegories of Reading* (Yale University Press, 1979) we read of "the radical figurality of language" on p. 202. On p. 10 de Man declares that "the rhetorical, figural potentiality of language" is equivalent to literature. The idea of language as "machine" is developed in the essay "Excuses" in the same volume (p. 298f.).

67 Lindsay Waters in his "Introduction" to Paul de Man's *Critical Writings 1953–1978* (Minnesota University Press, 1989), p. lvi.

phenomenological de Man to a later, deconstructive de Man, exploring rhetorical analysis. (There is a still earlier de Man, the young journalist on *Le Soir* up to 1942, whom I have no reason to comment on here; and perhaps even a later one, whom I will touch on towards the end: the post-hermeneutic critic in the essays on Kant, Schiller and Hegel.) "The Rhetoric of Temporality" is also the only text so far published[68] in which de Man refers to Kierkegaard; and if one were to choose a turning-point in the essay, itself a turning-point in de Man's writings, I would suggest the parenthetical phrase in which de Man claims "*repetition* (in the Kierkegaardian sense of the term)" to be the "meaning of the allegorical sign" (p. 207). *Repetition* as the characteristic of irony as well as of allegory is then called a temporal experience of "authentic" and "fundamental" dignity[69] – probably the last appearance of such terms in de Man's writings.

"The Rhetoric of Temporality" is organized in two parts, the first a historical study of the "symbol," where allegory is introduced as a polemical counterpart to "symbol," the second a more epistemological study of "irony." In a conclusion (p.222 ff.) the concepts are linked together in "their common discovery of a truly temporal predicament" (pp. 222). I made use of this discovery in the analysis of Kierkegaard above as the discovery of the temporality of the "instant": that the instantaneous *now* also has a precedent or a repetitive structure (to use Derrida's version). De Man takes his examples of allegory from Romantic literature, an epoch that is rumored to favor the symbol. But allegory, according to de Man, carries an insight that the symbol obstructs, i.e. a "negative" insight into an "authentically temporal predicament" (p. 208) – and we observe that not only "truly" and "authentic," but also "predicament" seem to be favorite terms.

De Man finds the predicament expressed in Kierkegaardian *repetition*, which he interprets as the view that the sign (i.e. the allegorical linguistic sign) refers to "meaning" not immediately, but only indirectly, by way of another sign, characterized by its "anteriority." Allegory therefore accentuates "distance," in contrast to the symbol, to which de Man ascribes the (hopeless) effort to reach the full and direct presence of meaning (and of meaning as presence).

---

68 There exists a not yet (1993) published lecture entitled "The Concept of Irony" referring to Kierkegaard's dissertation of that title.

69 On pp. 208, 214, 226 and 222 we find the words "authentic," "fundamental" and "truly" related to the temporality of "repetition."

The structure of his argument is well known from several of de Man's earlier essays from the 1950s, for instance "The Temptation of Permanence" quoted above, in which Heidegger's way of establishing a strong relation between *Dichtung* and truth (truth as presence) is criticized as deceptive in relation to the negative and differentiating, distancing insight that is possible and actually expressed in literature. De Man writes, for instance, that poetry as well as philosophical dialectics "excludes all permanent unity," but expresses, instead, "the movement of being."[70] In "The Rhetoric of Temporality" it is the "symbol" that is ascribed this deceptive zeal for "permanent unity," while the "repetition" of irony and allegory characterizes the "movement of being."

Kierkegaard's Constantin wanted us to remember kinesis; and Heidegger found the enigma of Being in its *movement*. Jan Rosiek has efficiently made the point that the interest shown by de Man in the 1950s in notions like *movement* and *becoming* was connected to the French "Hegel renaissance" – Kojève, Sartre, Blanchot, Hyppolite – and especially the movement of the spirit in Hegel's *Phänomenologie*.[71] In "The Rhetoric of Temporality" Hegel has been displaced in the sense that de Man declares Kierkegaardian "repetition" to be the very logic of the "movement of being." I will come back to the problematic question on whether or not Hegelian movement re-enters de Man's writings in his very last phase – in this case a linguistically purged Hegel. Not that grammar and linguistics are late inspirations for de Man. In "The Rhetoric of Temporality," allegory is defined linguistically as a sign repeating another (and temporally earlier) sign. And in 1957 de Man had already argued against a mimetic literature as having the (again hopeless) task of repeating an "original." Still, literature repeats; de Man finds the happy formula of poetical words repeating *themselves* since "the poetic language is not an originary language, but is derived from an originary language it does not know," etc.[72]

In the analysis of the concept of allegory in "The Rhetoric of Temporality" de Man goes one step further: he writes that allegory

70 De Man, "The Temptation of Permanence," in *Critical Writings 1953–1978*, pp. 35 and 38.

71 Jan Rosiek, *Figures of Failure. Paul de Man's Criticism 1953–1970* (Århus University Press, 1992).

72 De Man, "Criticism and the Theme of Faust," in *Critical Writings 1953–1978*, p. 87.

not only reminds us of "distance," but reaches its "negative" insight by establishing its langauge "in the void of this temporal difference" (p. 207). And de Man's linguistically sober definition of allegory suddenly acquires a mystical touch: grammar goes existential. How can language – and not just allegorical language, because allegorical language is here apparently an allegory of language in general – be "established" in a "void"? The expression carries a metaphorical suggestion of the very type that de Man criticizes as mystifyingly "symbolic." But it does not take much reading to discover that de Man in "The Rhetoric of Temporality" uses spatial and/or visual metaphors in order to suggest the opposite of space, i.e. the temporality of language. Most striking are his metaphors of mirrors and mirroring, which are established here in order to return in some of de Man's later essays.

The mirror becomes explicit at the end of the essay, where irony is linked to allegory in that common "temporal predicament." Irony is there called "the reversed mirror-image" of allegory (p. 225). Again a mystical touch – are not mirror-images always "reversed"? What, then, would the reversal of an already reversed mirror-image look like? The phrase gives in all circumstances a visual suggestion of the "temporal predicament" that includes a "reversal." (Remember de Man's interest, in an early criticism of Heidegger, quoted above, in the "retournement répété," the repeated reversal.)[73] The following phrases "temporalize" the mirror metaphor, so to speak, with a host of terms indicating suddenness: the ironic intervention in allegorical narration is called "instantaneous," it takes place "rapidly," "suddenly," "in one single moment." As an example we are given Baudelaire's prose poems, which are said to "climax in the single brief moment of a final *pointe*" (p. 225f.).

Pointe could of course mean the "point" of meaning as well as a temporal "instant," the graphical dot or grammatical full stop. Everything de Man writes on irony in "The Rhetoric of Temporality" emphasizes its being sudden, suggesting a break in temporality: time as instant breaking into time as sequence. With a word like *pointe* (supported by all the words for suddenness) he indicates a kind of time that is so limited in duration that it is no longer "time" but, instead, a break in sequential time, like a visual dot in the line of time. We recognize by now the ambition as well as the phenomenon in Plato's

---

73 De Man, "Heidegger's Exegesis of Hölderlin," p. 265.

to exaiphnes in *Parmenides,* in Kierkegaard's *Øieblikk* and in Heidegger's *Augenblick.*

"*Repetition* (in the Kierkegaardian sense of the term)" was de Man's suggestion as a solution to the problem of time, "repetition" as the link uniting time as sequence ("allegory") and time as instantaneous break ("irony"). Repetition is nothing less than what the younger de Man called the "movement of being."

The solution is explicitly Kierkegaardian and implicitly influenced by Heidegger's *Wiederholung,* I would guess (although without Heidegger's "resoluteness" and "fate"). But de Man has added an element that is not to be found in Heidegger, although it could be glimpsed in Kierkegaard's (or Constantin's) interest in the eye and the reversal and the allegorical complex Orpheus-Eros-Psyche. De Man's metaphor for this visual element is the mirror, or the "reversed mirror-image." De Man's *repetition* thus sticks to the "Kierkegaardian sense of the term," although with an emphasis on the eye and the reversal as reflection.

The meaning of the odd metaphor of "reversed mirror-image" is established with the help of Baudelaire's *De l'essence du rire,* where de Man starts his analysis of irony (and Baudelaire's *rire* is unqualifiedly identified with irony). De Man picks up Baudelaire's example of the man who is capable of laughing at himself when he falls in the street. Here we have the fall, again, doubling the individual in a *dédoublement,* i.e. into falling man and observing/laughing man. In the state that Baudelaire calls "le comique absolu" this doubling becomes permanent; according to de Man it is a split of the subject provoking uncanny giddiness: "irony is unrelieved *vertige,* dizziness to the point of madness" (p. 215).

Doubling, split and vertigo are all spatial phenomena that are invested with temporal irony by de Man. The intersection of space with time takes place at the "point" that is a point of turning or reversal as well as a point of "madness." When de Man, a bit further on in his argument, arrives at Baudelaire's "instantaneous", "rapid"" and "sudden" *pointe,* madness seems again not far from the point, so to speak. That *pointe* is "the instant at which the two selves [i.e. the individual in his *dédoublement*] are simultaneously present, juxtaposed within the same moment"; this moment is called "the moment of the present" (p. 226). This sounds both like a definition of schizophrenia and like an evocation of the Platonic *ousia,* which is usually translated (for example by Heidegger) as "presence." (And Heidegger could add that this would mean that *Seiendes* was "understood with regard to a

definite mode of time, the *present.*")[74] We may note here that this
sharp, thin and dividing point – *pointe* – that de Man ascribes to
"repetition" as the sudden reversal from time into space, is thin, but
still has a kind of extension or duration: it allows for repetition in the
form of reflection, doubling, mirroring. And it invites the "mode of the
present."

The only comment I have found on de Man's visual metaphors
associated with mirroring repetition is Jacques Derrida's in the essay
Psyché, in which he quotes de Man's assertion from "The Rhetoric of
Temporality" on the "truly temporal predicament" displayed by
irony and allegory. "The mirror is here the *predicament*," writes
Derrida, the mirror as "deadly and fascinating trap."[75]

The mirror as a trap? Could it be something like that "endless
succession of mirrors" evoked by Friedrich Schlegel in his already
quoted *Athenäum Fragment* No. 116 as an ideal state of poetic
reflection? Or, perhaps, the mirroring mirrors, once described like this
by Walter Benjamin: "When two mirrors look into each other, Satan
plays his most popular prank and opens in his own way (as his partner
does in the eyes of lovers) the perspective into eternity."[76] Derrida,
for his part, associates the trick of mirrors with the myth of Eros and
Psyche, which arises as an allegorical pattern also in de Man's
"Rhetoric of Temporality" immediately after the conclusion on irony
as the "reversed mirror-image" of allegory – although de Man
situates the myth as an allegorical pattern for Stendhal's *Chartreuse de
Parme* (although its relevance for his own argument comes out in his
title). According to Derrida, the blinding meeting (or non-meeting)
between Eros and Psyche creates grief ("deuil"). If the grief comes not
from the breaking of the mirror, but from the mirror itself, or the
mirroring ("la spécularization"), it is due to "an intervention of the
word ... The silvering [le tain], which prevents transparency and
authorizes the invention of the mirror, is a trace of language."[77] It is

74 Heidegger, *Sein und Zeit*, p. 25.
75 Jacques Derrida, *Psyché. Invention de l'autre* (Paris: Galilée, 1987), p. 28: "Le miroir
    est ici le *predicament* ... On est en proie au piège fatal et fascinant du miroir."
76 Walter Benjamin, *Das Passagen-Werk*, in Gesammelte Schriften, (Frankfurt-on-
    Main, 1982), vol. 5, p. 1049: "Blicken zwei Spiegel einander an, so spielt der
    Satan seinen liebsten Trick und öffnet auf seine Weise (wie sein Partner in den
    Blicken der Liebenden tut) die Perspektive ins Unendliche."
77 Derrida, *Psyché*, p. 31: "Car nous l'avons vu, si le deuil n'est pas annoncé par le
    bris du miroir mais survient comme le miroir lui-même que par l'intercession du

the word, according to Derrida, that makes immediate presence impossible and reflection or mirroring necessary. Again, with Derrida, it is the repeatability of the sign that is "primordial."

De Man started his essay by defining allegory by way of "*repetition* (in the Kierkegaardian sense of the term)" and ended with the "reversed mirror-image" of irony. The question is, then, whether or not "The Rhetoric of Temporality" is a real turning-point in de Man's writings; and if Kierkegaardian repetition is the point of turning within this turning. Or could the mirror-image be a "trap" making the "movement of being" into the "repeated reversal" ("retournement répété") evoked by a younger de Man in his criticism of Heidegger? Or is the "repeated reversal" a reminder of "*repetition* (in the Kierkegaardian sense of the term)" or of Constantin's kinesis?

This is probably like asking the confusing question whether de Man's later writing on irony is itself ironic. Or if his reflections on repetition are repetitive or if they reflect the "movement of Being." The real answer to such questions would probably be found by an analysis of the curiously repetitive structure of the essays typical of late de Man. I am not thinking only of their tendency to "always start again from scratch," as he writes in the preface to *The Rhetoric of Romanticism*, "and that their conclusions fail to add up to anything";[78] I am also thinking of their circular structure, with the end reflecting, repeating or duplicating the beginning: saying the same, but differently. Critics of de Man's writings have, to my knowledge, had little to say about this; they have been busy with ethics and epistemology. But even if de Man dissociated himself from rhetorical flair (for instance in the just mentioned preface to *The Rhetoric of Romanticism*), some simple observations cannot be wasted on this champion of rhetorics, who actually wrote his best essays in accordance with principles of repetition. This could even produce the "dizziness" he found in Baudelaire's *comique absolu*, and the "reversed mirror-image" of irony in "The Rhetoric of Temporality." One obvious example is the programmatic article "Semiology and Rhetoric", which starts the collection *Allegories of Reading* (1979).

Here we first get a seductively easygoing polemic against the

mot. C'est une invention et intervention du mot ... La tain, qui interdit la transparence et autorise l'invention du miroir, c'est une trace de langue."

78   De Man, *The Rhetoric of Romanticism* (Columbia University Press, 1984), p. viii.

opposition inside/outside, regarded as a compact metaphor and applied to literature and criticism. Result: "The recurrent debate opposing intrinsic to extrinsic criticism stands under the aegis of an inside/outside metaphor that is never being seriously questioned."[79] De Man then starts the "questioning" needed with a series of examples of growing complexity, in which he turns grammatical meaning against rhetorical meaning. First, we are led to think that the grammatical meaning (of a rhetorical question) suspends rhetorical meaning; and then (in a reading of Proustian "reading") that rhetorical meaning suspends grammatical meaning. The logical result of this is called *aporia*; the rhetorical result would be called irony. De Man speaks instead of a state of "suspended ignorance." This means that we are now "suspended" within the metaphor with which we started, not knowing what is "in" or what is "out"; we are *neither* "in" *nor* "out," but, rather, falling between. And, perhaps, while "falling," we may remember that the "fall" in "The Rhetoric of Temporality" was associated with *vertige* and irony, meaning that our "fall" is actually an effect of mirroring mirrors taking place within a "reversed mirror-image" (or was it "repeated reversal"?) of the very "reversal" with which we began.

"Semiology and Rhetoric" functions as a prelude to the whole collection *Allegories of Reading* and at its close a similar "reversal" is again "repeated," but now explicitly as irony. De Man then finishes his readings of Rousseau by summarizing his "main point" – *point* being, as mentioned above, all sorts of instantaneous points. The "main point," also called a "sudden revelation," is that de Man has discovered in Rousseau a "discontinuity," and this sudden and discontinuous "main point" is "disseminated" all over "the points of the figural line or allegory," thus becoming a continuous discontinuity, a permanent suddenness or "the permanent parabasis of an allegory." Becoming: irony. This irony repeats the "suspended ignorance" at the end of the first essay (in its turn a repetition of the ignorance of inside/outside at the beginning). The final irony suspends not only a compact metaphor or a temporary "ignorance," but actually the whole "line" of argument: irony is now nothing less than "the systematic undoing ... of understanding."[80]

Irony, which started out as a sudden, instantaneous and even capricious event, has now become permanent and systematic. This is

79 De Man, *Allegories of Reading*, p. 5.   80 Ibid. , p. 300f.

a remarkable reversal and a striking paradox that perhaps could be understood as if de Man has demonstrated – i.e. led us into – a trap: ironic "repetition" has been reversed into its own "reversed mirror-image." Why is it that the suddenness of irony must become repetitive, and that irony is not allowed even a temporary break of a "line"? Why has the instant to grow into permanence?

No direct answer is given, but we observe that de Man insists, already in "The Rhetoric of Temporality," on the stubborn permanence of the ironic break of "line" and even allows himself a dubious reading of the German *vorläufig* (as the word has been used to characterize romantic irony) in order to make his "point": that irony is not temporary, but "repetitive."[81] When de Man comes back to irony in the final essay of *Allegories of Reading*, "Excuses," irony is not only "repetitive," but "disseminated" all over the "line" of text that it simultaneously is said to break – a kind of visual magic that could be possible only in Schlegel's "endless succession of mirrors."

In another late essay, "Pascal's Allegory of Persuasion," we learn that Pascal uses zero in the line of numbers as an analogy of the ironical break of an allegorical "line". Zero is not a "negation" (i.e. cannot be dialectically mediated with the line of numbers), but is the "rupture" or "disjunction" of the line[82] – therefore analogous to the "parabasis" and "anacoluthon" used by de Man in the essays mentioned above as the rhetorical figures of irony.

The Pascal essay goes even further: de Man finds that the "rupture" of the line of numbers effected by zero (read, the ironic break of an allegorical "line") *cannot* "be located in a single point ... but that it is all-pervading." In "The Rhetoric of Temporality," the ironic effect depended, as we remember, on the sharp and dividing final *pointe*, which, in *Allegories of Reading*, has grown into the "main

---

81 De Man, "The Rhetoric of Temporality," p. 220: "Contrary to [Peter] Szondi's assertion, irony is not temporary [vorläufig] but repetitive," etc. As shown by Werner Hamacher (in *Reading de Man Reading*, p. 196), Szondi's *vorläufig* refers to a permanent *Vorspiel*: "The 'fore' – has taken leave of all after, provisional temporariness is absolute, and the future of happiness is given nowhere but in the promise of it."

82 De Man, "Pascal's Allegory of Persuasion," in Stephen Greenblatt (ed.), *Allegory and Representation* (Baltimore, 1981), p. 12. All quotations from this essay are from the same page.

point" of "discontinuity." In the Pascal essay the point seems to be gone (or is not "single" or cannot be found), while the ironic effect remains — Derrida would, no doubt, have found a "trace of language" there. The conclusion that ironic "disruption" is "all-pervading" seems to follow from the metaphor of mirroring mirrors and takes de Man to remarkable consequences, considering his earlier essays: in the Pascal essay he states that irony is no longer "susceptible ... to definition," it is not even "intelligible" and "it cannot be put to work as a device of textual analysis."

It follows that irony disappears as a concept or "device" from de Man's last essays. The *pointe* associated with a sudden ironical break disappears. "Repetition" in the sense of mirroring and reflection does not disappear, however. In "Autobiography as De-Facement" we read about a "specular moment," but this "moment" is not an "event" — that is, not a singular "point" and, therefore, not an ironic interruption or "undoing of understanding" — but rather a "part of all under-standing" including "knowledge of self."[83]

This epistemological idea, with its vaguely Freudian touch, could no doubt have been developed into a quite different "repetition" from the ironic sudden "point" or disrupting "zero" we met earlier, but still being a kind of "repetition" that could be associated with Kierkegaard. But the late, and so to speak, post-hermeneutical de Man has a suggestion of quite another "repetition" which seems far from any of the many Kierkegaardian senses of the term. Now it is "repetition" as mechanical repetition: no turning, no "point."

The term is now "stutter," cropping up a couple of times in de Man's late essays on "aesthetic ideology," and associated with something he calls "the essentially prosaic nature of art."[84] This "prosaic nature" he derives (as always) from a linguistic axiom: that the linguistic sign refers both to itself as sign and beyond itself as reference or meaning. Philosophical aesthetics, as de Man reads it in Kant and Hegel, operates on the level of meaning, but presupposes a level where the sign is "inscribed" as sign. The event of "inscription" (actually a development of, and a translation of, *Stiftung*, a central term in early German Romanticism) he calls the "prosaic materiality of the

83 De Man, "Autobiography as De-Facement," in *The Rhetoric of Romanticism* (1984), p. 70.
84 De Man, "Hegel on the Sublime," in Mark Krupnick (ed.), *Displacement. Derrida and After* (Bloomington, 1983), p. 152.

letter." This "materiality" is the basis or "bottom line" that aesthetics can neither do without nor make into meaning.[85] (And de Man may well be inspired not only by German Romantics here, but also by Derrida's discussion of *itération* as mentioned above.) De Man now states that the sign in its material aspect as "inscription" is already a "repetition" that cannot be used to do anything but perform its own "repetition", and with devastating results once you realize the mechanism: "Like a stutter, or a broken record, it [the inscription as 'principle of signification'] makes what it keeps repeating worthless and meaningless."[86]

It seems as if de Man has come to the end of his *via negativa*, and that the name of this end is "repetition" and, in the mechanical and duplicating sense expressed by the word "stutter," giving only auditory (and, maybe, some Nietzschean) associations. Stuttering has no "point" – and perhaps de Man situates it in "prosaic materiality" since it seems free from visuality. Stuttering is, in any case, devoid of anything like "intention" and definitely has no "existential" pathos, but is simply a reminder of language as "machine" and linguistic meaning as based on a "prosaic" and meaningless "inscription." Still, visuality – and perhaps a kind of irony and even a line of allegory – sneaks back into "repetition" by way of the metaphor used by de Man to illustrate his meaningless "stutter": the *broken record*. The record being broken by its own signs is a kind of visual intervention in the auditory scenery. But it is not just visual; it shows distinct traces of language. "Record" means a gramophone record, but it could also suggest a document or even a story, i.e. any sequence or line of events. Stuttering is an auditory and repetitive break in this record. But the break is visually repaired by its own expression. The metaphor "*broken record*" gives visuality to the "break," and even a kind of allegorical meaning to the "meaninglessness" referred to. By the symbolic power of the metaphor – and against what seems to be de Man's prosaic intentions with his "stutter" – the "break" in the record leads us back to the sudden "break" or "point" that de Man earlier associated with "repetition" and called irony.

Thus, irony comes ironically back to de Man's record at the very

85 De Man, "Phenomenality and Materiality in Kant," in Gary Shapiro and Alan Sica (eds.), *Hermeneutics: Questions and Prospects* (Amherst, University of Massachusetts Press 1984), p. 144.
86 De Man, "Hegel on the Sublime," p. 150.

moment when he drops all irony in order to promote "prosaic materiality." A reversal takes place when reversals are left out of consideration. The final irony is, however, that it is impossible to say if the irony of this reversal is an intended and controlled communication or if it just occurs as a result of uncontrollable linguistic mechanisms; i.e. if it undermines or underlines. Those who find the "materiality" of de Man's later essays gloomy or even "nihilistic" may, however, take comfort in the possibility (although it cannot be confirmed) that language is taking a kind of revenge – the poor language that de Man found established in a "void," and then never tired of criticizing for concealing this basic baselessness with the feigned meaning of symbols and metaphors. Language takes its revenge by providing de Man with a meaningful metaphor with symbolic dimensions exactly when he declares language to be a "stutter," a meaningless repetition of sounds. Or was it perhaps the "movement of being" that reminded us of its *retournement répété*, to echo the young de Man?

Perhaps (although it cannot be confirmed) this "movement of being" even creates a new path for history into the rhetoric of literary criticism; in that case "history" as a "*textual* process governed by laws that would be proper to the acts of inscription and reading rather than a natural process patterned on the chronological continuity," as Kevin Newmark has reminded us.[87] Derrida would contribute to this by underlining that the "iterability of the trace ... is the condition of historicity";[88] – and Heidegger would perhaps add that "the historicity of history has its essence in the returning to one's own."[89] *Retournement*, returning, iteration and even stuttering may all turn into versions of a *mimesis* gone linguistic, but also temporal and, therefore, historical; and as figurations of the *kinesis* that Constantin Constantius asked us to "consider seriously" as a preparation for the "easy" dialectic of "repetition (in the Kierkegaardian sense of the term)."

---

87 Kevin Newmark, *Beyond Symbolism. Textual History and the Future of Reading* (Cornell University Press, 1991), p. 224.

88 Derrida, in D. Attridge (ed.), *Acts of Literature*, p. 63.

89 Heidegger, "Die Geschichtlichkeit der Geschichte hat ihr Wesen in der Rückkehr zum Eigenen," etc., *Erläuterungen zu Hölderlins Dichtung* (Frankfurt-on-Main: Klostermann, 1981), p. 95.

❖❖❖

Index of subjects and names

❖❖❖

Index

Index

Virgil, 54, 92

Wahl, J., 123
Waters, L., 177, 178
Wetzel, M., 176
Wiederholung, 140, 153–67, 168, 170, 173

Williams, H., 119
Winckelmann, J. J., 46–48
Wulf, Ch., 2, 3, 5

øieblikk/et/ 136, 139, 140, 148, 153–54,
157, 159, 168, 173–74